new dimensions of freedom in america

Chandler Publications in
POLITICAL SCIENCE
VICTOR JONES, *Editor*

New
Dimensions
of Freedom
in America

EDITED BY

FREDERICK M. WIRT
Denison University

AND

WILLIS D. HAWLEY
University of California, Berkeley

CHANDLER PUBLISHING COMPANY
An Intext Publisher · Scranton, Pennsylvania 18515

To our second-born,
Sandy and Janet

Contents

new dimensions of freedom in america

Introduction

Recent events have moved Americans to examine—many for the first time—the meaning of liberty. Recurrent historical questions have now reappeared demanding answers: What is meant by freedom? Who should have it? Who should define it? How does such inquiry affect me? These questions, which have often been debated at levels far removed from average citizens, are now the substance of discussion in countless living rooms, offices, factories, clubs—in all those common places where people spend their lives. Hardly an American alive can have escaped being witness to, if not participant in, the events which have painted the television tubes of the last decade with the picture of expanding demands for civil rights and liberties. Every reader has seen some part of this development—Southern and Northern mobs, the rise and fall of police riot sticks, the awful loneliness of the little Negro girl going to school before hate-filled faces, the sometimes thundering denunciation of the United States Supreme Court for its latest decision. The pictures seem endless. For the viewer, depending upon his upbringing and values, these images are frightening or encouraging, enraging or thrilling, degrading or ennobling.

Even the dullest observer must conclude that the struggle for new dimensions of freedom has reached unusual intensity. For many "the time is out of joint" and threatening when not only criminals but also black militants, war resisters, writers on sex, and dissidents objecting to the traditional classroom prayer—or even to the Christmas pageant in the local school—refuse to keep their places and instead challenge the conventional wisdom which has been so comforting to the average American. In the face of these challenges, it seems difficult to remember that conflict over civil rights is not really new, and that the search for the meaning of liberty has been a continuing theme in American history.

Yet it is true that after midcentury, an unusual combination of groups and institutions has interacted in sensational events to focus our attention on a reinterpretation of what liberty means. In the process, there has taken place an extraordinary widening of that meaning, accompanied by a number of court decisions, legislative acts, and private group actions which have translated general prescriptions into meaningful particulars. In one sense, we are embarked upon a truly "noble experiment" testing whether we actually believe in, and can live with, the mandates of our ideals.

This book seeks to shed some light on the new meanings and problems of civil rights and on the dynamic quality of this experiment. It is intended to provide insight into the nature of the interaction between human behavior and social institutions by providing some commentary not only on the substantive issues in the current debate over the limits of liberty, but also on the context (social, political, and psychological) which influences how these issues are ultimately decided.

For example, there is more to civil rights than nine men in black robes handing us graven tablets embodying some transcendental wisdom of the ages. Judicial decisions are choices among competing values, often urged upon the Court by groups who are seeking the vast authority of that body to protect or promote ideas of what the good life requires. A Court decision, such as that upholding the Civil Rights Act of 1965, reinforces one significant group in society—Negroes—in its vision of how to secure its status while denying the legitimacy of the alternative vision of the Southern segregationist. This way of looking at the process requires us to analyze not merely authoritative laws but the contending groups—their values, power resources, and strategies.

Let us begin with values. We are all familiar, or think we are, with what this book will term the "Bright Tradition" of American values. Here are all the statements of the meaning of American life inseminated by philosophers in the Enlightenment, delivered in the trauma of the birth of the Republic, nurtured in many decades of Fourth of July speeches and school books, and ostensibly manifest in the life of adult America. Familiar symbols stimulate good feelings about our system, symbols which encapsulate this Bright Tradition: liberty, equality, justice, majority rule, minority rights—and the most powerful of all—democracy. These idealized values are associated with political institutions: the Constitution and its Bill of Rights, an august Supreme Court impartially defining and defending the tradition, and a Congress and Presidency implementing the values of the people. Many institutions other than the government contribute to the maintenance of these traditional values. As recent studies of the political attitudes of school children show, the school aids in causing them to view these values benevolently. The mass media do their part, as do public advertisers, speeches by public officials, and the sermons of ministers. Most importantly, the values of the Bright Tradition are transmitted and reinforced by the family.

Yet surely that cannot be all. Even if one knew no American history, one could see certain dilemmas inherent in the Bright Tradition. If men's lives are so arranged that they are free to do as much as their will and talent allow, how then is it possible for all men with differing talents to be equal? Or, if one insists on the primacy of equality, does this not imply the necessity to restrict the freedom of some whose individual talent and will would carry them beyond majoritarian standards? How is it logically possible for majority rule and minority rights to coexist? If the majority makes all decisions, then minorities have rights only to the degree the larger group permits. But if minorities have rights immune from encroachment by the majority, how then can the latter be said to rule?

The matter is further complicated by the fact that it is difficult to understand what is meant by a "majority," for there are few things on which there exists a majority which wishes something concrete to be done. In fact, most decisions in the public arena are made by combinations of minorities which coalesce to serve their immediate, collective ends and which represent only a small segment of the population. It may make little difference to the losing combination of minorities whether the decision is thrust upon them by another segment of minorities acting in the name of an apathetic majority or by a more or less unified majority. But in the process we do act on the principle that majorities make decisions. The problem of resolving these apparent contradictions will confront the reader throughout this book.

This book will also face the reader with the fact that the high values to which we all attest are often trampled, either by well-intentioned zeal or by plain old-fashioned inhumanity. In contrast to the Bright Tradition, Americans have what will be called here the "Dark Tradition," the occasions without number in our past when the majority has denied minorities their rights to life, liberty, and justice.

This "tradition" is not often acknowledged. The case of slavery and its injustices we know about and, overwhelmingly, regret. Less known is the treatment of the American Indian (past and present), by which we regularly, as a matter of *public* policy and at the urging of an overwhelming majority, stripped these people of their land, broke our treaties, and sought to exterminate them when they interfered—all with a casualness which today is hard to grasp.

In various times and places, we have slain members of religious minorities or otherwise deprived them of their rights to property, office, or worship. We have even had a sizable political movement—the Know-Nothings—which prior to the Civil War involved not only public denunciation of Roman Catholics but outright mob action to destroy them. Prior to 1850, Catholics in surprising numbers were killed for their beliefs; in Philadelphia one group of Catholics embattled inside their church faced cannon fire designed to break down the door. Nor has this suspicion or discrimination against the Roman Catholic wholly disappeared today, even after the election of John F. Kennedy.

Whole books have been written on the treatment of the immigrant, treatment which qualifies as part of the Dark Tradition. As each wave of newcomers entered, they mounted the bottom rung of a status ladder and, with successive generations, moved up to more acceptance. Their place on this ladder actually measured how much of the Bright Tradition they enjoyed. Many Irish-Americans still remember with bitterness the job-vacancy signs which specified that "No Irish need apply." On the West Coast this nativism took the form of societies seeking exclusion of the Orientals from the Bright Tradition—an exclusion written into our national immigration laws and manifest most blatantly during the internment of Americans of Japanese origin during World War II.

Probably the largest element of the population that has been excluded from the Bright Tradition has been the American woman, an exclusion still alive in popular attitudes and in certain practices.

All of this, and more, forms what we've termed the Dark Tradition, a dismal undercurrent of the bright mainstream of American freedom. From lynchings, church and home burnings, assassinations, bombings, economic boycotts, and whippings, to exclusion from the country club, there has been a variety of social-control techniques which are significant, if sorry, elements of American history. In looking back at these ugly times, we need to recognize that they are a part of what we have been and whence we have come. A frank confrontation of their reality helps us to understand something important about our total historical experience which we can apply to events of our times.

At a minimum, what can this Dark Tradition tell us? Clearly, not all minorities have shared in the best of our tradition of great liberal values. Men's attitudes and value preferences have differed strongly, and still do, on who is entitled to a full measure of liberty. Struggle, violent at times, seems a necessary requisite for obtaining one's share of the Bright Tradition. Freedom is not readily available to all members of society; noble statements of values, such as the Declaration of Independence or the Bill of Rights, are objectives we honor in the abstract, but they do not of themselves assure freedom. We come to the readings in this book with a keen awareness that the power possessed by a group or individual is an important determinant of the freedom enjoyed.

This book is concerned with the ways in which power residing in the state is used to affect the distribution of rights and property of its citizens who are concerned with preserving or furthering their income, safety, or deference. But we are also concerned with more subtle and sometimes more onerous restrictions on freedom which result from a society's effort to suppress unpopular ideas and practices.

What is to be done when the majority acts so as to invade the protection of a minority provided by the Constitution? What recourse does the minority have in the face of such encroachments? One answer has been that the Supreme Court will act to redress the evil done. But what if it does not—as it has not in many cases, such as the Court's failure until very recently to protect the rights of Negroes? Another answer is that one must rely ultimately upon contervailing forces to influence government or society to redress the balance. But what if the influence of the aggrieved minority on the government and on the majority is inadequate to protect its rights? Then, some argue, violence is necessary. When men are reduced to using spears in settling a problem, then a powerful consideration in determining the outcome is who has the most spears. Minorities invariably don't.

Another answer to the question of how minorities can be protected against the majority's suppression is that the former must rely on the essential and ultimate decency of the latter. This approach has the advantage of being consonant with the basic values of how policy is to be made in the democratic process; it relies on the majority to decide, after urging by interested parties. It is, however, cold comfort to members of the minority who suffer in the meantime. If, as in the case of the Negro, the process of majoritarian readjustment takes 100 years and more, it requires a powerful attachment to a total system of ideology to hold on while you are being trod upon. Yes, supporters of this view urge, but the alternative is less attractive than even this—minorities resorting to arms to overthrow the tyranny of the majority. It takes time to teach people to be humane, other-regarding, compassionate. We do treat the Indian better today than when we sent the cavalry after him or when we moved the Cherokees from Tennessee to the plains. We do now seem to understand that a man may be a Catholic and not be plotting overthrow of the government on order of the Holy See. We do now acknowledge that the brutal treatment of accused criminals is basically evil, not only because of what it does to the brutalized, but what it does to the people who brutalize. All true, of course, but cold comfort to those still denied their share of the Bright Tradition.

The questions of who should hold power and to what ends power should be employed are the two basic questions of all political theory. The answers to these are pursued as diligently today as when they fascinated Plato and Aristotle. In a real sense these two questions are what is pursued in this collection. How do we draw the line between the rights of the majority and the rights of the individual? What do we do when basic values are in conflict? For example:

—The right of a free press versus the right of a defendant to have a fair trial unaffected by undue publicity.

—The right of minorities to own property versus the right of the property owner to sell to whom he wishes.

—Helping maintain public order by not restricting police and prosecution versus ensuring the right to a fair trial by limiting police and prosecutors.

—Maintaining complete separation of church and state by denying all public aid to parochial schools versus providing the student in parochial schools with adequate facilities, transportation, and textbooks.

As these few issues illustrate, there are few easy answers to the questions of how and by whom freedom should be defined. Indeed, one of the aspects of democracy that many find so frustrating is that the concept of freedom seems to mean different things in different times and circumstances. The process of setting limits on the acts of individuals and groups that serve both the needs and the values of society never seems to end.

Finally, let us reconsider the basic premise which structures the context and elements of this book. It is that the search for a viable definition of freedom involves the competition of diverse and sometimes conflicting values. The results of the competition are determined not only by admonition or by appeal to sacred doctrine; also important in the outcome is the way in which government authoritatively allocates the values of society and the way in which society, by its actions, gives meaning to the letter and spirit of those allocations.

The Context of Freedom in America

Most of the articles in this volume deal with the prospects for preserving and expanding freedom. It is the editors' conviction that as far as this goal is concerned, Americans "have promises to keep." The gap between the promises of freedom and the reality has in our time provoked tension and even violence for both those impatient for and those resistant to social change. For observers to, and participants in, this tension, the future may seem apocalyptic. Among those most militant in expanding civil rights, it is often popular to conclude that we stand at Armageddon. It is useful, therefore, to begin a volume such as this by placing the scope of current freedom in historical perspective. This perspective leads us to suggest that, in the balance, there is room for some optimism that further progress can be made.

In the first article of this chapter, political scientist John Roche argues that "We've never had more freedom." It is important that Professor Roche came to this conclusion when examining the state of our liberty in the mid-1950's, after the uproar of McCarthyism and before the major struggle began to secure more freedom for Negroes. Few would deny that much, though occasionally faltering, progress has been made in the decade since. Roche demonstrates the existence of institutions, pressures, and concepts which made even the 1950's a far brighter period for the freedom of many than any earlier, purportedly "Golden Age." However, Professor Roche is quick to point out that we have no cause to rest content. It is a tired but true maxim that "eternal vigilance is the price of freedom." A large part of what this book is about is to suggest reasons for that vigilance and to illuminate the new dimensions of freedom which we have yet to secure.

The old saw that "ours is a nation of laws, not men," however worn, does reflect the considerable faith we seem to have that freedom can be (and is) protected by just laws and by a comprehensive system of judicial remedy. Many commentators on the course of freedom since World War II have concluded that the courts, and notably the Supreme

Court of the United States, can lay greater claim to the progress which liberty has made than can any other institution of government or society.[1]

Notable actions by the executive in recent years (such as President Truman's order to desegregate the armed forces and President Kennedy's order to end discrimination in public and federally financed housing) and the civil-rights legislation passed by the Congress were either foreshadowed or surpassed in consequence by actions of courts. In recent years the Supreme Court's decisions—concerning desegregation of schools and public facilities, freedom of religious worship, the rights of dissenters, and protection for the rights of those accused of crime—have set the tone of freedom's advance. These decisions were also stimulated by considerable public discussion and, in some cases, by public fears.

The drama of the Court's contributions to freedom may have dulled our awareness that the action of the courts often represents objectives not yet fully attained and deals with only a part of the problems of securing liberty. We shall see, in subsequent chapters of this book, that in many cases society has followed the Court's lead only at a distance or not at all, and that on still other questions of liberty the Court has yet to take a clear position (at least to the satisfaction of many civil-libertarians).

The second article in this chapter, written by the late Robert Jackson, an eminent Supreme Court Justice, discusses the role played by the Court in correcting injustice and expanding freedom, paying particular attention to the limitations on this role. Justice Jackson concludes by emphasizing the importance of an enlightened citizenry as the ultimate and most important source of individual freedom.

However, the idea of the public as the ultimate guardian of freedom provokes grave misgivings in some hearts. Many are apprehensive about the equalizing and conforming impulse of the majority (as was de Tocqueville) or society's capacity for the ruthless repression of dissent. Thus, in his famous essay, *On Liberty*, John Mill wrote:

Like other tyrannies, the tyranny of the majority was at first, and is still vulgarly, held in dread, chiefly as operating through the acts of the public authorities. But reflecting persons perceived that when society is itself the tyrant—society collectively, over the separate individuals who compose it—its means of tyrannizing are not restricted to the acts which it may do by the hands of its political functionaries. Society can and does execute its own mandates: and if it issues wrong mandates instead of right, or any mandates at all in things with which

---

[1]See, for example, Milton R. Konvitz, *Expanding Liberties: Freedom's Gains in Postwar America* (New York: Viking, 1966); and George W. Spicer, *The Supreme Court and Fundamental Freedoms* (2nd ed.; New York: Appleton, 1967)

it ought not to meddle, it practices a social tyranny more formidable than many kinds of political oppression, since, though not usually upheld by such extreme penalties, it leaves fewer means of escape, penetrating much more deeply into the details of life, and enslaving the soul itself.

Jackson's view of the importance of public opinion in securing freedom and Mill's warnings of the dangers of majority tyranny raise the question of just how broadly shared democratic principles are among Americans. This nation's history is replete with dramatic examples of prejudice and discrimination aimed at racial and religious minorities and of widespread intolerance of political dissenters. It is less than two decades since the heyday of McCarthyism, when the nation tolerated wide-reaching and arbitrary suppression of individual freedom in the name of national security. More recently, the wrath visited on civil-rights workers in both the South and the North, and attempts to suppress dissent to the country's Vietnam policy (and the not infrequent intolerance of the dissenters themselves), give testimony to weakness in the commitment to democratic principles of at least some large segments of this society.

While it is true that most Americans verbally endorse such principles as "free speech," "equality," or "due process," informed observers have long been aware that among Americans there was a credibility gap between these abstract notions of freedom and specific beliefs and behavior. The full breadth of this gap became increasingly clear as researchers began to make broader and more sophisticated use of public-opinion surveys. During the 1950's, especially, scholars turned up what seemed to many some alarming findings.[2] Among the most comprehensive efforts to assess the degree to which American values and beliefs are consistent with the basic assumptions of liberal democratic theory are those of Herbert McClosky and his associates. The third article in this chapter is excerpted from Professor McClosky's important article, "Consensus and Ideology in American Politics." Looking at the attitudes of the American people and their political leaders toward civil rights and liberties, McClosky makes it very clear that large numbers of us fall far short of fervent commitment to freedom for those who think and act unlike ourselves. Even among political leaders, sizable minorities are often reluctant to endorse specific applications of the "Democratic Creed." Among conclusions one may draw from this article, one of the most important is that political leadership, rather than public opinion, stands between the rights

---

[2]One of the most important of these studies is Samuel A. Stouffer's *Communism, Conformity, and Civil Liberties* (New York: Doubleday, 1955). See also James W. Prothro and Charles W. Grigg, "Fundamental Principles of Democracy: Bases of Agreement and Disagreement," *Journal of Politics*, 22 (1960), 276-294.

of minorities and the political and social suppression of dissent. Throughout this book we will examine other commentaries on the social and psychological context of freedom, and it will stand the reader in good stead to keep in mind the overview provided by McClosky's research.

While stressing that an enlightened public is essential if freedom is to be preserved and extended, we do not want to undervalue the importance of the courts and the law in securing civil rights and liberties. Professor William Muir has described well the necessity for both:

> Liberty depends upon heartfelt attitudes of men and women; in circumstances where there are no institutions to mediate between law and those people who harbor doubts about democratic attitudes, the law is rendered ineffectual. We can and should take steps to assure that such circumstances never occur by promoting numerous voluntary associations, social pluralism, better education, the upgrading of lawyers, and the training of judges. If these latter conditions obtain, then constitutions, laws, and courts can do their part—their highly flexible part—to engraft and preserve the attitudes upon which liberty depends.[3]

This, then is the theme to be pursued throughout these pages. Freedom is extremely fragile, and does not depend alone on even the most wise and solicitous system of justice. Freedom is, above all, a state of mind: a feeling of self-esteem and security which allows one to express his views and emotions with respect for others but without fear of arbitrary and unreasonable sanctions. Freedom is fostered by constitutional and legal protections but, more important, it requires a tolerant society which is, at the same time, confident of its capacity to withstand dissent and humble enough to entertain the possibility that it may be erring in its commitments and convictions. As one of America's great jurists, Learned Hand, observed: The spirit of liberty is one of doubt.

---

[3]William K. Muir. Jr., *Prayer in the Public Schools: Law and Attitude Change* (Chicago: The University of Chicago Press, 1967), p. 136.

JOHN P. ROCHE

We've Never Had More Freedom

About a year ago, the editors of the *New Republic* asked me to prepare a series of articles on the "State of Our Liberties." When we discussed the scope and direction of the series, it was my conviction that American freedom was on the downgrade, that our liberties today are considerably more circumscribed than they were, say, a century or a half-century ago, and the articles as then conceived were to reflect this viewpoint.

However, as I began working through material on the issues under examination, I became increasingly uncertain about my original framework of analysis. In fact, I began to wonder if the "Golden Age of American Freedom," which civil libertarians so confidently locate in the indefinite American past, were not just a myth. At this point, I started to stall off the editors' importune requests for my manuscript and launched an intensive investigation into the history of American non-conformism.

. . . Although I make no claim to originality, the net result is a substantial revision of much current liberal thinking on the subject of civil liberties. The core of my thesis is that American freedom has never been as firmly established or as broadly shared as is the case today. This thesis will seem overly sanguine to some. And so I should make it clear at once that I am not suggesting that the American Civil Liberties Union close up shop, nor am I justifying for one minute the many abuses of civil liberty that do occur. My optimism about the present, if optimism is the appropriate word, is founded on a pessimistic estimate of the past rather than on any conviction that we have achieved Nirvana. We still have a long way to go, and it will take continued struggle by thousands of dedicated individuals to keep the standard of freedom moving forward. Yet, there is no need to travel under the illusion that we are moving downhill from a mystical, unfettered past; on the contrary, it seems to me demonstrable that we are moving up the road from the lynching and the tar-pot toward the aspiration of impartial justice and the rule of law.

We are accustomed, when we consider our civil liberty, to extoll the "grass-roots" freedom of the early American scene—the New England town meeting, the spontaneous democracy of the frontier. We bewail the fact that the growth of the industrial state and the increasing bureaucratization of life have created an impersonal civilization in which individualism and liberty wither. Too often we forget that the other side of the direct democ-

Reprinted by permission of the author and the publisher from "We've Never Had More Freedom," *The New Republic*, 134 (January 23, January 30, February 6, 1956).

racy of the town meeting was the direct democracy of the lynching. That brilliant political sociologist Alexis de Tocqueville noted this ambivalence in his penetrating treatment of "The Unlimited Power of the Majority and its Consequences" in *Democracy in America*. Indeed, if one accepts majority rule as the touchstone of democracy, he must accept the lynching as a democratic institution, for in it we find the sovereignty in its starkest form.

Yet, until quite recently, democracy in the United States on the basic level of political decisions was rule of numbers pure and simple. True, this rule of numbers was frequently disguised by the forms of due process of law— "Give him a fair trial and hang him!" as the California gold-field slogan put it—but, unlike the situation in economic matters where the courts threw roadblocks in the way of direct democracy, there was little to protect the unpopular citizen from the wrath of this enraged neighbors. If worst came to worst and attempts were made to enforce individual rights on behalf of the non-conformist, a jury drawn from the vicinity could generally be counted upon (as in the recent Till Case) to redress the balance in favor of community sentiment.

What has confused historians looking back at the intellectual and social history of the United States is the fact that great diversity of opinion indubitably existed in the nation. From this they have drawn the erroneous conclusion that there was toleration of divergent opinions among the populace at large. It is my contention that the diversity of views was a consequence not of tolerance and mutual respect, but of the existence of many communities within the society each with its own rigid canons of orthodoxy.

In other words, if a man looked hard enough, he could probably find a community within the United States that shared his own peculiar views, and joining it, he could help impose his eccentricities on all within reach. The United States was the happy hunting ground of what David Riesman has acutely termed "vested heresies." There was no monolithic centralized state to fulfill the European model of authoritarianism, but there was decentralized authoritarianism aplenty. Of libertarianism, the respect for views considered fundamentally "wrong," there was little: the Populists, for example, were as ready to suppress economic orthodoxy as the economically orthodox were to expunge Populism.

Space does not permit extensive documentation of this hypothesis, but several examples can be quickly mentioned. First and foremost were the settlers of the Massachusetts Bay Colony who came to this country from Britain not to escape persecution, but to establish the religious absolutism that the laws of England would not permit. Massachusetts Bay, the "Zion in the Wilderness," was the archetype for hundreds of subsequent religious communities that have been established on the twin principles of freedom for Truth, and suppression for Error. The internal authoritarianism of such groups as the Mormons, Amish, Mennonites, and Brethren—at least in the Nineteenth Century—is clear.

Some confusion is created by the fact that our forefathers certainly seem more tolerant than we are. In part that may be because they did not necessarily share our convictions as to what was important. Thus from Jefferson's broad tolerance in religious matters is deduced a full belief in freedom of opinion. It would seem more accurate to say that Jefferson considered religion unimportant and was therefore willing to permit any nonsense to be spoken from a pulpit. However, in an area which Jefferson did consider important, he was prepared to excommunicate ideas. . . .

*   *   *   *

Sincere obeisance has always been paid to the principles of freedom of speech, press, assembly, and opinion by the great majority of Americans. But few generations have looked with kindness upon those who challenged the established order. There have always been incisive differences of viewpoint as to what constituted speech and opinion, and what constituted subversive action. The general outcome of this conflict, which was seldom publicly articulated, was that each community established certain key symbols to which it demanded unqualified allegiance of both idea and action. Outside of this myth-sector, broad differences of opinion were taken for granted. In the Old South, for example, there were few limitations on freedom of speech or press providing the individual concerned accepted the validity of slavery, but the non-conformist was shown no mercy. It is often forgotten that the first Jew (Benjamin) and the second Catholic (Mallory) to hold Cabinet rank in this country took their seats around the table with Jefferson Davis in 1861!

Freedom of opinion in general has thus been recognized and honored, but woe unto the non-conformist who laid profane hands on the Ark of the Covenant, who rejected a key myth, for by his action he has transmuted his offense from permissible difference of opinion to forbidden conspiracy against the *lares* and *penates* of the community. The house gods may vary from community to community, as they often did in the era before the economic consolidation of the nation and the communications revolution, but the reaction was the same: tar and feathers, the knout, the club, the noose—the latter sometimes reinforced by the ritual of trial by jury. The Non-Partisan League organizer in Minnesota, the Wobbly in Colorado, the abolitionist in Georgia, the Socialist in Oklahoma, the Catholic in Know-Nothing territory, and other crusaders for now forgotten enthusiasms, all felt the scourge of the great god numbers. Indeed, a close reading of American social history leaves one with the ineradicable conviction that tar and feathers was standard armament for "grass-roots democracy."

*   *   *   *

In recent years however there has been a distinct let-up in the force of direct democracy in the United States, and with it an easing of pressure against non-conformity. The Negro, the trade union organizer, the radical, even the Communist, have rights today that were non-existent, or at best fragmentary, 30 years ago.

It is my contention that two major developments are responsible. The first is the increasing power and jurisdiction of the national government over national life which has taken place as a concomitant, if not as a consequence, of the increasing industrialization and urbanization of the nation. The second is the rise of civil liberty elites, leadership groups, in American society that have initiated unceasing legal and educational campaigns on behalf of the rights of non-conformists. Let us examine these two propositions in some detail.

The national government was insulated against "direct democracy"—and by design. The Framers of the Constitution were superbly successful experimenters, but they sought to bar mob rule. The instrument of government they created was contrived above all to exorcise passion from political decision-making, to make impossible the sudden seizure of power by any faction, however well motivated. . . .

But an even more important factor is the social and economic consolidation that underlies this increase in national power. Here the outstanding characteristic is urbanization and the impersonalization of life that accompanies life in the metropolis and its suburbs. The growth of the city saw the disintegration of the rural system of social control, centered usually on that highly efficient intelligence service, the rural church. In the city it is quite possible to live differently, and believe differently, from one's neighbors without their even knowing, much less caring, about the deviation. While associations may be formed on a neighborhood basis, more frequently there are functional alignments: one's friends are the people one works with, who may be scattered all over town.

Moreover, except for the impersonal organ of the police, there are in the city no ready-made instruments of social control, of "direct democracy." Although such organizations as the American Legion may bid for the role with great vigor, they can seldom make a dent in the great wall of indifference. In sum, non-conformity, a psychological manifestation of strong individualism, is paradoxically sheltered by a blanket of urban anonymity.

*   *   *   *

And yet if civil liberty has gained from this process of urbanization and nationalization of political decision-making the gain has been accidental, a mere by-product of impersonal historical developments. In contrast the second factor in my analysis, the growth of civil liberty elites, involves human action and volition. Outstanding in this category of opinion-leaders have been the lawyers, closely followed by ministers, teachers, editors, and business men. Perhaps most important of all have been the professors of law, for as the law has become more and more an educated profession—as distinct from the old system of informal "reading" in a lawyer's office—that rigorous emphasis on procedural regularity and due process which is the mark of the expert teacher has permeated the consciousness of generations of students. Moreover, law today is the access-way to careers in labor, business, and politics even more than was the case a century ago, so business elites, labor elites, and political elites have been influenced by this climate of opinion.

More important perhaps has been the infiltration of national government decision-making groups by the legal elite. The great legal migration to Washington that took place in the 30's as the consequence of the mushroom-like growth of the national administration resulted in thousands of key jobs being held by firm advocates of due process of law and civil rights. The full impact of this legal colonization on the civil rights climate of the national government can only be imagined; in practice it meant that the thousands of basic, mundane decisions in which human rights were involved were suffused with a new direction. In addition, to throw in a really intangible factor, the ablest law school graduates become clerks to members of the judiciary, with all the potential influence that this anonymous function can imply. As de Tocqueville saw the legal profession of his day as a real check on the excesses of local democracy, so today we can see the lawyers as a force for regularized—even pettifogged—procedures of national governmental operation and for the maintenance of the myth of impartial justice, a myth never fully fleshed, but nonetheless vital as a goal for collective aspirations.

But the improvement of the civil liberties climate has also been due to the passionate efforts of crusading individuals and groups. It is almost true to say that the American Civil Liberties Union invented civil rights, for before this organization came on the scene after World War I, there was little articulated interest in or concern for the problem except among the oppressed. Much the ACLU did directly, but above all, it supplied a formula—a public relations "package"—a body of civil rights doctrine, around which could be mobilized the teachers, trade unionists, ministers, editors, and others who had previously lived in atomistic impotence. . . . For every dues-paying member, there were probably a hundred non-members, frequently in key opinion-forming positions in their communities, who followed the Union's leadership, rallied to its campaigns, and passed on its position to their opinion-constituents.

In this article, I have suggested that the concept of civil liberties as we think of it today is a modern development on the American scene. Roughly prior to World War I, an American's civil rights were a coefficient of his sub-culture. If he remained among his co-believers, his rights were secure (and he was secure in his right to enforce his opinions on non-believers in his bailiwick), while if he travelled among heathens, he expressed himself at his peril. In practice, the great bulk of Americans had substantial freedom because they lived and died among their co-opinionists in a context where unquestioned and unquestioning allegiance was rendered to the vital myths of the group.

Some may question [my thesis] on the ground that it rests on the analysis of extreme cases, of radically deviant opinions, and is therefore unrepresentative. But in a discussion of civil liberties, it is the extreme situations which determine the theoretical framework; the fact that Democrats respect the rights of Republicans is not analytically meaningful, for neither group challenges the vital myths of the other—indeed, they share the same body of myths with minor variations. The touchstone of an authentic civil libertarian is his attitude toward one who denigrates the house gods. Unless one is willing to defend the rights of the person whose views (and this is a discussion of views, not overt acts) are not ranked as "opinion," but as subversion or sacrilege, he can not in justice claim to defend civil liberty.

*   *   *   *

[In] an earlier period one could often speak accurately of a reign of terror, whereas today, in view of the changes in American life . . . the terrorists are usually equipped with a papier-mâché guillotine.

Authentic reigns of terror were launched in the Nineteenth Century to say nothing of such earlier campaigns as those conducted by God's Massachusetts agents against the Quakers in the colonial period. The dominant white, rural, Protestant sub-culture was constantly at war with other sub-cultures who rejected their key social symbols. Take, for instance, the nativist movement which in the 1840's and 50's spawned a powerful political wing in the Know-Nothings, with a platform of virulent anti-Catholic sentiments. The nativists did not simply propagandize for their viewpoint; they organized murderous and destructive riots in the patronage system, local federal officials are always potential candidates for state office, so state office-holders must never permit them to get a unique hold on the public attention. This is true even when the same party controls both the state and national government, for then factional battles in primaries have to be reckoned with; it is more true when different parties control these two governments. Needless to add, once this institutional competition gets under way, there is no effective check on how extreme it will become except the danger of committing the mortal sin of American politics—boring the sovereign people.

Another factor to be considered is that the national government is far more responsive to the views of civil liberty elites than are state and local governments. This is not necessarily due to superior enlightenment (although the high percentage of "enlightened" lawyers in key jobs in Washington discussed [earlier] fits into the picture here); superior vulnerability is probably a better explanation. When the *New York Times* thunders editorially against the Veterans Administration for depriving legless veteran James Kutcher of his disability pension, the VA quakes, but all the admonitory *Times* pronouncements in the world will hardly disturb the Board of Selectmen of East Siwash. There is *one* national government; there are thousands of local governments. Although it may seem that I am here contradicting my earlier assertion that the national government is more insulated from extremism than other governments, in fact the two propositions are supplementary rather than opposed. The various segments of the national government are highly vulnerable to pressure, the administration being the most poorly insulated, but it is virtually impossible for the same pressure complex to dominate *all* segments—the President, the Congress, and the courts.

*   *   *   *

While today most of the sting has gone from direct democracy, and nothing of equal coercive impact has developed on the national scene to replace it, the character of persecution has also changed. Typically the deviant in contemporary America faces restrictions of a bureaucratic nature: he is denied security clearance, he is discharged without honor from the army, and so on. It is surely no consolation to the employee discharged from government in a Kafkaesque proceeding to hear that in 1919 he might have been beaten to death with a tire-chain. And yet, compared with the segment of American society that lived in rightless limbo half a century ago, the segment that is today maltreated is minute, and this segment has a good chance of receiving at least the elements of due process of law.

But if the present position of the non-conformist has improved, his future situation is not necessarily so cheerful. As was suggested earlier, the decline of local democracy has ameliorated the condition of the individual deviant, but it has also contributed to an increasing concentration of power in the central government. It is now conceivable that we could have a nationwide reign of terror, whereas in the Nineteenth Century this was literally impossible. While no prophet of gloom, and certainly no advocate of such an anachronism as states' rights, I think we should notice carefully one instance of what the national government can do: the "unconstitutional" imprisonment in concentration camps of the West Coast American-Japanese in World War II. (I put unconstitutional in quotes because the Supreme Court, Justice Black speaking, found the Constitution flexible enough to permit this incarceration.) This was a case in which the fragmentation of power which normally operates in the national government went into hibernation, and President Roosevelt, the Congress *without dissent*, and the courts put the Nisei away for possessing not enemy beliefs, but enemy chromosomes.

A similar potential can be seen in the security program. During the Civil War, Northern "security risks" could flee to honor in the South, and *vice versa*, but today a man found to be a risk in New York is barred from broad categories of employment throughout the nation. He can no longer find security in a sympathetic sub-culture. The great power for good of the national government has as an inevitable concomitant a great power for evil. From my point of view there are no inexorable forces at work moving the United States toward authoritarianism, but the liberal community must realize that the instruments of national power it so casually bestowed upon the national government in the period 1935-52 are capable of employment against its interests. "The sword cares not who wields it, nor whose blood it sheds." . . .

*   *   *   *

The literature about individual violations of rights is abundant, so I shall not attempt an instance by instance, area by area, study. What I plan to do is investigate two major tendencies in American public policy. First, the enlargement of the political sector; and, second, the withering of decency. However, before I begin the discussion of these trends, it is essential that I define what I mean by democracy, for this definition is fundamental to my subsequent analysis.

Democratic government is by far the most difficult system to implement and operate yet conceived. The supreme danger that confronts it is a perpetual tendency to drift in the direction of majoritarianism. But majority rule is not democracy; to identify the two is to confuse the instrument with the premise. Once one identifies the two, he divorces himself from the democratic tradition and enters another which either overtly or covertly asserts that power is its own justification. The essence of this approach to democracy is that the fists of the majority, like Frederick the Great's cannon, are inscribed *ultima ratio regnum*—the ultimate justification of the state.

To the democrat, power is not self-legitimatizing. On the contrary, power is only legitimate to the extent that it forwards certain ethical, philosophical or religious ends. The basic purpose of power is to make possible a maximum development of human potentialities, and this purpose is in turn founded upon the unverifiable assumption that men are capable of rising to a level of unselfish dedication to each other and to the common weal.

Moreover, the democrat is denied the comforting crutch of certainty. While he holds his convictions *on the level of action* firmly enough to die for them on occasion, *on the level of thought* he is constantly engaged in questioning, in searching for better answers. It is his fate to be constantly battling for what he knows to be at best a half-truth, to be making a full action commitment on the basis of incomplete evidence.

To achieve working answers to everyday problems, the democrat accepts majority decisions as binding on the actions of the community. However, no decision is ever final. In the event that new evidence appears, a new trial is in order, and it is the dynamic function of the non-conformist to urge new trials, to submit new evidence, to demand a public hearing for a different view. Thus in a healthy democracy the majority and the non-conformist depend upon each other, and each supplies a vital component to the whole. Stability is provided by the majority, while vitality flows from the non-conformist. Consequently, the democrat protects the rights of the non-conformist not merely as an act of decency, but more significantly as an imperative for himself and the whole society.

This is the idea, and if, as I have suggested, we in the United States have tarnished it somewhat, even tarnished it has a grandeur which no elitist theory can approach. It is toward this great dream of power as the ethical instrument of a self-governing community—not as the whim of a prince, a priest or a proletariat, nor the passions of a majority—that I believe American public policy must be directed.

A major threat to the achievement of this goal seems to me to stem from the enlargement of the political sector. It is characteristic of totalitarian states that no sector of national life can exist free from political control. . . .

. . . [Faced] with worldwide assault from Communism, free societies have been forced to review their own definition of "political." For example, it is patent that 19th Century cliches about freedom of organization cannot suffice to deal with a political party that is also a foreign intelligence service and a potential rebel army. Similarly, insurance companies, sport clubs, trade unions, children's camps, have turned up which defy the classic definition of these organizations by having political rather than private objectives.

Faced with this strange and frightening phenomenon, the American people have moved in two directions to counteract the dangers they fear: first, they have rushed to set up a security program, or programs, based more on principles of vengeance than security; and, second, they have injected political criteria into areas where these principles have no meaning.

In short, they have tended to defend themselves by imitating the tactics of the enemy, by enlarging the political sector.

*   *   *   *

The second direction in which we have moved is toward applying political criteria in areas where they are senseless, if not pernicious. Many examples of this sort can be found on the American scene: harmonica players are denied a hall because of alleged subversive connections, boxers are required to take loyalty oaths before putting on the gloves, unemployed workers are refused compensation because of ties with Communist unions, etc. Most actions of this sort are merely silly and—as I suggested [earlier] —there is certainly no reign of terror loose in the nation, but silly or not, their cumulative effect is dangerous.

Consequently we should make all possible efforts to limit the political sector. In dealing, for example, with Communist public school teachers, I feel the key level of examination is not that of Party membership, but that of teaching. It is my personal conviction that Communists make bad teachers because of the closed quality of their minds, to say nothing of their penchant for illegitimate extra-curricular activities such as organizing secret student cells, but this proposition is a matter to be tested and adjudicated in individual instances.

The second broad tendency which seems to me to threaten our liberties is what I have called the withering of decency. The assault against Communism has in the United States begun to resemble a campaign against rabid foxes—in word, if not in deed—and many seem to have forgotten a basic truth that can only be overlooked at great peril to an individual and a national soul: that Communists are human beings.

It has always been characteristic of public hysteria, reigns of terror, purges and the like that the enemy is dehumanized; he becomes a *thing*. . . .

*   *   *   *

We all know from personal experience how easy it is to be carried away by frenzy and join the haters—the human capacity to hate is proof of a sort for the doctrine of Original Sin—and we all have regretted our dalliance. It is probably to prevent our hasty judgments from haunting us forever that we have built elaborate procedural labyrinths into our law, and it is to prevent such frenzied aberrations from poisoning the future that we have built delay into our political institutions. As the Massachusetts *Body of Liberties* (1641) succinctly put the matter: "Our duty and desire is to do nothing suddainlie which fundamentally concerne us."

However, we cannot expect our institutions alone to preserve our spiritual chastity; on the contrary, these institutions can in the long haul be no stronger than the morality that supports them. This is why it is so important that our political leaders *be* leaders, be willing to stick their necks out in the cause of decency. . . .

*   *   *   *

I have attempted an over-all appraisal of the state of American liberties as of 1956. Perhaps because I do not share the conviction of many American historians that the history of the United States has been the unfolding of Anglo-Saxon virtues and the assimilation to them of benighted Irish, Jews, Poles or Asians, I take a somewhat more jaundiced view in these articles of the American past than is customary. As a descendant of immigrants who were *not* greeted by Grover Whalen, but by signs reading "No Irish Need Apply," I may have an unduly prejudiced view of inter-group relations in the 19th Century. But whatever biases I may have, I submit that the evidence is clear: in the United States today, ethnic, political, religious non-conformists have more leeway, have a better life-expectancy, than was ever before the case. As the United States has emerged from the radical internal transformations that accompanied the industrial revolution, we seem to have achieved a new maturity, a willingness to live and let live, and a growing acceptance of legal procedures. As I have suggested in this final [section], great dangers confront us and those who cherish liberty must fight a many-fronted war if we are to maintain and enlarge our heritage. But in these fights we can draw some comfort from looking back at the great distance we have travelled and from the knowledge that while the American standard may be tattered, we have achieved a level of individual freedom that hundreds of millions of human beings can only conceive of as a remote, impossible aspiration.

ROBERT H. JACKSON

The Supreme Court as a Guardian of Liberty

That the Supreme Court, in some instances, can interpose judicial authority between political forces and those whose liberty they would over-

Reprinted by permission of the publishers from Robert H. Jackson, *The Supreme Court in the American System of Government*, pp. 24-25, 61, 75-77, 79-82, Cambridge, Mass.: Harvard University Press, Copyright, 1955, by William Eldred Jackson and G. Bowdoin Craighill, Jr., Executors. Footnotes have been omitted. Editors' title.

ride is a great distinction from those governments abroad which have been subverted by dictatorship. But I have tried to point out that while our judiciary is an effective instrument for applying to the case of an individual the just laws enacted by representatives of a freedom-respecting society, it has grave jurisdictional, procedural, and political shortcomings. These counsel against leaving the protection of liberty wholly to the judiciary, while heedlessly allowing the elected branches of the Government to be constituted without regard to their members' attitudes toward liberty.

Let us take the factor of delay. Since the Court may pronounce a judgment of unconstitutionality only in deciding a case or controversy, obviously it cannot take the initiative in checking what the Justices may know to be constitutional violations. It has no self-starting capacity and must await the action of some litigant so aggrieved as to have a justiciable case. Also, its pronouncement must await the decision in the lower courts. Often it is years after a statute is put on the books and begins to take effect before a decision on a constitutional question can be heard by the Supreme Court. The Smith Act of 1940 was held constitutional for the first time in 1951, and the Alien Registration Act, also of 1940, was passed on in 1952. The run of constitutional litigation, like that of all litigations, is slow and costly.

Such delays often mean that the damage is done before the remedy for invasion of civil liberties is available. For example: In 1951 the Court cast serious doubt upon the legality of the Attorney General's list of subversive organizations promulgated in 1947. But the list had long been widely circulated and accepted, and despite the Court's views it has never ceased to be used in the press, in the executive department, by and before congressional committees, and even in courts to prejudice individuals in their liberty, position, and good name.

Then, too, many of the most vital acts of government cannot be challenged at all by the case and controversy route, because the questions are political or involve the spending power, foreign affairs, or the war power. The Supreme Court is a tribunal of limited jurisdiction, narrow processes, and small capacity for handling mass litigation; it has no force to coerce obedience, and is subject to being stripped of jurisdiction or smothered with additional Justices any time such a disposition exists and is supported strongly enough by public opinion. I think the Court can never quite escape consciousness of its own infirmities, a psychology which may explain its apparent yielding to expediency, especially during war time.

* * * *

The political function which the Supreme Court, more or less effectively, may be called upon to perform comes to this. In a society in which rapid changes tend to upset all equilibrium, the Court, without exceeding its own limited powers, must strive to maintain the great system of balances upon which our free government is based. Whether these balances and checks are essential to liberty elsewhere in the world is beside the point; they are indispensable to the society we know. Chief of these balances are: first, between the Executive and Congress; second, between the central goverment and the states; third, between state and state; fourth, between authority, be it state or national, and the liberty of the citizen, or between the rule of the majority and the rights of the individual.

*   *   *   *

Perhaps the most delicate, difficult and shifting of all balances which the Court is expected to maintain is that between liberty and authority. It is not so easy as some people believe to determine what serves liberty best by way of restriction of authority. For example, the removal of the Japanese from the West Coast during the War, which seemed to me plainly unconstitutional as applied to citizens, was rationalized as a service to ultimate liberty. And I suppose no one would be more likely than Abraham Lincoln to win recognition by common vote as the greatest servant of freedom; yet President Lincoln, at the outset of his administration, suspended the writ of habeas corpus and resorted to wholesale arrest without warrant, detention without trial, and imprisonment without judicial conviction. Private mail was opened, and Cabinet officers simply sent telegrams ordering persons to be arrested and held without communication or counsel. The power was given to generals of various of the northern states to suppress newspapers and suspend the writ. President Lincoln, in his famous letter to Erastus Corning and others, defended his conduct, saying all that ever could be said and what always will be said in favor of such policies in time of emergency. Those policies were sharply but unavailingly condemned in May of 1861 by the aged Chief Justice Taney, and he has said all that can be said on the other side. Had Mr. Lincoln scrupulously observed the Taney policy, I do not know whether we would have had any liberty, and had the Chief Justice adopted Mr. Lincoln's philosophy as the philosophy of the law, I again do not know whether we would have had any liberty.

Lord Acton has said that liberty is a term of two hundred definitions. About all I am sure of is that it is something never established for the future, but something which each age must provide for itself. I think we are given the rough outlines of a free society by our Bill of Rights. Liberty is not the mere absence of restraint, it is not a spontaneous product of majority rule, it is not achieved merely by lifting underprivileged classes to power, nor is it the inevitable by-product of technological expansion. It is achieved only by a rule of law.

But we must bear in mind that in the protection of individual or minority rights, we are often impinging on the principle of majority rule. Judicial opinions rarely face this dilemma. Let us take, for example, a community engaged largely in steel work, many of whose inhabitants are employed on night shifts and get their rest by day. Acting through regularly chosen representatives, the municipality duly enacts a regulation that precludes doorbell ringing in the distribution of literature or goods. A religious faction insists upon ringing doorbells to summon the occupant to the door to receive religious tracts that attack his religion and seek to convert him to the faith of the caller. If the Court holds that the right of free speech includes the right to enter upon private property and summon the owner to the door, it necessarily holds that a majority of a community are without the right to protect their hours of rest against such religiously inspired aggression.

In case after case in which so-called civil rights are involved, the question simmers down to one of the extent to which majority rule will be set aside. This issue has been debated, but it has by no means been settled, and views shift as the occasion for judicial intervention shifts from case to case. About all we need to note, unless we were to go into a lengthy discussion of the particular cases of application of the power, is that the power of the Court to protect individual or minority rights has on the other side of the coin the power to restrain the majority. Some profound political philosophers, among them Mr. Jefferson, doubted the advisability of such intervention. Mr. Jefferson asked where else we may "find the origin of *just* powers, if not in the majority of the society? Will it be in the minority? Or in an individual of that minority?" Perhaps we should say that it is only to be found in the law, in rationally and dispassionately devised rules which limit the majority's control over the individual and the minority. But even with the best draftsmanship possible such rules cannot but leave many questions for interpretation.

*   *   *   *

. . . Judicial power to nullify a law duly passed by the representative process is a restriction upon the power of the majority to govern the country. Unrestricted majority rule leaves the individual in the minority unprotected. This is the dilemma and you have to take your choice. The Constitution-makers made their choice in favor of a limited majority rule.

*   *   *   *

If an organized society wants the kind of justice that an independent, professional judicial establishment is qualified to administer, our judiciary is certainly a most effective instrument for applying law and justice to individual cases and for cultivating public attitudes which rely upon law and seek justice. But I know of no modern instance in which any judiciary has saved a whole people from the great currents of intolerance, passion, usurpation, and tyranny which have threatened liberty and free institutions. The Dred Scott decision did not settle the question of the power to end slavery, and I very much doubt that had Mr. Justice McLean not dissented in that case it would have done any more to avoid war. No court can support a reactionary regime and no court can innovate or implement a new one. I doubt that any court, whatever its powers, could have saved Louis XVI or Marie Antoinette. None could have avoided the French Revolution, none could have stopped its excesses, and none could have prevented its culmination in the dictatorship of Napoleon. In Germany a courageous court refused to convict those whom the Nazi government sought to make the scapegoats for the Reichstag fire, clandestinely set by the Nazis themselves, and other courts decreed both the Nazi and the Communist parties to be illegal under German law. Those judgments fell on deaf ears and became dead letters because the political forces at the time were against them.

It is not idle speculation to inquire which comes first, either in time or importance, an independent and enlightened judiciary or a free and tolerant society. Must we first maintain a system of free political government to assure a free judiciary, or can we rely on an aggressive, activist judiciary to guarantee free government? While each undoubtedly is a support for the other, and the two are frequently found together, it is my belief that the attitude of a society and of its organized political forces, rather than its legal machinery, is the controlling force in the character of free institutions.

I am a fairly consistent reader of British newspapers. I have been repeatedly impressed with the speed and certainty with which the slightest invasion of British individual freedom or minority rights by officials of the government is picked up in Parliament, not merely by the opposition but by the party in power, and made the subject of persistent questioning, criticism, and sometimes rebuke. There is no waiting on the theory that the judges will take care of it. In this country, on the contrary, we rarely have a political issue made of any kind of invasion of civil liberty. On the contrary, district attorneys who have been rebuked by the courts are frequently promoted by the public. The attitude seems to be, leave it to the judges. Years after the event takes place, the judges make their pronouncement, often in the form of letting some admittedly guilty person go, and that ends the matter. In Great Britain, to observe civil liberties is good

politics and to transgress the rights of the individual or the minority is bad
politics. In the United States, I cannot say that this is so. Whether the political
conscience is relieved because the responsibility here is made largely a
legal one, I cannot say, but of this I am sure: any court which undertakes
by its legal processes to enforce civil liberties needs the support of an enlightened and vigorous public opinion which will be intelligent and discriminating as to what cases really are civil liberties cases and what questions
really are involved in those cases. I do not think the American public is
enlightened on this subject.

*   *   *   *

HERBERT McCLOSKY

Consensus and Ideology in American Politics*

The belief that consensus is a prerequisite of democracy has, since de
Tocqueville, so often been taken for granted that it is refreshing to find the
notion now being challenged. Prothro and Grigg,[1] for example, have
questioned whether agreement on "fundamentals" actually exists among
the electorate, and have furnished data which indicate that it may not.
Dahl,[2] reviewing his study of community decision-makers, has inferred that
political stability does not depend upon widespread belief in the superiority

---

*This is a revised version of a paper initially prepared for delivery at the Annual
Meeting of the American Political Science Association, Washington D. C., September 1962.
The research on which it is based has been processed and analyzed through the Survey Research Center, University of California, Berkeley. Major support for the research was
made available by the Social Science Research Council; supplementary support was given
by the Rockefeller Foundation and the Institute of Social Sciences, University of California. I am indebted to my research assistant, Beryl L. Crowe, for assistance in the preparation of the research materials. This article may be referred to as number A22 in the Survey
Research Center's publication series.
    [1]James W. Prothro and C. W. Grigg, "Fundamental Principles of Democracy: Bases
of Agreement and Disagreement," *Journal of Politics*, Vol. 22 (Spring, 1960), pp. 276-94.
    [2]Robert A. Dahl, *Who Governs?* (New Haven, 1961), ch. 28.

Reprinted by permission of the author and the publisher from "Consensus and Ideology
in American Politics," *The American Political Science Review*, 58 (June, 1964), pp. 361-
382. Footnotes have been renumbered to run in sequence, and appendixes have been
omitted.

of democratic norms and procedures, but only upon their *acceptance*. From the findings turned up by Stouffer,[3] and by Prothro and Grigg, he further conjectures that agreement on democratic norms is greater among the politically active and aware—the "political stratum" as he calls them—than among the voters in general. V. O. Key,[4] going a step further, suggests that the viability of a democracy may depend less upon popular opinion than upon the activities and values of an "aristocratic" strain whose members are set off from the mass by their political influence, their attention to public affairs, and their active role as society's policy makers. "If so, any assessment of the vitality of a democratic system should rest on an examination of the outlook, the sense of purpose, and the beliefs of this sector of society."

Writers who hold consensus to be necessary to a free society have commonly failed to define it precisely or to specify what it must include. Even Tocqueville[5] does not go deeply enough into the matter to satisfy these needs. He tells us that a society can exist and, a *fortiori*, prosper only when "the minds of all the citizens [are] rallied and held together by certain predominant ideas; . . . when a great number of men consider a great number of things from the same aspect, when they hold the same opinions upon many subjects, and when the same occurrences suggest the same thoughts and impressions to their minds"—and he follows this pronouncement with a list of general principles he believes Americans hold in common. Elsewhere, he speaks of the "customs" of the American nation (its "habits, opinions, usages, and beliefs") as "the peculiar cause which renders that people able to support a democratic government." But nowhere does he set forth explicitly the nature of the agreement upon which a democratic society presumably depends.

Later commentators have not clarified matters much. Some, like A. Lawrence Lowell,[6] have avoided Tocqueville's emphasis upon shared ideas, customs, and opinions in favor of the less demanding view that popular

[3]Samuel A. Stouffer, *Communism, Conformity, and Civil Liberties* (New York, 1955).

[4]V. O. Key, "Public Opinion and the Decay of Democracy," *Virginia Q. Rev.*, Vol. 37 (Autumn, 1961), pp. 481-94. See also David B. Truman, "The American System in Crisis," *Political Science Quarterly*, Vol. 74 (Dec., 1959), pp. 481-97. John Plamenatz, "Cultural Prerequisites to a Successfully Functioning Democracy: a Symposium," this REVIEW, Vol. 50 (March, 1956), p. 123.

[5]Alexis de Tocqueville, *Democracy in America* (ed. Phillips Bradley, New York, 1945), II, p. 8; I, pp. 392, 322. The difficulty of specifying the values which underlie democracy, and on which consensus is presumed to be required, is illustrated in the exchange between Ernest S. Griffith, John Plamenatz, and J. Roland Pennock, cited above, pp. 101-37. The problem of certifying the "fundamentals" of democratic consensus is directly discussed by Pennock, pp. 132-3. See also Peter Bachrach, "Elite Consensus and Democracy," *Journal of Politics*, Vol. 24 (August, 1962), pp. 449-52.

[6]A. L. Lowell, *Public Opinion and Popular Government* (New York, 1926), p. 9.

government requires agreement mainly "in regard to the legitimate character of the ruling authority and its right to decide the questions that arise." Consensus, in this view, becomes merely a synonym for legitimacy. Others speak of consensus as a sense of solidarity or social cohesion arising from a common ethos or heritage, which unites men into a community.[7] Political scientists have most frequently employed the term to designate a state of agreement about the "fundamental values" or "rules of the game" considered essential for constitutional government. Rarely, however, have writers on consensus attempted to state what the fundamentals must include, how extensive the agreement must be, and *who* must agree. Is agreement required among all men or only among certain of them? Among the entire electorate or only those who actively participate in public affairs? Is the same type of consensus essential for all democracies at all times, or is a firmer and more sweeping consensus needed for periods of crisis than for periods of calm, for newer, developing democracies than for older stable ones?

While certain of these questions are beyond the scope of this paper (no one, in any event, has done the systematic historical and comparative research needed to answer them satisfactorily), something might be learned about the relation of ideological consensus to democracy by investigating the subject in at least one major democracy, the United States. In the present paper I wish to explore further some of the questions raised by the writers I have cited and to present research findings on several hypotheses relating to those questions.

I. HYPOTHESES AND DEFINITIONS

We expected the data to furnish support for the following hypotheses, among others:

—That the American electorate is often divided on "fundamental" democratic values and procedural "rules of the game" and that its understanding of politics and of political ideas is in any event too rudimentary at present to speak of ideological "consensus" among its members.

—That, as Prothro and Grigg report for their samples, the electorate exhibits greater support for general, abstract statements of democratic belief than for their specific applications.

—That the constituent ideas of American democratic ideology are principally held by the more "articulate" segments of the population, including

---

[7]*Cf.*, for example, Louis Wirth, *Community Life and Social Policy* (Chicago, 1956), pp. 201-3, 381-2. For a critique of "consensus theory" and the several definitions of consensus see Irving L. Horowitz, "Consensus, Conflict, and Cooperation: a Sociological Inventory," *Social Forces*, Vol. 41 (Dec., 1962), pp. 177-188.

the political influentials; and that people in these ranks will exhibit a more meaningful and far reaching consensus on democratic and constitutional values than will the general population.

—That consensus is far from perfect even among the articulate classes, and will be evidenced on political questions more than on economic ones, on procedural rights more than on public policies, and on freedom more than equality.

—That whatever increases the level of political articulateness—education, S.E.S., urban residence, intellectuality, political activity, etc.—strengthens consensus and support for American political ideology and institutions.

Whether a word like ideology can properly be employed in the American context depends, in part, on which of its many connotations one chooses to emphasize. Agreement on the meaning of the term is far from universal, but a tendency can be discerned among contemporary writers to regard ideologies as *systems* of belief that are elaborate, integrated, and coherent, that justify the exercise of power, explain and judge historical events, identify political right and wrong, set forth the interconnections (causal and moral) between politics and other spheres of activity, and furnish guides for action.[8] While liberal democracy does not fulfill perfectly the terms of this definition, it comes close enough, in my opinion, to be considered an ideology.[9] The elements of liberal democratic thought are not nearly so vague as they are sometimes made out to be, and their coalescence into a single body of belief is by no means fortuitous. American democratic "ideology" possesses an elaborately defined theory, a body of interrelated assumptions, axioms, and principles, and a set of ideals that serve as guides for action. Its tenets, postulates, sentiments, and values inspired the great revolutions of the seventeenth and eighteenth centuries, and have been repeatedly and explicitly set forth in fundamental documents, such as the Constitution, the Declaration, and the Federalist Papers. They have been restated with remarkable unanimity in the messages of Presidents, in political speeches, in the pronouncements of judges and constitutional commentators, and in the writings of political theorists, historians, and publicists.

[8] *Cf.* Daniel Bell, *The End of Ideology* (Glencoe, 1960), pp. 369-75; Edward Shils, "Ideology and Civility: on the Politics of the Intellectual," *Sewanee Review*, Vol. 66 (Summer, 1958), pp. 450-1; Louis Wirth, *op. cit.*, pp. 202-3.

[9] A persuasive case for considering liberal democracy as an ideology is made by Bernard Williams, "Democracy and Ideology," *Political Science Quarterly*, Vol. 32 (October-December, 1961), pp. 374-84. The nature of ideology in America and some of the other questions addressed in the present paper are discussed by Robert G. McCloskey, "The American Ideology," in Marian D. Irish (ed.), *Continuing Crisis in American Politics* (Englewood Cliffs, N. J., 1963), pp. 10-25.

They are so familiar that we are likely to see them not as a coherent union of ideas and principles embodying a well-defined political tendency, but as a miscellany of slogans and noble sentiments to be trotted out on ceremonial occasions.

Although scholars or Supreme Court justices might argue over fine points of interpretation, they would uniformly recognize as elements of American democratic ideology such concepts as consent, accountability, limited or constitutional government, representation, majority rule, minority rights, the principle of political opposition, freedom of thought, speech, press, and assembly, equality of opportunity, religious toleration, equality before the law, the rights of juridical defense, and individual self-determination over a broad range of personal affairs. How widely such elements of American liberal democracy are approved, by whom and with what measure of understanding, is another question—indeed, it is the central question to be addressed in this paper. But that they form an integrated body of ideas which has become part of the American inheritance seems scarcely open to debate.[10]

The term consensus will be employed in this paper to designate a state of agreement concerning the aforementioned values. It has principally to do with shared beliefs and not with feelings of solidarity, the willingness to live together, to obey the laws, or to accept the existing government as legitimate. Nor does it refer to an abstract or universal state of mind, but to a measurable state of concurrence around values that can be specified. Consensus exists in degree and can be expressed in quantitative form. No one, of course, can say how close one must come to unanimity before consensus is achieved, for the cutting point, as with any continuous variable, is arbitrary. Still, the term in ordinary usage has been reserved for fairly substantial measures of correspondence, and we shall take as a minimal requirement for consensus a level of agreement reaching 75 per cent. This figure, while also arbitrary, recommends itself by being realistically modest (falling as it does midway between a bare majority and unanimity), and by having been designated in this country and elsewhere as the extraordinary majority required for certain constitutional purposes.

---

[10]See Gunnar Myrdal, *An American Dilemma: The Negro Problem and American Democracy* (New York, 1944), ch. 1. For a comprehensive review of the American value system and evidence concerning its stability over time, see Clyde Kluckhohn, "Have There Been Discernible Shifts in American Values during the Past Generation?" in E. E. Morison (ed.), *The American Style: Essays in Value and Performance* (New York, 1958), pp. 145-217. Kluckhohn concludes (p. 152) that despite some changes, the American value system has been "remarkably stable" since the 18th century and remains "highly influential in the life of the United States."

Since I shall in subsequent pages frequently (and interchangeably) employ such terms as the "articulate minority," the "political class," the "political elite," the "political influentials," and the "political stratum," I should also clarify what they are intended to signify. I mean them to refer to those people who occupy themselves with public affairs to an unusual degree, such as government officials, elected office holders, active party members, publicists, officers of voluntary associations, and opinion leaders. The terms do not apply to any definable social class in the usual sense, nor to a particular status group or profession. Although the people they designate can be distinguished from other citizens by their activity and concerns, they are in no sense a community, they do not act as a body, and they do not necessarily possess identical or even harmonious interests. "Articulates" or "influentials" can be found scattered throughout the society, at all income levels, in all classes, occupations, ethnic groups, and communities, although some segments of the population will doubtless yield a higher proportion of them than others. I scarcely need to add that the line between the "articulates" and the rest of the population cannot always be sharply drawn, for the qualities that distinguish them vary in form and degree and no single criterion of classification will satisfy every contingency.

The data for the present inquiry have been taken from a national study of political actives and supporters carried out in 1957-58. I have in a previous paper described the procedures of that study in some detail,[11] and will not trouble to repeat that description here. Perhaps it will suffice for present purposes merely to note the following: national surveys were carried out on two separate samples, the first a sample of over 3,000 political "actives" or "leaders" drawn from the delegates and alternates who had attended the Democratic and Republican conventions of 1956; the second a representative national sample of approximately 1,500 adults in the general population drawn by the American Institute of Public Opinion (Gallup Poll). Gallup interviewers also delivered and introduced the questionnaire to all respondents, discussed its contents with them, and furnished both oral and written instructions for its self-administration and completion. . . .

The party actives may be considered an especially pure sample of the "political stratum," for every person in the sample has marked himself off from the average citizen by his greater political involvement. Although the general population sample may be regarded as a sample of "inarticulates," to be compared with the sample of leaders, there are within it, of course,

---

[11]Herbert McClosky, Paul J. Hoffmann, and Rosemary O'Hara, "Issue Conflict and Consensus Among Party Leaders and Followers," this REVIEW, Vol. 44 (June, 1960), pp. 406-27.

many persons who by virtue of education, profession, organizational activities, etc. can be classified as "articulates." We shall for certain purposes consider them in this light in order to provide further tests for our hypotheses.

Both samples received the same questionnaire—a lengthy instrument containing questions on personal background, political experience, values, attitudes, opinions, political and economic orientation, party outlooks, and personality characteristics. Many of the questions were direct inquiries in the standard form, but most were single sentence "items" with which the respondent was compelled to express his agreement or disagreement. While each of these items can stand alone and be regarded in its own right as an indicator of a person's opinions or attitudes, each of them is simultaneously an integral element of one of the 47 "scales" that was expressly fashioned to afford a more refined and reliable assessment of the attitude and personality predispositions of every respondent. Each of the scales (averaging approximately nine items) has been independently validated either by empirical validation procedures employing appropriate criterion groups, or by a modified Guttman reproducibility procedure (supplemented, in some instances, by a "face validity" procedure utilizing item ratings by experts).

Data on the *scale* scores are presented in Table IV and are to be distinguished from the "percentage agree" scores for *individual items* presented in the remaining tables.

II. FINDINGS

"Rules of the game" and democratic values. Although the so-called "rules of the game" are often separated from other democratic values, the distinction is to some extent arbitrary. One might, for example, reasonably regard as "rules of the game" many of the norms governing free speech, press, social and political equality, political toleration, and the enforcement of justice. For convenience, nevertheless, we shall treat separately those responses that stand out from the general body of democratic attitudes by their particular emphasis upon fair play, respect for legal procedures, and consideration for the rights of others. A sample of items expressing these values is presented in Table I.

The responses to these items show plainly that while a majority of the electorate support the "rules of the game," approval of such values is significantly greater and more uniform among the influentials. The latter have achieved consensus (as we have defined it) on eight of the twelve items and near consensus on three of the remaining four items. The electorate, by contrast, does not meet the criterion for consensus on a single item.

TABLE I. POLITICAL INFLUENTIALS VS. THE ELECTORATE: RESPONSE TO ITEMS EXPRESSING "RULES OF THE GAME"*

Items	Political Influentials (N = 3020)	General Electorate (N = 1484)
	% Agree	
There are times when it almost seems better for the people to take the law into their own hands rather than wait for the machinery of government to act.	13.3	26.9
The majority has the right to abolish minorities if it wants to.	6.8	28.4
We might as well make up our minds that in order to make the world better a lot of innocent people will have to suffer.	27.2	41.6
If congressional committees stuck strictly to the rules and gave every witness his rights, they would never succeed in exposing the many dangerous subversives they have turned up.	24.7	47.4
I don't mind a politician's methods if he manages to get the right things done.	25.6	42.4
Almost any unfairness or brutality may have to be justified when some great purpose is being carried out.	13.3	32.8
Politicians have to cut a few corners if they are going to get anywhere.	29.4	43.2
People ought to be allowed to vote even if they can't do so intelligently.	65.6	47.6
To bring about great changes for the benefit of mankind often requires cruelty and even ruthlessness.	19.4	31.3
Very few politicians have clean records, so why get excited about the mudslinging that sometimes goes on?	14.8	38.1
It is all right to get around the law if you don't actually break it.	21.2	30.2
The true American way of life is disappearing so fast that we may have to use force to save it.	12.8	34.6

*Since respondents were forced to make a choice on each item, the number of omitted or "don't know" responses was, on the average, fewer than one percent, and thus has little influence on the direction or magnitude of the results reported in this and subsequent tables.

Although the *scales* (as distinguished from individual *items*) cannot appropriately be used to measure *consensus*, comparison of the scores on those scales which most nearly embody the "rules of the game" furnishes additional evidence that the political class responds to such norms more favorably than does the electorate. The proportion scoring high[12] on a scale of "faith in direct action" (a scale measuring the inclination to take the law into one's own hands) is 26.1 per cent for the active political minority and 42.5 per cent for the general population. On a scale assessing the willingness to flout the rules of political integrity, the proportions scoring high are 12.2 per cent and 30.6 per cent respectively. On "totalitarianism," a scale measuring the readiness to subordinate the rights of others to the pursuit of some collective political purpose, only 9.7 per cent of the political actives score high compared with 33.8 per cent of the general population.

These and other results which could be cited support the claim advanced by earlier investigators like Prothro and Grigg, and Hyman and Sheatsley,[13] that a large proportion of the electorate has failed to grasp certain of the underlying ideas and principles on which the American political system rests. Endorsement of these ideas is not unanimous among the political elite either, but is in every instance greater than that exhibited by the masses.

The picture changes somewhat when we turn from "rules of the game" to items which in a broad, general way express belief in freedom of speech and opinion. As can be seen from Table II, support for these values is remarkably high for both samples. Both groups, in fact, respond so overwhelmingly to abstract statements about freedom that one is tempted to conclude that for these values, at least, a far-reaching consensus has been achieved.[14] These results become even more striking when we consider that the items in the table are not mere cliches but statements which in some instances closely paraphrase the arguments developed in Mill's essay, *On Liberty*. We cannot, therefore, dismiss them as mere responses to familiar, abstract sentiments which commit the respondent to nothing in particular.

Still, as can readily be discerned from the items in Table III, previous investigators have been partially correct, at least, in observing that the principles of freedom and democracy are less widely and enthusiastically

---

[12]"High" refers to a score made by the upper third of the popular distribution on the scale in question. For example, in the case of the "political indulgence" scale approximately one-third (actually 30.6%) received scores of five or above. Hence, anyone making a score of five or above on this scale is considered to have scored high on "political indulgence." "Low" refers to scores made by the lower third of the distribution.

[13]Prothro and Grigg, *loc. cit.*; Herbert Hyman and Paul B. Sheatsley, "The Current Status of American Public Opinion," in Daniel Katz *et al.* (eds.), *Public Opinion and Propaganda* (New York, 1954), pp. 33-48.

[14]*Cf.* Robert Lane's report on his "Eastport" sample, in *Political Ideology* (New York, 1962), pp. 461-2.

TABLE II. POLITICAL INFLUENTIALS VS. THE ELECTORATE: RESPONSES TO
ITEMS EXPRESSING SUPPORT FOR GENERAL STATEMENTS OF
FREE SPEECH AND OPINION

Items	Political Influentials (N = 3020)	General Electorate (N = 1484)
	% Agree	
People who hate our way of life should still have a chance to talk and be heard.	86.9	81.8
No matter what a person's political beliefs are, he is entitled to the same legal rights and protections as anyone else.	96.4	94.3
I believe in free speech for all no matter what their views might be.	89.4	88.9
Nobody has a right to tell another person what he should and should not read.	81.4	80.7
You can't really be sure whether an opinion is true or not unless people are free to argue against it.	94.9	90.8
Unless there is freedom for many points of view to be presented, there is little chance that the truth can ever be known.	90.6	85.2
I would not trust any person or group to decide what opinions can be freely expressed and what must be silenced.	79.1	64.6
Freedom of conscience should mean freedom to be an atheist as well as freedom to worship in the church of one's choice.	87.8	77.0

favored when they are confronted in their specific, or applied, forms.[15] As Dahl remarks, it is a "common tendency of mankind . . . to qualify universals in application while leaving them intact in rhetoric."[16] This observation, of course, also holds for the political articulates, but to a lesser degree. Not only do they exhibit stronger support for democratic values than does the electorate, but they are also more consistent in applying the general principle to the specific instance.[17] The average citizen has greater diffi-

[15]See Hyman and Sheatsley, op. cit., pp. 40-2; Prothro and Grigg, op. cit.
[16]Robert A. Dahl, loc. cit. For data on the failure of some people to perceive the relevance of democratic principles for concrete situations see G. D. Wiebe, "The Army-McCarthy Hearings and the Public Conscience," Public Opinion Quarterly, Vol. 22 (Winter 1958-59), pp. 490-502.
[17]See also Stouffer, op. cit., ch. 2.

TABLE III. POLITICAL INFLUENTIALS VS. THE ELECTORATE: RESPONSE TO
ITEMS EXPRESSING SUPPORT FOR SPECIFIC APPLICATIONS OF
FREE SPEECH AND PROCEDURAL RIGHTS

Items	Political Influentials (N = 3020)	General Electorate (N = 1484)
	% Agree	
Freedom does not give anyone the right to teach foreign ideas in our schools.	45.5	56.7
A man oughtn't to be allowed to speak if he doesn't know what he's talking about.	17.3	36.7
A book that contains wrong political views cannot be a good book and does not deserve to be published.	17.9	50.3
When the country is in great danger we may have to force people to testify against themselves even if it violates their rights.	28.5	36.3
No matter what crime a person is accused of, he should never be convicted unless he has been given the right to face and question his accusers.	90.1	88.1
If a person is convicted of a crime by illegal evidence, he should be set free and the evidence thrown out of court.	79.6	66.1
If someone is suspected of treason or other serious crimes, he shouldn't be entitled to be let out on bail.	33.3	68.9
Any person who hides behind the laws when he is questioned about his activities doesn't deserve much consideration.	55.9	75.7
In dealing with dangerous enemies like the Communists, we can't afford to depend on the courts, the laws and their slow and unreliable methods.	7.4	25.5

culty appreciating the importance of certain procedural or juridical rights, especially when he believes the country's internal security is at stake.

Findings which underscore and amplify these conclusions are yielded by a comparison of the scale scores. The data presented in Table IV confirm that the influentials not only register higher scores on all the pro-democratic scales (faith in freedom, faith in democracy, procedural rights, tolerance), but are more likely to reject anti-democratic sentiments as well. Although they are themselves an elite of a sort, they display greater faith in the capacity of the mass of men to govern themselves, they believe more firmly in political equality, and they more often disdain the "extreme"

TABLE IV. POLITICAL INFLUENTIALS VS. THE ELECTORATE: PERCENTAGES SCORING HIGH AND LOW ON DEMOCRATIC AND ANTI-DEMOCRATIC ATTITUDE SCALES*

Scale	Political Influentials (N = 3020)	General Electorate (N = 1484)	Scale	Political Influentials (N = 3020)	General Electorate (N = 1484)
	(%s down)			(%s down)	
Faith in Democracy			Elitism		
% High*	40.1	18.5	% High	22.8	38.7
% Low	14.4	29.7	% Low	41.0	22.4
Procedural Rights			Totalitarianism		
% High	58.1	24.1	% High	9.7	33.8
% Low	12.3	31.3	% Low	60.1	28.4
Tolerance			Right Wing		
% High	61.3	43.1	% High	17.5	33.1
% Low	16.4	33.2	% Low	45.3	28.9
Faith in Freedom			Left Wing		
% High	63.0	48.4	% High	6.7	27.8
% Low	17.1	28.4	% Low	68.7	39.3
Ethnocentrism			California F-Scale		
% High	27.5	36.5	% High	14.7	33.5
% Low	46.9	36.3	% Low	48.0	23.5

*For explanation of % High and Low see footnote 12. The middle group has been omitted from this table. Differences between the influentials and the electorate on all the scales in this table are, by Kolmogorov-Smirnov and chi-square tests, statistically significant at or beyond the .01 percent level of significance.

beliefs embodied in the Right Wing, Left Wing, totalitarian, elitist, and authoritarian scales. Their repudiation of anti-democratic attitudes is by no means unanimous either, but their responses are more uniformly democratic than are those expressed by the electorate.

Equalitarian values. If Americans concur most strongly about liberty in the abstract, they disagree most strongly about equality. Examples of equalitarian values are presented in Table V. Both the political stratum and the public divide sharply on these values, a finding which holds for political, as well as for social and economic equality. Both are torn not only on the empirical question of whether men are *in fact* equal but also on the normative issue of whether they should be *regarded* as equal. Neither comes close to achieving consensus on such questions as the ability of the people to rule themselves, to know their best interests in the long run, to understand the issues, or to pick their own leaders wisely. Support for these equalitarian features of "popular" democracy, however, is greater among the elite than among the masses.

The reverse is true for the values of economic equality. Among the political stratum, indeed, the weight of opinion is against equality—a result strongly though not exclusively influenced by the pronounced economic conservatism of the Republican leaders in the sample. Support for economic equality is only slightly greater among the electorate. The pattern, furthermore, is extremely spotty, with some policies strongly favored and others as strongly rejected. Thus approval is widespread for public policies (such as social security) that are designed to overcome gross inequalities, but is equally strong for certain features of economic life that promote inequality, such as private enterprise, economic competition, and unlimited pursuit of profit.[18] On social and ethnic equality, both samples are deeply split.

In short, both the public and its leaders are uncertain and ambivalent about equality. The reason, I suspect, lies partly in the fact that the egalitarian aspects of democratic theory have been less adequately thought through than other aspects, and partly in the complications connected with the concept itself. One such complication arises from the historical association of democracy with capitalism, a commingling of egalitarian and inegalitarian elements that has never been (and perhaps never can be) perfectly reconciled. Another complication lies in the diffuse and variegated

---

[18]These inferences are drawn not only from the few items presented in Table V, but from data previously reported by H. McClosky, P. J. Hoffmann, and R. O'Hara, *op. cit.*, p. 413; and from the responses to dozens of items in the present study that express attitudes and opinions toward the private enterprise system, taxes, private property, profits, socialism, etc. On the whole, little enthusiasm is registered among either the elite or the masses for a drastic revision of the economy or a major redistribution of the wealth.

TABLE V. POLITICAL INFLUENTIALS VS. THE ELECTORATE: RESPONSES TO ITEMS EXPRESSING BELIEF IN EQUALITY

Items	Political Influentials (N=3020)	General Electorate (N=1484)
	% Agree	
Political Equality		
The main trouble with democracy is that most people don't really know what's best for them.	40.8	58.0
Few people really know what is in their own best interest in the long run.	42.6	61.1
"Issues" and "arguments" are beyond the understanding of most voters.	37.5	62.3
Most people don't have enough sense to pick their own leaders wisely.	28.0	47.8
It will always be necessary to have a few strong, able people actually running everything.	42.5	56.2
Social and Ethnic Equality		
We have to teach children that all men are created equal but almost everyone knows that some are better than others.	54.7	58.3
Just as is true of fine race horses, some breeds of people are just naturally better than others.	46.0	46.3
Regardless of what some people say, there are certain races in the world that just won't mix with Americans.	37.2	50.4
When it comes to the things that count most, all races are certainly not equal.	45.3	49.0
The trouble with letting certain minority groups into a nice neighborhood is that they gradually give it their own atmosphere.	49.8	57.7
Economic Equality		
Labor does not get its fair share of what it produces.	20.8	44.8
Every person should have a good house, even if the government has to build it for him.	14.9	28.2
I think the government should give a person work if he can't find another job.	23.5	47.3
The government ought to make sure that everyone has a good standard of living.	34.4	
There will always be poverty, so people might as well get used to the idea.	40.4	59.4

nature of the concept, a result of its application to at least four separate domains: political (*e.g.*, universal suffrage), legal (*e.g.*, equality before the law), economic (*e.g.*, equal distribution of property or opportunity), and moral (*e.g.*, every man's right to be treated as an end and not as a means). Accompanying these are the confusions which result from the common failure to distinguish equality as a *fact* from equality as a *norm*. ("All men are created equal," for example, is taken by some as an empirical statement, by others as a normative one.) Still other complications arise from the differential rewards and opportunities inevitable in any complex society, from the differences in the initial endowment individuals bring into the world, and from the symbolism and fears that so often attend the division of men into ethnic compartments. All these confound the effort to develop a satisfactory theory of democratic equality, and further serve to frustrate the realization of consensus around egalitarian values.

*   *   *   *

Coherence and consistency of attitudes. So far we have explored the question of ideology and consensus mainly from the point of view of agreement on particular values. This, however, is a minimum criterion. Before one can say that a class or group or nation has achieved consensus around an ideology, one should be satisfied that they understand its values in a coherent and correct way. It is a poor consensus in which generalities and slogans are merely echoed with little appreciation of their significance. It seemed appropriate, therefore, to compare the influentials and voters concerning their information and understanding, the relation of their opinions to their party preferences, and the consistency of their views on public affairs.

To begin with, the influentials are more likely than the electorate to have opinions on public questions. For example, 28 per cent of the public are unable (though a few may only be *unwilling*) to classify themselves as liberal, middle of the road, or conservative; while only 1.1 per cent of the articulates fail to make this classification. Forty-eight per cent of the voters, compared to 15 per cent of the actives, do not know in which direction they would turn if the parties were reorganized to reflect ideological differences more clearly. Forty-five per cent of the electorate but only 10.2 per cent of the influentials cannot name any issue that divides the parties. By ratios of approximately three or four to one the electorate is less likely to know which level of government they are mainly interested in, whether they prefer their party to control Congress or the presidency, whether they believe in party discipline and of what type, whether control of the parties should rest at the national or local levels, and so on.

As these and other of our findings suggest, active political involvement heightens one's sense of intellectual order and commitment. This inference is further supported by the data on partisanship. One example may suffice to illustrate the point: when the articulates and the electorate are ranged on a scale assessing their orientation toward 14 current liberal-conservative issues, the political actives tend to bunch up at the extreme ends of the distribution (the Democratic actives at the "liberal" end, the Republican actives at the "conservative" end), while the rank and file supporters of both parties fall more frequently into the middle or conflicted category. The political influentials, in short, display issue orientations that are more partisan and more consistent with their party preferences.

Essentially the same effect is achieved among the general population by increases in education, economic status, or other factors that raise the level of articulateness. College-educated Democrats and Republicans, for example, disagree more sharply on issues than grade school Democrats and Republicans do. Partisan differences are greater between the informed than between the uninformed, between the upper-class supporters of the two parties than between the lower-class supporters, between the "intellectuals" in both parties than between those who rank low on "intellectuality."

Increases in political knowledge or involvement, hence, cause men not so much to waver as to choose sides and to identify more unswervingly with one political tendency or its opposite. Inarticulateness and distance from the sources of political decision increase intellectual uncertainty and evoke political responses that are random rather than systematic. We are thus led by the findings to a pair of conclusions that may at first appear contradictory but that in reality are not: the political class is more united than the electorate on fundamental political values but divides more sharply by party affiliation on the issues which separate the two parties. [19] Both facts—the greater consensus in the one instance and the sharper cleavage in the other—testify to its superior ideological sophistication.

Not only are the articulates more partisan, but they are also more consistent in their views. Their responses to a wide range of political stimuli are to a greater extent intellectually patterned and informed. They are, for example, better able to name reference groups that correspond with their party affiliation and doctrinal orientation: approximately twice as many active Democrats as ordinary Democratic voters name liberal, Democratically oriented organizations as groups they would seek advice from (e.g., trade unions, Farmers Union, etc.); and by equally large or larger ratios they *reject* as sources of advice such conservative or Republican oriented organizations as the NAM, the Farm Bureau, and the Chamber of Commerce. With some variations, similar findings emerge when Republican leaders are compared with Republican voters. If we also take into account

---

[19] See also V.O. Key, *Public Opinion and American Democracy* (New York, 1961), pp. 51-2.

the liberal or conservative issue-orientation of the respondents, the differential ability of party leaders and followers to recognize reference groups becomes even more pronounced. Clearly, the political stratum has a better idea than the public has of who its ideological friends and enemies are. The capacity to recognize sympathetic or hostile reference groups is not highly developed among the public at large.

Compared with the influentials, ordinary voters also show up poorly in their ability to classify themselves politically. For example, among Democratic actives who score as "liberals" in their views on issues, 82.2 per cent correctly describe themselves as "liberals," while 16.7 per cent call themselves "middle of the roaders" and only 1.1 per cent misclassify themselves as "conservatives." Among Democratic *voters* who actually hold liberal views, only 37.0 per cent are able to label themselves correctly. The disparity is less striking between Republican leaders and followers but bears out no less conclusively that most voters lack the sophistication to recognize and label accurately the tendency of their own political views. Even their choice of party is frequently discrepant with their actual ideological views: as we reported in a previous paper,[20] not only do Democratic and Republican voters hold fairly similar opinions on issues, but the latter's opinions are closer to the opinions of Democratic leaders than to those of their own leaders.

Data we have gathered on patterns of support for individual political leaders yield similar conclusions: the articulates are far better able than the electorate to select leaders whose political philosophy they share. Often, in fact, voters simultaneously approve of two or more leaders who represent widely different outlooks—for example, Joseph McCarthy and Dwight D. Eisenhower. In a similar vein, a surprisingly large number of voters simultaneously score high on a Right Wing scale and a liberal issues scale, or hold other "discrepant" outlooks. Such inconsistencies are not unknown among the political actives either, but they are much less frequent. Not only does the public have less information than the political class but it does not succeed as well in sorting out and relating the information it does possess.[21]

Most of the relationships reported in the foregoing have been tested with education, occupation, and sometimes with other demographic variables controlled, but the introduction of these factors does not change the direc-

[20] McClosky, Hoffmann, and O'Hara, *op. cit.*
[21] For other findings on the state of ideological development among the electorate, see Angus Campbell, Philip E. Converse, Warren E. Miller and Donald E. Stokes, *The American Voter* (New York, 1960), chs. 8-10.

tion of the findings, although it sometimes affects the magnitude of the scores.

Comparisons of scores for the two samples have also been made with "acquiescent" response-set controlled. Acquiescence affects the results, but does not eliminate the differences reported or alter the direction or significance of the findings. . . .

III. SUMMARY AND DISCUSSION

Several observations can be offered by way of summarizing and commenting upon the data just reported:

1. American politics is widely thought to be innocent of ideology, but this opinion more appropriately describes the electorate than the active political minority. If American ideology is defined as that cluster of axioms, values and beliefs which have given form and substance to American democracy and the Constitution, the political influentials manifest by comparison with ordinary voters a more developed sense of ideology and a firmer grasp of its essentials. This is evidenced in their stronger approval of democratic ideas, their greater tolerance and regard for proper procedures and citizen rights, their superior understanding and acceptance of the "rules of the game," and their more affirmative attitudes toward the political system in general. The electorate displays a substantial measure of unity chiefly in its support of freedom in the abstract; on most other features of democratic belief and practice it is sharply divided.

The political views of the influentials are relatively ordered and coherent. As liberals and conservatives, Democrats and Republicans, they take stands on issues, choose reference groups, and express preferences for leaders that are far more consistent than the attitudes and preferences exhibited by the electorate. The latter's opinions do not entirely lack order but are insufficiently integrated to meet the requirements of an ideology.[22] In contrast to the political elite, which tends to be united on basic values but divided on issues by party affiliation (both of which testify to a measure of ideological sophistication), the voters divide on many basic political values and adopt stands on issues with little reference to their party affiliation.

---

[22] For a similar conclusion on this point, see V. O. Key, *Public Opinion and American Democracy* (New York, 1961), pp. 41, 49. The second chapter of this volume contains an excellent discussion of opinion consensus among the electorate, and touches on a number of the points dealt with in this paper. Evidence on the infrequency of "ideological" thinking among the voters is presented in Campbell, Converse, Miller and Stokes, *op. cit.*, p. 249. By the criteria used the authors were able to classify only 3.5% of the voters as "ideologues" and 12% as "near-ideologues."

The evidence suggests that it is the articulate classes rather than the public who serve as the major repositories of the public conscience and as the carriers of the Creed. Responsibility for keeping the system going, hence, falls most heavily upon them.[23]

2. Why should consensus and support for democratic ideology be stronger among the political stratum than among the electorate? The answer plainly has to do with the differences in their political activity, involvement and articulateness.

Some observers complain that Americans have little interest in political ideas because they are exclusively concerned with their own personal affairs. Evidence is becoming available, however, that political apathy and ignorance are also widespread among the populations of other countries and may well be endemic in all societies larger than a city-state. It is difficult to imagine any circumstance, short of war or revolutionary crisis, in which the mass of men will evince more interest in the community's affairs than in their own concerns. This is not because they are selfish, thoughtless, or morally deficient, but because the stimuli they receive from public affairs are relatively remote and intangible. One can scarcely expect ordinary men to respond to them as intensely as they respond to the more palpable stimuli in their own everyday lives, which impinge upon them directly and in ways they can understand and do something about. The aphorism which holds man to be a political animal may be supportable on normative grounds but is scarcely defensible as a description of reality. Political apathy seems for most men the more "natural" state. Although political matters are in a sense "everyone's concern," it is just as unreasonable to hope that all men will sustain a lively interest in politics as it would be to expect everyone to become addicted to chamber music, electronics, poetry, or baseball. Since many voters lack education, opportunity, or even tangible and compelling reasons for busying themselves with political ideas, they respond to political stimuli (if they respond at all) without much reflection or consistency. Their life-styles, furthermore, tend to perpetuate this state of affairs, for they are likely to associate with people like themselves whose political opinions are no more informed or consistent than their own. As inarticulates, they are also inclined to avoid the very activities by which they might overcome their indifference and develop a more coherent point of view.

Many voters, in addition, feel remote from the centers of political decision and experience an acute sense of political futility. They know the political world only as a bewildering labyrinth of procedures and unceas-

[23]V. O. Key, "Public Opinion and the Decay of Democracy," *loc. cit.*

ing turmoil in which it is difficult to distinguish the just from the wicked, the deserving from the undeserving. The political questions about which they are asked to have opinions are complex and thorny; every solution is imperfect and exacts its price; measures that benefit some groups invariably aggrieve others. The principles which govern the political process seem vague, recondite and impossible to relate to actual events. All this obviously deters voters from developing ideologically, from acquiring insights into the subtleties of the democratic process, and from achieving consensus even on fundamental values.

Although the influentials face some of the same obstacles, they are better able to overcome them. As a group they are distinguished from the mass of the electorate by their above-average education and economic status, their greater political interest and awareness, and their more immediate access to the command posts of community decision. Many of them participate not only in politics but in other public activities as well. This affords them, among other benefits, a more sophisticated understanding of how the society is run and a more intimate association with other men and women who are alert to political ideas and values. Political concepts and abstractions, alien to the vocabulary of many voters, are for the elite familiar items of everyday discourse.

Consider also that the political stratum is, by almost every social criterion we have examined, more homogeneous than the electorate. This promotes communication among them and increases their chances of converging around a common body of attitudes.[24] As Newcomb[25] has remarked, "The actual consequences of communication, as well as the intended ones, are consensus-increasing." Among many segments of the general population, however, communication on matters of political belief either occurs not at all or is so random and cacophonous as to have little utility for the reinforcement of political values. If Louis Wirth is correct in observing that "the limits of consensus are marked by the range of effective communication,"[26] it becomes easier to understand why the active minority achieves consensus more often than the voters do.

Compared with the electorate, whose ordinary members are submerged in an ideological babble of poorly informed and discordant opinions, the members of the political minority inhabit a world in which political ideas

---

[24] For additional data on the homogeneity of social characteristics and values among American elite groups, see James N. Rosenau, "Consensus-Building in the American National Community: Hypotheses and Supporting Data," *Journal of Politics*, Vol. 24 (November, 1962), pp. 639-661.
[25] Theodore M. Newcomb, "The Study of Consensus," in R. K. Merton *et al.* (eds.), *Sociology Today* (New York, 1959), pp. 277-92.
[26] *Op. cit.*, p. 201.

are vastly more salient, intellectual consistency is more frequently demanded, attitudes are related to principles, actions are connected to beliefs, "correct" opinions are rewarded and "incorrect" opinions are punished. In addition, as participants in political roles, the actives are compelled (contrary to stereotype) to adopt opinions, to take stands on issues, and to evaluate ideas and events. As *articulates* they are unavoidably exposed to the liberal democratic values which form the main current of our political heritage. The net effect of these influences is to heighten their sensitivity to political ideas and to unite them more firmly behind the values of the American tradition. They may, as a result, be better equipped for the role they are called upon to play in a democracy than the citizens are for *their* role.

The findings furnish little comfort for those who wish to believe that a passion for freedom, tolerance, justice and other democratic values springs spontaneously from the lower depths of the society, and that the plain, homespun, uninitiated yeoman, worker and farmer are the natural hosts of democratic ideology. The mystique of the simple, unworldly, "natural" democrat has been with us since at least the rise of Christianity, and has been assiduously cultivated by Rousseau, Tolstoy, Marx, and numerous lesser writers and social reformers. Usually, the simpler the man, the lower his station in life, and the greater his objective need for equality, the more we have endowed him with a capacity for understanding democracy. We are thus inclined to give the nod to the farmer over the city man, the unlearned over the educated, the poor man over the man of wealth, the "people" over their leaders, the unsophisticated over the sophisticated. Yet every one of these intuitive expectations turns out, upon investigation, to be questionable or false. Democratic beliefs and habits are obviously not "natural" but must be learned; and they are learned more slowly by men and women whose lives are circumscribed by apathy, ignorance, provincialism and social or physical distance from the centers of intellectual activity. In the absence of knowledge and experience—as we can readily observe from the fidgety course of growth in the newly emerging nations—the presuppositions and complex obligations of democracy, the rights it grants and the self-restraints it imposes, cannot be quickly comprehended. Even in a highly developed democratic nation like the United States, millions of people continue to possess only the most rudimentary understanding of democratic ideology.

3. While the active political minority affirms the underlying values of democracy more enthusiastically than the people do, consensus among them is far from perfect, and we might well inquire why this is so.

Despite the many forces impelling influentials toward agreement on basic ideological values, counteracting forces are also at work to divide them.

Not all influentials are able to comprehend democratic ideas, to apply them to concrete contexts, or to thread their way through the complexities of modern political life. Nor is communication perfect among them either, despite their greater homogeneity. Many things divide them, not least of which are differences in education, conflicting economic and group interests, party competition, factional cleavages and personal political ambitions.

In demonstrating that the influentials are better prepared than the masses to receive and reflect upon political ideas, we run the risk of over-stating the case and of exaggerating their capacity for ideological reasoning. Some members of the political class obviously have no more intellectual concern with politics than the masses do; they are in it for "the game," for personal reasons, or for almost any reason except ideology.

Then, too, while most democratic ideas are in their most general form simple enough for almost all members of the elite to understand, they become considerably more puzzling when one sets out to explicate them, to relate them to each other, or to apply them to concrete cases. Only a few of the complications need to be cited to illustrate the point; several of the ideas, such as equality, are either inherently vague or mean different things in different contexts. Some democratic (or constitutional) values turn out in certain situations to be incompatible with other democratic values (e.g., the majority's right to make and enforce the laws at times clashes with individual rights, such as the right to stand on one's religious conscience). As this suggests, democratic ideas and rules of the game are ordinarily encountered not in pure form or in isolation but in substantive contexts that are bound to influence the ways in which we react to them.[27] Many businessmen who consider the regulation of business as an unconstitutional invasion of freedom look upon the regulation of trade unions as a justifiable curb upon lawlessness; trade unionists, needless to say, lean to the opposite view.

Consider, too, what a heavy burden we place upon a man's normal impulses by asking him to submit unconditionally to democratic values and procedures. Compliance with democratic rules of the game often demands an extraordinary measure of forbearance and self-discipline, a willingness to place constraints upon the use of our collective power and to suffer opinions, actions, and groups we regard as repugnant. The need for such self-restraint is for many people intrinsically difficult to comprehend and still more difficult to honor. Small wonder, then, that consensus around democratic values is imperfect, even among the political influentials who are well situated to appreciate their importance.

---

[27] For a discussion of this point, see Peter Bachrach, "Elite Consensus and Democracy," *Journal of Politics*, Vol. 24 (August, 1962), pp. 439-52.

4. We turn now to the most crucial question suggested by the research findings, namely, what significance must be assigned to the fact that democratic ideology and consensus are poorly developed among the electorate and only imperfectly realized among the political influentials?

Our first and most obvious conclusion is that contrary to the familiar claim, a democratic society can survive despite widespread popular misunderstanding and disagreement about basic democratic and constitutional values. The American political system survives and even flourishes under precisely these conditions, and so, we have reason to think, do other viable democracies. What makes this possible is a more conjectural question, though several observations can be offered by way of answering it.

Democratic viability is, to begin with, saved by the fact that those who are most confused about democratic ideas are also likely to be politically apathetic and without significant influence. Their role in the nation's decision process is so small that their "misguided" opinions or non-opinions have little practical consequence for stability. If they contribute little to the vitality of the system, neither are they likely to do much harm. Lipset[28] has pointed out that "apathy undermines consensus," but to this one may add the corollary observation that apathy also furnishes its own partial corrective by keeping the doubters from acting upon their differences. In the United States, at least, their disagreements are *passive* rather than *active*, more the result of political ignorance and indifference than of intellectual conviction or conscious identification with an "alien" political tendency. Most seem not even to be aware of their deviations from the established values. This suggests that there may, after all, be some utility in achieving agreement on large, abstract political sentiments, for it may satisfy men that they share common values when in fact they do not. Not only can this keep conflicts from erupting, but it also permits men who disagree to continue to communicate and thus perhaps to convert their pseudo-consensus on democratic values into a genuine consensus.

I do not mean to suggest, of course, that a nation runs no risks when a large number of its citizens fail to grasp the essential principles on which its constitution is founded. Among Americans, however, the principal danger is not that they will reject democratic ideals in favor of some hostile ideology, but that they will fail to understand the very institutions they believe themselves to be defending and may end up undermining rather than safeguarding them. Our research on "McCarthyism," for example, strongly suggests that popular support for the Senator represented less a

---

[28]Seymour Martin Lipset, *Political Man* (New York, 1960), p. 27. Chapter I of this volume provides a stimulating and valuable discussion of the relation of conflict and consensus to the operation of democracy.

conscious rejection of American democratic ideals than a misguided effort to defend them. We found few McCarthy supporters who genuinely shared the attitudes and values associated with his name.[29]

Whether consensus among the influentials is either a necessary or sufficient condition for democratic stability is not really known. Since the influentials act, make public decisions, are more organized, and take political ideas more seriously, agreement among them on constitutional values is widely thought to be essential for viability. At present, however, we do not have enough information (or at least we do not have it in appropriately organized form) to state with satisfactory precision what the actual relation is between elite consensus and democratic stability. Some democratic governments, e.g., Weimar Germany, crumbled when faced with ideological conflicts among their political classes; others, e.g., post-war Italy and France, have until now managed to weather pronounced ideological cleavages. The opinion has long prevailed that consensus is needed to achieve stability, but the converse may be the more correct formulation, i.e., that so long as conditions remain stable, consensus is not required; it becomes essential only when social conditions are disorganized. Consensus may strengthen democratic viability, but its absence in an otherwise stable society need not be fatal or even particularly damaging.

It should also be kept in mind that the existence of intellectual disagreements—even among the influentials—does not necessarily mean that they will be expressed or acted upon. In the United States (and doubtless elsewhere as well), numerous influences are at work to prevent ideological cleavages from assuming an important role in the nation's political life. This is certainly the tendency of such political institutions as federalism, checks and balances, separation of powers, bicameralism, the congressional committee system, the judiciary's practice of accommodating one discrepant law to another, and a system of elections more often fought around local issues and personalities than around urgent national questions. Our two-party system also functions to disguise or soften the genuine disagreements that distinguish active Democrats from active Republicans. The American social system contributes to the same end, for it is a model of the pluralistic society, a profuse collection of diverse groups, interests and organizations spread over a vast and variegated territory. Consensus in such a society becomes difficult to achieve, but by the same token its absence can also more easily be survived. The complexities of a highly pluralistic social and political order tend to diminish the impact of intellectual differences, to compel

---

[29] Herbert McClosky, "McCarthyism: The Myth and the Reality," unpublished paper delivered at the American Psychological Association, New York, September, 1957. See also Wiebe, loc. cit.

compromise, and to discourage the holders of divergent views from crystal-
lizing into intransigent doctrinal camps. Thus it seems, paradoxically
enough, that the need for consensus on democratic rules of the game increases as the conflict among competing political tendencies becomes sharper, and declines as their differences become more diffused. Italy by this
reasoning, has greater need of consensus than the United States, but has
less chance of achieving it. A democratic nation may wisely prefer the American model to the Italian, though what is ideally desired, as Lipset observes,[30] is a balance between cleavage and consensus—the one to give
reality and force to the principle of opposition, the other to furnish the secure framework within which that principle might be made continuously effective. Countervailing power within a structure of shared political values
would, by this logic, be the optimal condition for the maintenance of a democratic society.

5. But even giving this much weight to consensus may exaggerate the
role which intellectual factors play in the attainment of democratic stability.
The temptation to assign a controlling influence to the place of ideas in the
operation of democracy is very great. Partly this results from our tendency
to confuse the textbook model of democracy with the reality and to assume
the high order of rationality in the system that the model presupposes (*e.g.*,
an alert citizenry aware of its rights and duties, cognizant of the basic rules,
exercising. consent, enjoying perfect information and choosing governers
after carefully weighing their qualifications, deliberating over the issues,
etc.). It is not my purpose to ridicule this model but to underscore the observation that it can easily mislead us into placing more weight than the
facts warrant upon cognitive elements—upon ideas, values, rational choice,
consensus, etc.—as the cementing forces of a democratic society. An *ad
hominem* consideration may also be relevant here: as intellectuals and students of politics, we are disposed both by training and sensibility to take
political ideas seriously and to assign central importance to them in the
operation of the state. We are therefore prone to forget that most people
take them less seriously than we do, that they pay little attention to issues,
rarely worry about the consistency of their opinions, and spend little or no
time thinking about the values, presuppositions, and implications which
distinguish one political orientation from another. If the viability of a
democracy were to depend upon the satisfaction of these intellectual activities, the prognosis would be very grim indeed.

Research from many different lines of inquiry confirms unequivocally
that the role heretofore assigned to ideas and to intellectual processes in
general has been greatly exaggerated and cannot adequately explain many

[30] Lipset, *op. cit.*, pp. 21-2.

political phenomena which, on *a priori* grounds, we have expected them to explain. Witness, for example, the research on the non-rational factors which govern the voting decision, on the effects—or rather the non-effects —of ideology on the loyalty and fighting effectiveness of German and American soldiers, on the differences between the views of party leaders and followers, on the influence of personality on political belief, and on group determinants of perception.[31] We now have evidence that patriotism and the strength of one's attachment to a political community need not depend upon one's approval of its intellectual, cultural, or political values. Indeed our present research clearly confirms that the men and women who express "patriotism" in extreme or chauvinistic form usually have the least knowledge and understanding of American democratic ideals, institutions, and practices.

Abundant anecdotal data from the observation of dictatorial and other nations further corroborates the conclusion that men may become attached to a party, a community, or a nation by forces that have nothing to do with ideology or consensus. Many of these forces are so commonplace that we often neglect them, for they include family, friends, home, employment, property, religion, ethnic attachments, a common language, and familiar surroundings and customs. These may lack the uplifting power of some political doctrines, but their ability to bind men to a society and its government may nevertheless be great. This observation, of course, is less likely to hold for the intelligentsia than for the inarticulates, but even the political behavior of intellectuals is never governed exclusively by appeals to the mind.

The effect of ideas on democratic viability may also be diminished by the obvious reluctance of most men to press their intellectual differences to the margin and to debate questions that may tear the community apart. So long as no urgent reason arises for bringing such differences to the surface, most men will be satisfied to have them remain dormant. Although there are men and women who are exceptions to this generalization, and who cannot bear to leave basic questions unresolved, they are likely to be few, for both the principles and practices of an "open society" strongly reinforce tolerance for variety, contingency and ambiguity in matters of belief and

---

[31] *Cf.*, for example, Campbell, *et al.*, *op. cit.*; Bernard R. Berelson, Paul F. Lazarsfeld, and William N. McPhee, *Voting* (Chicago, 1954), especially ch. 14; Edward A. Shils and Morris Janowitz, "Cohesion and Disintegration in the German Wehrmacht in World War II," *Public Opinion Quarterly*, Vol. 12 (1948), pp. 280-315; Herbert McClosky, "Conservatism and Personality," this REVIEW, Vol. 52 (March, 1958), pp. 27-45; T. W. Adorno *et al.*, *The Authoritarian Personality* (New York, 1950), ch. XVII; Richard Crutchfield, "Conformity and Character," *American Psychologist*, Vol. 10 (1955), pp. 191-198.

conscience. As our data on freedom of opinion suggest, few Americans expect everyone to value the same things or to hold identical views on public questions. The tendency to ignore, tolerate, or play down differences helps to create an illusion of consensus which for many purposes can be as serviceable as the reality.[32]

6. To conclude, as we have in effect, that ideological awareness and consensus are overvalued as determinants of democratic viability is not to imply that they are of no importance. While disagreements among Americans on fundamental values have tended to be passive and, owing to apathy and the relative placidity of our politics, easily tolerated; while they do not follow party lines and are rarely insinuated into the party struggle; and while no extremist movement has yet grown large enough to challenge effectively the governing principles of the American Constitution, this happy state of affairs is not permanently guaranteed. Fundamental differences could *become* activated by political and economic crises; party differences could *develop* around fundamental constitutional questions, as they have in France and other democracies; and powerful extremist movements are too familiar a phenomenon of modern political life to take for granted their eternal absence from the American scene.

Obviously a democratic nation also pays a price for an electorate that is weakly developed ideologically. Lacking the intellectual equipment to assess complex political events accurately, the unsophisticated may give support to causes that are contrary to their own or to the national interest. In the name of freedom, democracy, and the Constitution, they may favor a McCarthy, join the John Birch Society, or agitate for the impeachment of a Supreme Court Justice who has worked unstintingly to uphold their constitutional liberties. They may also have difficulty discriminating political integrity from demagoguery, maturity and balanced judgment from fanaticism, honest causes from counterfeits. Our findings on the attitudes shown by ordinary Americans toward "extreme" political beliefs (Left Wing beliefs, Right Wing beliefs, totalitarianism, isolationism, etc.) verify that the possibilities just cited are not merely hypothetical. Those

---

[32]Robert G. McCloskey, *loc. cit.*, suggests that the American political tradition is marked by "ambivalence" toward certain of our fundamental values and that this may discourage the achievement of "consensus" in the usual sense. He believes, however, that Americans have learned to live with, and even to ignore, inconsistencies in the value system, in keeping with our "pragmatic spirit." Whether this ability is uniquely American or whether it is characteristic of all "open," democratic societies is a question well worth investigating. It could, conceivably, be a natural outgrowth of democratic ideology itself, no element of which can be conceived and enforced absolutely without infringing other elements. On this last point, see Sidney Hook, *The Paradoxes of Freedom* (Berkeley, 1962), pp. 14-62.

who have the least understanding of American politics subscribe least enthusiastically to its principles, and are most frequently "misled" into attacking constitutional values while acting (as they see it) to defend them.

There is, however, reason to believe that ideological sophistication and the general acceptance of liberal democratic values are increasing rather than declining in the United States. Extreme ideological politics of the type associated with Marxism, fascism and other doctrinaire networks of opinion may be waning, as many sociologists believe,[33] but the same observation does not hold for the influence of democratic ideas. On the contrary, democratic ideology in the United States, linked as it is with the articulate classes, gives promise of growing as the articulate class grows. Many developments in recent American life point to an increase in "articulateness": the extraordinary spread of education, rapid social mobility, urbanization, the proliferation of mass media that disseminate public information, the expansion of the middle class, the decline in the size and number of isolated rural groups, the reduction in the proportion of people with sub-marginal living standards, the incorporation of foreign and minority groups into the culture and their increasing entrance into the professions, and so on. While these developments may on the one side have the effect of reducing the tensions and conflicts on which extreme ideologies feed, they are likely on the other side to beget a more articulate population and a more numerous class of political influentials, committed to liberal democracy and aware of the rights and obligations which attend that commitment.

---

[33] Cf., Daniel Bell, *The End of Ideology* (Glencoe, 1960), pp. 369-375; S. M. Lipset, *op. cit.*, pp. 403-47; Edward Shils, *loc. cit.*

Freedom of Expression

There is substantial consensus that freedom of expression is an essential ingredient of democracy. Even opponents of a particular idea or the way it is expressed put their opposition to particular cases in which "liberty" has become "license," while maintaining that they are in fact defending freedom. In totalitarian societies, special interpretations of "freedom of expression" are wrenched out of the context of democratic philosophy so as to support the elites' suppression in the name of "freedom." Thus it is that the special importance of freedom to democracy finds testimony in the efforts of all oligarchies to silence the press or to make it a mouthpiece for the regime's version of the truth. In such cases, repression is justified as necessary for maintaining security. Note the wisdom of William Pitt's observation almost two centuries ago: "Necessity is the plea for every infringement of human freedom. It is the argument of tyrants, it is the creed of slaves."

Within democratic states, too, there are frequent and seemingly inexorable pressures to restrict freedom of expression. Ideas that deviate from accepted norms invariably cause some people feelings of discomfort and anxiety, if not wrath. Even when the idea being expressed hasn't a remote chance of popular acceptance, the temptation is often very compelling to suppress such a challenge to one's notions of the way things should be. Whether the alleged threat is to youth, religion, or the state, democratic nations know this tension between the urge to speak out and the fear of free expression.

However, as John Roche has argued in Chapter I, it has become increasingly difficult to restrict freedom of expression in this country. The Supreme Court nationalizes standards of official toleration, interest groups support dissenters' claims to free expression, greater education brings greater toleration, and a more extensive communication system transmits tolerant standards while it inhibits the intolerant. It is not accidental that television cameramen have been targets of attack by the intolerant in social conflicts concerning race or the nation's defense policies. Often the presence of the mass media has turned aside the disgruntled official or citizen about to silence a vocal dissenter.

The Supreme Court has played an especially vital role in reducing restrictions on free expression. Book, newspaper, and film censorship have been all but voided by recent decisions. The meaning of obscenity, if not clarified, has been subjected to greater discussion, which has led to a confrontation between older, more absolute concepts of the role of sex in human relations and newer, more flexible concepts. As a result of Court action the threat to newspaper editors of libel proceedings, with their insidious consequence of inhibiting expression, has become almost a thing of the past. The freedom to form groups in order to express one's interests, the defense of a professor from certain kinds of state interference in his associations and belief, the protection of a street speaker against heavy-handed police action, the freedom to picket and demonstrate peaceably—these and more have found protection in the Supreme Court's expanding definition of the freedom of expression.[1]

But if the Court has moved to widen the range of permissible expression, it has not eliminated the problems of defining remaining restrictions. One can escape these problems by adopting the "absolutist" view that the First Amendment means precisely what it says: "Congress shall make no law . . . abridging the freedom of speech, or of the press . . . ." For the absolutist, no limits are deemed desirable or necessary. In recent years, Supreme Court Justices Hugo Black and William O. Douglas have at one time or another enunciated this view. But others on the bench and the general public have refused to accept this absolutist view, believing instead that under specified circumstances some limits on expression are justifiable because other and higher values will be served thereby. Thus the Supreme Court has *not* placed under automatic protection "fighting words" (those familiar terms of Anglo-Saxon origin), obscenity, incitement to violence, all picketing and demonstrations, or malicious libel. It has felt that to permit such expression would cause other social values to suffer, such values as the maintenance of order and morality.

Both the absolutist and the balancing criteria, however, create problems. Granting permission for the expression of any viewpoint includes, by definition, the expression of the outrageous, offensive, threatening, and subverting. As Herbert McClosky shows in his article in Chapter I, Americans will not countenance this blanket permission. Moreover, as Justice Jackson explained, the Court is futile when it pushes too far.

---

[1]For a review of these developments, see Milton R. Konvitz, *Expanding Liberties: Freedom's Gains in Postwar America* (New York: Viking, 1966), Chaps. II-V.

As for the balancing test, men clearly will differ over the priority they assign the social values which are to be weighed. For example, libertarian Justices Earl Warren and Hugo Black clash on the priority that should be assigned to the right to oppose segregation by use of a sit-in: Warren emphasizes the value of such expression, while Black stresses the resultant public inconvenience and the rights of the property owners concerned. On the other hand, Warren is more concerned with the need to restrain obscene publications than is Black, who believes the potential danger of such material is less than the dangers of restricting its dissemination. Balancing, then, is no simple problem in mechanics.

But despite the difficulties the Court has experienced in balancing competing values, it continues to lower barriers against the freedom of expression. In the selections in this chapter, we will focus heavily on this trend.

We begin with Thomas I. Emerson's analysis of the uses and limits of free expression. Emerson has organized the extensive philosophical writing on the freedom's value into four major purposes. Further, he discusses the difficulties involved in constructing a theory of its limitations. His interpretations indicate the problems currently facing the nation of setting new limits.

We look next at the issue which has been the center of controversy about expression from our earliest history. The first controversies dealt with the restriction of "sacrilege" and later "sedition." In the mid-nineteenth century, obscenity became the focus of controversy, and innumerable restrictions were passed in the name of morality. In the past several decades, the Supreme Court has been wrestling (the term is not exaggerated) to define obscenity. While the Court has declined to protect obscenity under the First Amendment, it has nevertheless weakened antiobscenity laws by insisting on more permissive definitions. While some criteria of definition seem to have appeared in the past decade, the Court members have been sorely tried in the effort. At one point in the mid-1960's, Justice Potter Stewart opined: "I shall not today attempt further to define ['hard-core pornography'], and perhaps I could never succeed in intelligibly doing so. But I know it when I see it, and the motion picture involved in this case is not that." (*Jacobellis* v. *Ohio*, 1964) This statement, although hardly clarifying the subject, does illustrate the Court's confusion. The next selection, which was prepared by the staff of *The University of Chicago Law Review*, provides a recent survey of Court decisions on libel and obscenity.

The obscenity controversy reaches deep into the community, for the possibility that certain books and films will undermine moral values is, as we have said earlier, highly disturbing to many groups. Those opposing censorship are many, and their opposition is often vehement; H. L. Mencken once described censors as "blue-nosed smut-snifters." Likewise, those supporting censorship have been equally vitriolic; "corrupters of youth" is among the milder epithets they assign to the purveyors of material of which they disapprove. But many in this controversy are far from the kind of zealot characterized by these exaggerated charges.

To what extent, if any, does expression produce antisocial effects such as delinquency? Sociologists John H. Gagnon and William Simon survey the available evidence on this query, much of which seems to be negative, although little research—if any—explores the long-run cumulative effect which may operate in ways which some fear.[2] Fear of such effect upon the young moved the Supreme Court in the spring of 1968 to uphold a New York law designed to protect the young from obscene literature. This opinion and the dissent of Justice Fortas are presented here to show the nature of this controversy.[3]

If the content of expression is controversial, so recently have been the modes of expression—demonstrations and civil disobedience. By and large, contemporary Americans enjoy substantial freedom from legal sanctions to peacefully protest unjust policies and laws. But what if peaceful protest fails to convince a majority of voters or public officials of the need to change the allegedly unwise or immoral policy or law? What obligations does the protester have to society, and how do these obligations compare with his obligations to his own conscience? In short, must an individual obey or long tolerate a law he believes to be immoral? This is not an easy question, and the limits on and wisdom of civil disobedience have become increasingly important issues in the 1960's.

Those who practice civil disobedience are quick to remind us that the American Revolution was a dramatic precedent for their way of resisting laws and policies they consider oppressive. Moreover, even the most casual observer must acknowledge that civil disobedience to racial segregation in the late 1950's and 1960's has been a preeminent factor in securing and enforcing civil-rights legislation on behalf of racial minorities. Thus the question: What is the role of civil disobedience in a democratic society?

Here, as elsewhere in the field of liberty, different answers to such a question rest on different moral assumptions about what the

---

[2] A more technical discussion of this research is Robert B. Cairns, James C. N. Paul, and Julius Wishner, "Sex Censorship: The Assumptions of Anti-Obscenity Laws and the Empirical Evidence," *Minnesota Law Review* (1962), pp. 1009-1041. For a statistical statement of the volume of ostensibly obscene literature, see Charles J. Rogers, "Police Control of Obscene Literature," *Journal of Criminal Law, Criminology, and Police Science* (December, 1966), pp. 430-482.

[3] A good review of the problems of defining "variable obscenity" may be found in *Note*, "Constitutional Problems in Obscenity Legislation Protecting Children," *Georgetown Law Journal* (Summer, 1966), pp. 1379-1414.

community may legitimately do to restrain those in the minority. Whether and when civil disobedience can be justified is one of the ancient concerns of political theory, from Sophocles' *Antigone* through Thoreau's essay *On the Duty of Civil Disobedience* to Martin Luther King's *Letter from Birmingham City Jail.* Thoreau put the case for civil disobedience quite succinctly: "Under a government which imprisons any unjustly, the true place for a just man is also a prison." Others, however, argue that one cannot remedy alleged evils by disobeying the law in the name of morality while democratic methods of change remain open.

This debate has not been limited to exchanges among philosophers. The general public has consistently and, it seems, increasingly shown opposition to the practice of civil disobedience. Nor have the courts been uninvolved. From 1965 to 1967, the Supreme Court began to reject the legitimacy of specific acts of civil disobedience; in the fall of 1967, for example, the late Reverend King eventually served a minor jail sentence for disobeying a local-court injunction prohibiting demonstrations. Further, those who protested the draft and the Vietnam War by violating the law were arrested and prosecuted with little legal acknowledgement that their ethical commitment justified their acts.

The intimate union of law and morality is illustrated in the concluding selections of this chapter on freedom of expression. A legal analysis reviews current Supreme Court decisions on the use of pickets, sit-ins, parades, and the like, and decisions on their limits. Then some of the tone of the moral conflict is sensed in a series of opposing statements by five Americans on the rightness of civil disobedience.

Through the several articles in this chapter, we seek to understand the new areas into which freedom of expression is moving. While the Court may seem to be providing hard lines of definition of limits, on closer review we see it makes actually quite small moves when contenders ask for large moves. Although this may leave unanswered many critical questions, many observers feel that in such incremental tacking maneuvers, the Supreme Court best maintains its authority while exerting a cumulative influence.

The articles in this chapter illustrate well the difficulties in protecting both the rights of the individual and the moral and political stability of society. John Stuart Mill's answer to this problem was that "the sole end for which mankind are warranted, individually or collectively, in interfering with the liberty of action of any of their number, is self-protection." But, clearly, this "solution" raises as many questions as it answers, as Mill's attempt to apply this principle clearly shows.[4]

---

[4]See John Stuart Mill, *On Liberty* (1849), Chaps. I, IV, and V especially.

In short, the question of what criteria we may use to restrict the individual's freedom of expression remains unanswered, and it seems that it will always be so. How would you specify the proper line between freedom and order? Consider your answers to the following questions, and see if you can identify a common line which unifies your answers.

—Should public employees be prohibited from taking full part in partisan political activities?

—Should someone be allowed to urge in a public place the alleged delights of drugs such as LSD?

—Should the explicit depiction of sexual relations in a motion picture open to the public be permitted?

—Should a university open its recruiting facilities to a firm which makes weapons for a war when many students, feeling the war is immoral, wish to prevent recruitment?

—Should a board of trustees of a state university forbid the hiring and require the firing of any professor who urges violation of the law (such as blocking access to induction centers as a method of protesting the draft)?

—Should a state pass laws forbidding a bookseller from knowingly selling obscene material to a minor?

—Should a union of public employees, like their counterparts in private industry, be allowed to strike, even if it means, for example, that garbage goes uncollected?

THOMAS I. EMERSON

Toward a General Theory of the First Amendment

The right of the individual to freedom of expression has deep roots in our history. But the concept as we know it now is essentially a product of the development of the liberal constitutional state. It is an integral part of the great intellectual and social movement beginning with the Renaissance

From *Toward a General Theory of the First Amendment*, pp. 3-22, 24-25, by Thomas I. Emerson. © Copyright 1963, 1966 by Thomas I. Emerson. Reprinted by permission of Random House, Inc. Footnotes have been omitted.

which transformed the Western world from a feudal and authoritarian society to one whose faith rested upon the dignity, the reason and the freedom of the individual. The theory in its modern form has thus evolved over a period of more than three centuries, being applied under different circumstances and seeking to deal with different problems. It is sufficient for our purposes to restate it in its final, composite form, as it comes to us today.

The values sought by society in protecting the right to freedom of expression may be grouped into four broad categories. Maintenance of a system of free expression is necessary (1) as a method of assuring individual self-fulfillment, (2) as a means of attaining the truth, (3) as a method of securing participation by the members of the society in social, including political, decision-making, and (4) as a means of maintaining the balance between stability and change in the society. We consider these in their affirmative aspects, without regard at this time to the problems of limitation or reconciliation with other values.

INDIVIDUAL SELF-FULFILLMENT

The right to freedom of expression is justified first of all as the right of an individual purely in his capacity as an individual. It derives from the widely accepted premise of Western thought that the proper end of man is the realization of his character and potentialities as a human being. Man is distinguished from other animals principally by the qualities of his mind. He has powers to reason and to feel in ways that are unique in degree if not in kind. He has the capacity to think in abstract terms, to use language, to communicate his thoughts and emotions, to build a culture. He has powers of imagination, insight and feeling. It is through development of these powers that man finds his meaning and his place in the world.

The achievement of self-realization commences with development of the mind. But the process of conscious thought by its very nature can have no limits. An individual can neither tell where it may lead nor anticipate its end. Moreover, it is an *individual* process. Every man is influenced by his fellows, dead and living, but his mind is his own and its functioning is necessarily an individual affair.

From this it follows that every man—in the development of his own personality—has the right to form his own beliefs and opinions. And it also follows that he has the right to express these beliefs and opinions. Otherwise they are of little account. For expression is an integral part of the development of ideas, of mental exploration and of the affirmation of self. The power to realize his potentiality as a human being begins at this point and must extend at least this far if the whole nature of man is not to be thwarted.

Hence suppression of belief, opinion and expression is an affront to the dignity of man, a negation of man's essential nature. What Milton said of licensing of the press is equally true of any form of restraint over expression: it is "the greatest displeasure and indignity to a free and knowing spirit that can be put upon him."

The right to freedom of expression derives secondly from basic Western notions of the role of the individual in his capacity as a member of society. Man is a social animal, necessarily and probably willingly so. He lives in company with his fellow men; he joins with them in creating a common culture; he is subject to the necessary controls of society and particularly of the state. His right to express his beliefs and opinions in this role as a member of his community follows from two fundamental principles. One is that the purpose of society and of its more formal aspect, the state, is to promote the welfare of the individual. Society and the state are not ends in themselves; they exist to serve the individual. The second is the principle of equality, formulated as the proposition that every individual is entitled to equal opportunity to share in common decisions which affect him.

From these concepts there follows the right of the individual to access to knowledge; to shape his own views; to communicate his needs, preferences and judgments; in short, to participate in formulating the aims and achievements of his society and his state. To cut off his search for truth, or his expression of it, is thus to elevate society and the state to a despotic command and to reduce the individual to the arbitrary control of others. The individual, in short, owes an obligation to cooperate with his fellow men, but that responsibility carries with it the right to freedom in expressing himself.

Two basic implications of the theory need to be emphasized. The first is that it is not a general measure of the individual's right to freedom of expression that any particular exercise of the right may be thought to promote or retard other goals of the society. The theory asserts that freedom of expression, while not the sole or sufficient end of society, is a good in itself, or at least an essential element in a good society. The society may seek to achieve other or more inclusive ends—such as virtue, justice, equality, or the maximum realization of the potentialities of its members. These problems are not necessarily solved by accepting the rules for freedom of expression. But, as a general proposition, the society may not seek to solve them by suppressing the beliefs or opinions of individual members. To achieve these other goals it must rely upon other methods: the use of counter-expression and the regulation or control of conduct which is not expression. Hence the right to control individual expression, on the ground that it is judged to promote good or evil, justice or injustice, equality or inequality, is not, speaking generally, within the competence of the good society.

The second implication, in a sense a corollary of the first, is that the theory rests upon a fundamental distinction between belief, opinion and communication of ideas on the one hand, and different forms of conduct on the other. For shorthand purposes we refer to this distinction hereafter as one between "expression" and "action." As just observed, in order to achieve its desired goals, a society or the state is entitled to exercise control over action—whether by prohibiting or compelling it—on an entirely different and vastly more extensive basis. But expression occupies a specially protected position. In this sector of human conduct, the social right of suppression or compulsion is at its lowest point, in most respects nonexistent.

This marking off of the special area of expression is a crucial ingredient of the basic theory for several reasons. In the first place, thought and communication are the fountainhead of all expression of the individual personality. To cut off the flow at the source is to dry up the whole stream. Freedom at this point is essential to all other freedoms. Hence society must withhold its right of suppression until the stage of action is reached. Secondly, expression is normally conceived as doing less injury to other social goals than action. It generally has less immediate consequences, is less irremediable in its impact. Thirdly, the power of society and the state over the individual is so pervasive, and construction of doctrines, institutions and administrative practices to limit this power so difficult, that only by drawing such a protective line between expression and action is it possible to strike a safe balance between authority and freedom.

ATTAINMENT OF TRUTH

In the traditional theory, freedom of expression is not only an individual but also a social good. It is, to begin with, the best process for advancing knowledge and discovering truth.

Considered in this aspect, the theory starts with the premise that the soundest and most rational judgment is arrived at by considering all facts and arguments which can be put forth in behalf of or against any proposition. . . . Conversely, suppression of information, discussion, or the clash of opinion prevents one from reaching the most rational judgment, blocks the generation of new ideas, and tends to perpetuate error. This is the method of the Socratic dialogue employed on a universal scale.

The process is a continuous one. As further knowledge becomes available, as conditions change, as new insights are revealed, the judgment is open to reappraisal, improvement, or abandonment.

The theory demands that discussion must be kept open no matter how certainly true an accepted opinion may seem to be. Many of the most widely acknowledged truths have turned out to be erroneous. Many of the most significant advances in human knowledge—from Copernicus to Einstein—

have resulted from challenging hitherto unquestioned assumptions. No opinion can be immune from challenge.

The process also applies regardless of how false or pernicious the new opinion appears to be. For the unaccepted opinion may be true or partially true. And there is no way of suppressing the false without suppressing the true. Furthermore, even if the new opinion is wholly false, its presentation and open discussion serves a vital social purpose. It compels a rethinking and retesting of the accepted opinion. It results in a deeper understanding of the reasons for holding the opinion and a fuller appreciation of its meaning.

The only justification for suppressing an opinion is that those who seek to suppress it are infallible in their judgment of the truth. But no individual or group can be infallible, particularly in a constantly changing world.

It is essential to note that the theory contemplates more than a process for arriving at an individual judgment. It asserts that the process is also the best method for reading a general or social judgment. . . . Through the acquisition of new knowledge, the toleration of new ideas, the testing of opinion in open competition, the discipline of rethinking its assumptions, a society will be better able to reach common decisions that will meet the needs and aspirations of its members.

PARTICIPATION IN DECISION-MAKING

The third main function of a system of freedom of expression is to provide for participation in decision-making through a process of open discussion which is available to all members of the community. . . .

This development was partly due to acceptance of the concept that freedom of expression was a right of the individual, as discussed previously. But it was also inherent in the logic of free expression as a social good. In order for the process to operate at its best, every relevant fact must be brought out, every opinion and every insight must be available for consideration. Since facts are discovered and opinions formed only by the individual, the system demands that all persons participate. . . .

But in addition to these reasons, the right of all members of society to form their own beliefs and communicate them freely to others must be regarded as an essential principle of a democratically organized society. The growing pressures for democracy and equality reinforced the logical implications of the theory and demanded opportunity for all persons to share in making social decisions. This is, of course, especially true of political decisions. But the basic theory carried beyond the political realm. It embraced the right to participate in the building of the whole culture, and included freedom of expression in religion, literature, art, science and all areas of human learning and knowledge.

In the field of political action, as just mentioned, the theory of freedom of expression has particular significance. It is through the political process that most of the immediate decisions on the survival, welfare and progress of a society are made. It is here that the state has a special incentive to repress opposition and often wields a more effective power of suppression. Freedom of expression in the political realm is usually a necessary condition for securing freedom elsewhere. It is in the political sector, therefore, that the crucial battles over free expression are most often fought.

As the general theory makes clear, freedom of discussion in public affairs serves an important function regardless of whether the political structure of a nation is democratic or not. Every government must have some process for feeding back to it information concerning the attitudes, needs and wishes of its citizens. It must, therefore, afford some degree of freedom at least to some of its citizens, to make known their wants and desires. Indeed, in a more formal aspect—as a petition for redress of grievances—this right of communicating to the government in power was one of the earliest forms of political expression. The Magna Carta and the Bill of Rights of 1689, for instance, were promulgated in response to such petitions. In general, the greater the degree of political discussion allowed, the more responsive is the government, the closer is it brought to the will of its people, and the harder must it strive to be worthy of their support.

The crucial point, however, is not that freedom of expression is politically useful, but that it is indispensable to the operation of a democratic form of government. Once one accepts the premise of the Declaration of Independence—that governments derive "their just powers from the consent of the governed"—it follows that the governed must, in order to exercise their right of consent, have full freedom of expression both in forming individual judgments and in forming the common judgment. . . .

*   *   *   *

BALANCE BETWEEN STABILITY AND CHANGE

The traditional doctrine of freedom of expression, finally, embodies a theory of social control. The principle of open discussion is a method of achieving a more adaptable and at the same time more stable community, of maintaining the precarious balance between healthy cleavage and necessary consensus. This may not always have been true, and may not be true of many existing societies. But where men have learned how to function within the law, an open society will be the stronger and more cohesive one.

The reasons supporting this proposition can only be stated here in summary form. In the first place, suppression of discussion makes a rational judgment impossible. In effect it substitutes force for logic. Moreover, coercion of expression is likely to be ineffective. While it may prevent social change, at least for a time, it cannot eradicate thought or belief; nor can it promote loyalty or unity. As Bagehot observed, "Persecution in intellectual countries produces a superficial conformity, but also underneath an intense, incessant, implacable doubt."

Furthermore, suppression promotes inflexibility and stultification, preventing the society from adjusting to changing circumstances or developing new ideas. . . .

Again, suppression of expression conceals the real problems confronting a society and diverts public attention from the critical issues. . . . Further, suppression drives opposition underground, leaving those suppressed either apathetic or desperate. It thus saps the vitality of the society or makes resort to force more likely. . . .

The argument that the process of open discussion, far from causing society to fly apart stimulates forces that lead to greater cohesion also rests upon the concept of political legitimation. Stated in narrower and perhaps cruder terms, the position is that allowing dissidents to expound their views enables them "to let off steam." . . . It operates, in short, as a catharsis throughout the body politic.

The principle of political legitimation, however, is more broadly fundamental. It asserts that persons who have had full freedom to state their position and to persuade others to adopt it will, when the decision goes against them, be more ready to accept the common judgment. They will recognize that they have been treated fairly, in accordance with rational rules for social living. They will feel that they have done all within their power, and will understand that the only remaining alternative is to abandon the ground rules altogether through resort to force, a course of action upon which most individuals in a healthy society are unwilling to embark. In many circumstances they will retain the opportunity to try again and will hope in the end to persuade a majority to their position. Just as in a judicial proceeding where due process has been observed, they will feel that the resulting decision, even though not to their liking, is the legitimate one.

In dealing with the problem of social control, supporters of free expression likewise emphasize that the issue must be considered in the total context of forces operating to promote or diminish cohesion in a society. By and large, they theorize, a society is more likely to be subject to general inertia than to volatile change. Hence resistance to the political order is unlikely to reach the stage of disorder unless a substantial section of the population is living under seriously adverse or discriminatory conditions. Only a government which consistently fails to relieve valid grievances need fear the outbreak of violent opposition. Thus, given the inertia which so often characterizes a society, freedom of expression, far from causing upheaval, is more properly viewed as a leavening process, facilitating necessary social and political change and keeping a society from stultification and decay.

Moreover, the state retains adequate powers to promote political unity and suppress resort to force. For one thing, it shares the right to freedom of expression with its citizens. While there may be some limits on this power, the state is normally in a much better position to obtain information and in a much more authoritative position from which to communicate its official views than the ordinary citizen or group of citizens. More importantly, the state possesses the authority to restrict or compel action. The right with which we are concerned, as already noted, extends only to expression; when the stage of action is reached, the great power of the state becomes available for regulation or prohibition. And finally, the state has not only the power but also the obligation to control the conditions under which freedom of expression can function for the general welfare. This includes not only responsibility for eliminating grievances which may give rise to disorder but also a responsibility for maintaining economic and social conditions under which the ground rules of democracy can operate.

Proponents of the theory acknowledge that the process of full discussion, open to all, involves some risks to the society that practices it. At times there may be substantial delay in the working out of critical problems. There can be no ironclad guarantee that in the end a decision beneficial to society will be reached. The process, by encouraging diversity and dissent, does at times tend to loosen the common bonds that hold society together and may threaten to bring about its dissolution. The answer given is that the stakes are high and that the risks must be run. No society can expect to achieve absolute security. Change is inevitable; the only question is the rate and the method. The theory of freedom of expression offers greater possibilities for rational, orderly adjustment than a system of suppression. Moreover, they urge, as the lesson of experience, that the dangers are usually imaginary; that suppression is invoked more often to the prejudice of the general welfare than for its advancement. To this they add that the risks are the lesser evil, that the alternatives are worse, that the only security worth having is that based on freedom.

Thus the theory of freedom of expression involves more than a technique for arriving at better social judgments through democratic procedures. It comprehends a vision of society, a faith and a whole way of life. The theory grew out of an age that was awakened and invigorated by the idea of a new society in which man's mind was free, his fate determined by his own powers of reason, and his prospects of creating a rational and enlightened civilization virtually unlimited. It is put forward as a prescription for attaining a creative, progressive, exciting and intellectually robust community. It contemplates a mode of life that, through encouraging toleration, skepticism, reason and initiative, will allow man to realize his full potentialities. It spurns the alternative of a society that is tyrannical, conformist, irrational and stagnant. It is this concept of society that was embodied in the first amendment.

It is not within the scope of this book to demonstrate the soundness of the traditional theory underlying freedom of expression, or its viability under modern conditions. The writer believes that such a demonstration can be made. But the significant point here is that we as a nation are presently committed to the theory, that alternative principles have no substantial support, and that our system of freedom of expression must be based upon and designed for the realization of the fundamental propositions embodied in the traditional theory.

* * * *

In constructing and maintaining a system of freedom of expression, . . . [the] crucial issues have revolved around the question of what limitations, if any, ought to be imposed upon freedom of expression in order to reconcile that interest with other individual and social interests sought by the good society. . . . The crux of the problem is that the limitations, whatever they may be, must be applied by one group of human beings to other human beings. In order to take adequate account of this factor it is necessary to have some understanding of the forces in conflict, the practical difficulties in formulating limitations, the state apparatus necessary to enforce them, the possibility of distorting them to attain ulterior purposes, and the impact of the whole process upon achieving an effective system of free expression.

The starting point is a recognition of the powerful forces that impel men toward the elimination of unorthodox expression. Most men have a strong inclination to suppress opposition even where differences in viewpoint are comparatively slight. But a system of free expression must be framed to withstand far greater stress. The test of any such system is not whether it tolerates minor deviations but whether it permits criticism of the fundamental beliefs and practices of the society. And in this area the drives to repress, both irrational and rational, tend to become overwhelming.

The human propensity to curb unwanted criticism has long been noted by the theorists of freedom of expression . . . [and] has also been stressed in modern studies of the authoritarian personality. An attack upon cherished premises tends to create anxiety, especially in those who have a a strong inner need for certainty. The deviant opinion is felt as a threat to personal security. And the response tends to be fear, hatred or a similar emotion, from which springs a compulsion to eliminate the source of the danger. In such circumstances it is natural to turn to the state for protection against the supposed evil. Such factors play a prominent part in the formulation of restrictions upon expression and, equally important, in their administration.

It is necessary to take into account not only the psychology of the orthodox but also the psychology of the dissenter. Persons who stand up against society and challenge the traditional view often have strong feelings for the issues they raise. Others may be influenced by inner tensions which make it difficult for them to "adjust" to the prevailing order. In any event, the dissent is often not pitched in conventional terms; nor does it follow customary standards of polite expression. This tends to increase the anxiety and hostility of the orthodox and thus compounds the problem.

Apart from these inner compulsions at work in a system which undertakes to limit freedom of expression, difficulties arise at the more rational level. To many people their immediate and personal affairs are the most vivid and most compelling. Those who currently dominate a society naturally cling to their economic, political and social position of advantage. Vested interests in the status quo or in the continuing ignorance of other people tend to take precedence over the broader interests of society as a whole. Forces of this nature vigorously resist the expression of new ideas or the pressures of the underprivileged who would change existing conditions in the society.

* * * *

That full understanding and readiness to accept the theory of freedom of expression tends to be an acquired attitude is apparent from the entire history of free expression. It has been common for individuals and groups who demanded freedom of expression for themselves to insist that it be denied to others. Until the nineteenth century most of the theoretical supporters of freedom of expression took this position. And even those who urged a broader view have sought to impose restrictions upon their opponents when they achieved power. . . .

Similar attitudes prevail in our own times. Studies of public support for freedom of expression reveal an alarmingly high proportion of the population who are unwilling to apply the basic principles of the theory in practice. . . .

Taking all these factors into account, it is clear that the problem of maintaining a system of freedom of expression in a society is one of the most complex any society has to face. Self-restraint, self-discipline and maturity are required. The theory is essentially a highly sophisticated one. The members of the society must be willing to sacrifice individual and short-term advantage for social and long-range goals. And the process must operate in a context that is charged with emotion and subject to powerful conflicting forces of self-interest.

These considerations must be weighed in attempting to construct a theory of limitations. A system of free expression can be successful only when it rests upon the strongest possible commitment to the positive right and the narrowest possible basis for exceptions. And any such exceptions must be clear-cut, precise and readily controlled. Otherwise the forces that press toward restriction will break through the openings, and freedom of expression will become the exception and suppression the rule.

A second major element in the problem is the inherent difficulty of framing limitations on expression. Expression in itself is not normally harmful, and the objective of the limitation is not normally to suppress the communication as such. Those who seek to impose limitation on expression do so ordinarily in order to forestall some anticipated effect of expression in causing or influencing other conduct. It is difficult enough to trace the effect of the expression after the event. But it is even more difficult to calculate in advance what its effect will be. The inevitable result is that the limitation is framed and administered to restrict a much broader area of expression than is necessary to protect against the harmful conduct feared. In other words, limitations of expression are by nature an attempt to prevent the possibility of certain events occurring rather than a punishment of the undesired conduct after it has taken place. To accomplish this end, especially because the effect of the expression is so uncertain, the prohibition is bound to cut deeply into the right of expression.

Moreover, the infinite varieties and subtleties of language and other forms of communication make it impossible to construct a limitation upon expression in definite or precise terms. . . . In order to accomplish what the framers of the limitation seek, the limitation must be couched in a sweeping generalization. This means, of course, that a wide area of expression is brought within the reach of the limitation and enormous discretionary power placed in the hands of those who administer it.

This brings us to a third factor in the dynamics of limitation—the apparatus required for administration and enforcement. Those who are assigned this task already have or soon develop a tendency to pursue it with zeal. At the very least they have a job to do, the continued existence of which depends upon their activeness in performing it. Often their efficiency and possibility of advancement are measured in terms of their success, which means success in restricting expression. Prosecution of unpopular opinion is frequently an important avenue of political advancement and hence has a special appeal for the politically ambitious. While there has been little study of the psychology of the censor, security officer and investigator, experience demonstrates that many of those attracted to these positions are likely to be more than ordinarily influenced by the fears, prejudices or emotions which furnish the driving force for suppression. Much of the day-to-day work of administration is controlled by persons in the lower echelons of a bureaucracy, where narrow adherence to rigid rules, fear of superiors, and sensitivity to pressures carry the application of restrictions to their extreme limits. And accompanying techniques of enforcement in the area of expression—the investigations, surveillance, searches and seizures, secret informers, voluminous files on the suspect—all tend to exercise a repressive influence on freedom of expression.

Other features of the administration of a limitation on expression press in the same direction. Thus the very bringing of a prosecution or other governmental proceeding, even where it is not successful, or the simple fact of investigating, can have the most serious impact. The essential point is that the forces inherent in any system of administration tend to drive to excess, and the mere existence of an enforcement apparatus is in itself restrictive.

A fourth element in the practical administration of limitations on freedom of expression is that the objectives of the limitation are readily subject to distortion and to use for ulterior purposes. Many persons do not easily separate the conduct or threatened conduct of those who express unwanted ideas from their expression of hated and feared opinions. Thus opposition to the conduct or to the potential conduct readily merges into suppression of opinion. The irresistible drive is not only to oppose the action sought by the minority group but to suppress their advocacy of it. Frequently prosecution of unpopular opinion is used as a screen for opposing necessary social change. And often the limitation becomes a weapon in a political struggle, employed primarily for partisan advantage.

Finally, in analyzing limitations on freedom of expression, there must be taken into account the whole impact of restriction on the healthy functioning of a free society. Limitations are seldom applied except in an atmosphere of public fear and hysteria. This may be deliberately aroused or may simply be the inevitable accompaniment of repression. Under such circumstances the doctrines and institutions for enforcing the limitations are subjected to intense pressures. Moreover, while some of the more hardy may be willing to defy the opposition and suffer the consequences, the more numerous are likely to be unwilling to run the risks. Similarly, persons whose cooperation is needed to permit the full flow of open discussion—those who own the means of publication or the facilities for communication—are likely to be frightened into withholding their patronage and assistance.

*   *   *   *

. . . The lesson of experience, in short, is that the limitations imposed on discussion, as they operate in practice, tend readily and quickly to destroy the whole structure of free expression. They are very difficult to keep in hand; the exceptions are likely to swallow up the theory. Maintenance of a system of free expression, therefore, is not an easy task. This is especially true as we confront the conditions of today. We have tended over the years to refine and delineate more carefully the restrictions we seek to impose. But the new problems arising out of modern industrial society make the issue more delicate and troublesome than at any time in our history.

THE UNIVERSITY OF CHICAGO LAW REVIEW

Dirty Words and Dirty Politics

Two kinds of speech that traditionally have not been accorded first amendment protection are libel and obscenity. Before 1964, libel law had developed a series of intricate rules designed to compensate damaged reputations and at the same time to allow specified classes of expression to pass untrammelled. However, in *New York Times Co. v. Sullivan,* the Supreme Court subjected the common law tests for libel to the scrutiny of the first amendment, adding the element of intent to what had previously been a two part test encompassing falsity and harm to reputation. The effect of the decision was to give more complete protection to those criticizing the government in print and, at the same time, to define narrowly the exceptions to that protection by which a plaintiff might recover damages for defamation.

In obscenity law, as developed since 1957, the Court employed a somewhat similar three part test to pare away from communications dealing candidly with sex those materials which were deemed obscene and without any redeeming social importance. Beginning with *Roth v. United States,* the Court struck a constitutional balance between the positive social value of discussions of sex and the ill effect that such materials might have on

Reprinted by permission of The University of Chicago Law Review from "Dirty Words and Dirty Politics: Cognitive Dissonance in the First Amendment," *The University of Chicago Law Review,* 34 (Winter, 1967), pp. 367-379, 383-386. All footnotes but one have been omitted.

society. In the spring of 1966, however, the Court in three obscenity decisions set about reordering the balance in order to make more precise the standards set out in *Roth* and subsequent cases. As in *Times*, the key to rebalancing was the element of defendant's intent. The use of the intent element in these cases, however, was markedly different from the use of intent in *Times* and in previous obscenity cases; much confusion has followed.

I. THE MULTI-THRESHOLD TEST IN LIBEL

At common law, two discrete elements are necessary to a cause of action for libel: the writings must be false and defamatory of the plaintiff. The defendant has the burden of proving the truth of any defamatory remarks as legal justification for their publication. Since the harm against which libel law guards is injury to plaintiff's reputation—his character as others view him—mere falsity is not sufficient to make out a case. The plaintiff must also show that the statements taken as a whole defame him in the eyes of others, that they tend to hold him up to hatred, ridicule, or contempt.

The two elements of falsity and defamatory harm satisfied, plaintiff's case is complete. Libel law in a majority of jurisdictions does not require proof of an element of intent or negligence; absolute liability is the standard. However, in raising a defense of privilege, the defendant may open up the question of his intent. Two categories of privilege may be pleaded by a defendant, defeasible and absolute, but only for the former is intent relevant.

Defeasible privilege is most important in the freedom it gives journalists and other critics in their discussions of public figures and public issues. The "fair comment" rule grants a qualified privilege to discussion not only of politicians and public officials, but also of writers, sports figures, entertainers, and others whose activities or beliefs make them public figures. Under this rule, error as to opinion is privileged, but, in a majority of jurisdictions, error as to fact is not. The obvious policy of the rule is to encourage open discussion and criticism of issues and people in the public eye, albeit with factual accuracy rigorously required. Further justification lies in the notion that most people who might be defamed under the rule have voluntarily exposed their works or themselves in certain capacities to the public. Their reputations are, to some extent, public property.

The most significant limitation on this and other defeasible privileges is the intent with which the defamer publishes his remarks. A showing of malice, that the defendant published his remarks out of ill will for the plaintiff, will generally defeat the privilege. Similarly, defendant's disbelief in his own opinions, excessive vehemence in his defamation, or unnecessary communication of the remarks to persons having no legitimate interest in them, all work to defeat the privilege. The plaintiff must show that defendant abused the policy behind the privilege, that is, that the defendant was not attempting to obtain truth for his readers by open discussion of public issues and public figures.

In the *Times* case, the Court decided that such limited privilege, combined with the basic elements of falsity and defamatory harm, did not sufficiently protect the freedom of the press to report on public issues and to comment on the activities of public officials. . . .

* * * *

While the Court's decision in *Times* did not end the significance of truth and defamatory harm in the test for libel of public officials, it forcefully indicated their inadequacy as insulators of a constitutionally desirable degree of uninhibited discussion. Thus, while truth and defamatory harm were retained as thresholds which must be met to put the statement inside the common law boundary of libel, the Court in *Times* added a third— "actual malice"—as another independent hurdle in a multi-threshold test designed to increase protection of first amendment freedoms.

As defined in *Times*, "actual malice" exists when a statement is shown to have been made "with knowledge that it was false or with reckless disregard of whether it was false or not." . . .

[The] new actual malice threshold greatly altered the impact of the truth element in this area of libel law. . . . [The] Court has in effect shifted the burden of proof with regard to truth; it will be very difficult for a plaintiff to prove malice without first proving the falsity of the statement in question. Hence, of the "three 'galloping presumptions' of damage, falsity, and malice," at least two, falsity and malice, have been harnessed.

It should be noted that *Times* has affected only a portion of libel law and does not even cover the full scope of situations to which the fair comment privilege applies. Subsequent cases, however, have expanded the definition of "public official" to such an extent that the multi-threshold test of *Times* may ultimately replace fair comment altogether. Such a result would substantially reduce the number of libel suits and would greatly enlarge the scope of social criticism through the press. But whatever the breadth of its future application, the central thrust of the Court's approach in *Times* remains. The new test adds a third and independent threshold to those already in existence, establishing a multi-threshold test further to protect the public interest in free and open discussion of public officials.

II. PORNOGRAPHY PER SE, PRURIENT APPEAL,
   AND PANDERING

Obscenity law as it has evolved from the Court's 1957 decision in *Roth* has focused on three elements—patent offensiveness, harmful effect on audience, and the distributor's intent—which may be viewed as establishing a multi-threshold test analogous to that developed for libel in *Times*. In obscenity, as in libel, the three part test has been applied to determine what speech is within the protection of the first amendment and what may be regulated. Parallels drawn between the elements of these tests may be used further to evaluate the multi-threshold approach to speech problems.

The first threshold in obscenity is that the publication must be intrinsically indecent, regardless of its use or its audience. "[S]ex and obscenity are not synonymous." The standard was clarified in *Manual Enterprises, Inc. v. Day*, where it was held that materials had to be "patently offensive" in order to be found obscene. Without this initial threshold test, the Court argued, many of our most respected works of art and literature would be taken from the reading public. "[S]uch a construction (of the statute) . . . would doubtless encounter constitutional barriers."

The "effect" element constitutes the second threshold. Material is obscene when, "to the average person, applying contemporary community standards, the dominant theme of the material taken as a whole appeals to prurient interest." The Court is concerned here with the effect that obscene materials have on their audience—the harm which the legislature is presumably attempting to prevent through its imposition of criminal sanctions. As in defamation, the publication must be taken as a whole, a reaction against the old rule of *Regina v. Hicklin*. A second reaction to the *Hicklin* test is the requirement that prurient appeal be measured by the standard of the "normal person." This standard also reflects the Court's decision in *Butler v. Michigan*, in which a state law banning for all readers any books tending to influence minors adversely was held unconstitutional. The first amendment does not allow abridgement of the freedom to listen for everyone when there is reason only to regulate for a few.

Just as libelous statements must be found defamatory in the eyes of those to whom they are addressed, publications in obscenity litigation must be shown to be "obscene" in the eyes of their audience. In this respect the Court continued to be tied to the idea of a national audience as a result of *Butler* and *Roth* until the 1966 cases, where, in the *Mishkin* decision, the Court adopted the Lockhart and McClure concept of "variable obscenity:"

We adjust the prurient-appeal requirement to social realities by permitting the appeal of this type of material to be assessed in terms of the sexual interests of its intended and probable recipient group.

The adjustment of the audience rule not only introduced social realities; it also helped the Court to find something obscene for the first time since the *Roth* case was decided. The Court realized in obscenity what the law of libel has recognized for a long time—that the materials have their ill effect not in the abstract, but in the eyes of their recipients.

The flip side of the prurient interest coin, the "privilege" in obscenity law, is the requirement that the publication in question be "utterly without redeeming social value." The "social value" test has greater force than a privilege in defamation, however, in that it is an element that must be proved in addition to prurient appeal in order to meet the ill effect theshold. Recognizing that much literature can be found to appeal to someone's prurient interest, the Court has built in this safeguard to further isolate those materials it deems socially harmful. Any publication that in some way contributes to art, literature, or thought is protected, regardless of its appeal to prurient interest. "Ceaseless vigilance" must be employed to protect open discussion of "sex, a great and mysterious motive force in human life, . . . indisputably . . . a subject of absorbing interest to mankind through the ages; it is one of the vital problems of human interest and public concern." Hence, a state may not ban materials for advocating sexually provocative ideas. Nor may a novel with even minimal literary value be banned. The Court has apparently extended the same kind of protection to literature and the arts that it gave to political discussion in *Times;* Professor Kalven's plea that "beauty has constitutional status too" appears to have been heard.

Before 1966 the question of intent had never played a very important role in obscenity prosecutions, simply because the Court was usually concerned with whether the materials in question were to be banned, and not with the fate of the publishers and distributors. The so-called "social value" privilege had been absolute, the burden falling on the prosecution to show that the materials had no social value. The Court's only word on the subject of intent came in *Smith v. California,* where a bookseller was convicted of selling obscene literature under a state absolute liability statute. The Court held the statute unconstitutional on the ground that it would require all sellers to be closely familiar with the contents of all their books and to become their own censors. To avoid risk of prosecution, sellers would probably take many books off their shelves that might conceivably run afoul of the obscenity statute, thus depriving the public of much worthwhile reading. The Court ruled that any such statute would have to include some element of scienter, although it did not specify how this provision should be drawn. The requirement of a mens rea element here is not as a limit to privilege, as in defamation, but rather as a further protection for distributors of materials dealing with sex. In this sense the Court's use of the intent element was similar to its use in *Times*: rather than making the defendant prove good intent to justify his actions, the defendant's mens rea [guilty intent] becomes a third, independent threshold for the prosecution to meet.

III. "COMMERCIAL EXPLOITATION": A NEW ELEMENT

The 1966 obscenity cases subverted the thrust of the multi-threshold test. The Court began in *Memoirs* where, after finding the controversial novel *Fanny Hill* not obscene in a neutral context, it delivered the following dictum:

Evidence that the book was commercially exploited for the sake of prurient appeal, to the exclusion of all other values, might justify the conclusion that the book was utterly without redeeming social importance.

In its holding, the Court relied on the point that evidence at trial had shown the novel to have "some" redeeming social value. Its dictum suggested that the novel could be the subject of further prosecutions should evidence arise of distributors marketing the book solely on its "prurient appeal." In clarifying this point, the Court stated:

It is not that in such a setting the social value test is relaxed so as to dispense with the requirement that a book be *utterly* devoid of social value, but rather that, as we elaborate in *Ginzburg v. United States*, . . . where the purveyor's sole emphasis is on the sexually provocative aspects of his publications, a court could accept his evaluation at face value.

*   *   *   *

In *Ginzburg*, the Court's entire attention was on the element of intent or "commercial exploitation." The Court assumed without deciding that Ginzburg's three publications could not be proved obscene standing apart from the context in which they had been sold. In fact, in the case of one publication, . . . the Court admitted that an earlier distribution to a list of physicians and psychiatrists had been of some social value. However, the Court found that Ginzburg had played up the "sexually provocative" aspects of the publications in his advertising circulars. Small portions of the advertising had noted the social value of the publications, but the Court rejected this as mere "pretense." It inferred that Ginzburg had intended the publications to be bought solely for their prurient appeal. The Court concluded:

We perceive no threat to First Amendment guarantees in thus holding that in close cases evidence of pandering may be probative with respect to the nature of the material in question and thus satisfy the *Roth* test.

The Court added that it was not banning the publications per se: "All that will have been determined is that questionable publications are obscene in a context which brands them as obscene . . . ."

The hint in *Ginzburg*, as well as in *Memoirs*, is that pandering enters the equation when the social importance of the materials is at a minimum, a fact which presumably indicates a "close case." *Mishkin* suggests that it should lend weight to evidence of prurient appeal. This would tend to narrow the problem, although from all the Court tells us in *Ginzburg*, evidence of pandering may relate to the determination of the patent offensiveness threshold as well.

[Section IV has been omitted.]

V. *TIMES v. GINZBURG*: SOME DISTINCTIONS

Having applied the threshold approach of libel to obscenity, it is necessary to point out some significant differences between the two areas of law and the way in which the multi-threshold test affects them. While the similarities between the two based on their common foundation in the first amendment are striking, their individual peculiarities lend force to the conclusion that obscenity defendants should, at the very least, be given the same protection that is now given in libel law.

It is significant initially to note that the defendant won in *Times*, while in two of the three obscenity cases the publishers were convicted. In instituting the "variable obscenity" theory in *Ginzburg* and its two companion cases, it is strikingly apparent that the Court considered the cases against a background markedly different from that in *Times*, where the overriding emphasis was on further protection of speech. Perhaps this attitude of restraint reflected in the new decisions was caused by an unarticulated desire on the part of the Court to redraw the boundaries of obscenity law in order to obtain more convictions.

However, a more persuasive reason for this different perspective may be that the Court takes a more protective attitude toward communications involving politics than toward communications dealing with sex. With the issues of seditious libel and censorship by the government of its critics lurking in the background, the Court had little difficulty in coming to the defense of an institution such as the *New York Times* in a somewhat spurious libel suit. The defense of a New York smut salesman has less appeal to judicial sensibilities. Whereas free and open political debate is an absolute essential of the democratic system, it is more difficult to find a comparable compulsion for wide-open discussion of sex. Yet in *Burstyn* [*v. Wilson* (1952)] the Court conceded no constitutional difference between entertainment and the reporting of politics, and it would therefore appear that the law calls for equal treatment of these two areas of speech.

A significant difference between libel and obscenity is that in libel one is generally dealing with ideas and the reporting of facts, while in obscenity litigation the materials are questioned for the form in which they present themes or images; the courts are dealing with questions of tastes and esthetics in obscenity, not with accuracy as to facts and opinions. Many writers and artists are attempting to convey images through their work, the final impression of the work being created in the mind of the individual recipient. In this context, the notion of "social value" is somewhat inimical to the issues at hand. Despite the Court's effort to make social value interchangeable with "literary or scientific or artistic value," it is obviously extremely difficult to determine whether a given primary audience finds a magazine utterly without social (literary) value; what may be of literary value to the uneducated man may be utterly worthless to the Ph.D.[1] Where the critical questions turn on the means and form of expression rather than its content, there is a clear danger of turning the rule into a "gentlemen's privilege," where an educated court and expert witnesses may be unable to see what some may regard as literary merit. Certainly under the rules of *Ginzburg* and *Mishkin*, where social value was determined by the circumstances of distribution, such discrimination against those with less sophisticated literary tastes is inevitable. The conclusion to be drawn from these considerations involving the inherent difficulty of determining what is obscene is that the test for such a determination should be overbroad in order sufficiently to protect marginal materials. In fact, there would appear to be more compelling reason for building this prophylactic protection into an obscenity test than there is for its existence in a libel formula since the more objective nature of libel determinations make them less prone to error.

The last point that sets obscenity apart from libel is that in *Ginzburg* a man was sent to prison for five years; in *Times*, a newspaper was threatened with a money judgment. The fact that much of obscenity law involves criminal prosecution and the possibility of a prison sentence would seem to demand that the defendant's right to free expression be as fully protected as possible, for not only is a source of expression being restricted, but

---

[1]Concomitantly, Shakespeare must be deemed to be totally lacking in social or literary importance to those unable to comprehend his works.

Also worth noting here is the data developed by the (Kinsey) Institute for Sex Research "showing that, generally, better educated persons are more responsive to pornography because they are more imaginative and better able to conceptualize than persons of low social and educational status; the latter are less likely to get excited about a picture with which they can 'do nothing.'" Magrath, *The Obscenity Cases: Grapes of Roth*, 1966 SUP. CT. REV. 7, 65-66.

For the argument that pornography may be a useful medium for modern writing see Michelson, *Apology for Pornography*, The New Republic, Dec. 10, 1966, p. 21.

It is interesting to note that the social value test is implicit in *Times* whereas it is explicit in obscenity law. The relatively objective *Times* rule tends to exclude materials of no social value but does not use that rather vague term as a criterion of the test. . . .

its publisher is being imprisoned. Thus it is probable that pressure on publishers to observe a safer margin will result in the operational illegality of legitimate materials dealing with sex because of the threat of greater sanctions.

SOME CONCLUDING OBSERVATIONS

Any constitutional test for obscenity must focus on the protection of expression concerning sex that is of only marginal value in order to protect that of real importance. It is always easy to find zealous censors, less easy to find those who will support speech unpopular with the majority. To counteract this tendency, the *Times* opinion offers an admirable model.

The difficulties with defining a clearcut rule for obscenity are manifold. The standards of the community toward discussion of sexual matters change so rapidly that any rule must be subject to almost continuous reevaluation. Standards vary so widely among groups in society that what shocks one person bores the next and is a source of "psychic autoeroticism" to yet another. Moreover, any judgment as to the obscenity of a work necessarily involves subjective determination of the taste with which it was written. The danger here, of course, is that the tastes of one group will be imposed on others. Finally, it is difficult to identify and to measure the social and individual harm the law wishes to punish. It is perhaps for some of these reasons that Justices Black and Douglas have been moved to vote for the unconstitutionality of all obscenity regulation.

But a persistent majority of the Court has insisted on the constitutionality of some regulation of pornographic materials. Again, *Times* offers an admirable model for the construction of a rule. The rule must overprotect all speech to protect that which is valuable. The test must rely on the most objective elements possible. It must be as precise as possible, both to serve notice on those who may be criminally prosecuted and to guarantee consistency in the courts. For these purposes, the multi-threshold test in *Times* seems most suitable. The Court should first require determination of whether the material is inherently indecent. Here, it would be better not to apply the variable obscenity theory, but rather to judge the offensiveness of the material by contemporary national standards . . . . Second, the test should include an ill effect or harm threshold, which will define what about the material is harmful enough to put it beyond first amendment protection. If this harm is the titillation of sexually immature minds, it should be so stated. In this instance, it is sensible to again borrow from libel law in judging the effect by determining its impact on the actual primary audience. Evidence of the intended audience may be helpful here, but surely not conclusive. A counterbalance to the ill effect element should be required proof that the material has no value to the primary audience other than its capacity to bring about the harm or ill effect proscribed. The third independent threshold should be the intent of the publisher or distributor of the materials to exploit the weakness of the primary recipient group for the particular ill effect defined. This element should be independent and should not be a tool for determining or redirecting the burden of proof for either of the other two thresholds. The defendant must have known that the primary recipient group was susceptible, that the material would have the ill effect defined upon the group, and that members of the group would buy the material primarily to receive the defined ill effect.

Such a test is not altogether inconsistent with *Ginzburg* and its companion cases. Virtually every portion of this test is suggested by one or more of the Justices. What is basically different, and what is crucial to the success of the test, is that each threshold be independent of the other two.

JOHN H. GAGNON *and* WILLIAM SIMON

Pornography—Raging Menace or Paper Tiger?

*   *   *   *

TWO FACES OF PORNOGRAPHY

The court apparently considers pornography to have two major dimensions. The first can be defined as dealing with sexual representations that are offensive to public morality or taste, which concerned the court most importantly in the Ginzburg case. The second centers on the effect of pornography on specific individuals or classes, which is the focus of most public discussions and prior court decisions on pornography. This dimension was mentioned only twice in the array of decisions of 1966, but much of the confusion in discussions of pornography reflects a difficulty in distinguishing between these dimensions or a tendency to slip from one to the other without noting the change.

The first dimension—offenses to a public morality—not only appears more objective, but also has a cooler emotional tone. The problem becomes

Reprinted by permission of the authors and the publisher from "Pornography—Raging Menace or Paper Tiger?" TRANS-ACTION Magazine (July-August, 1967), pp. 41-48. Copyright © 1967 by Washington University, St. Louis, Mo.

one of tolerating a public nuisance, or defining what constitutes a public nuisance. This issue becomes complex because the heterogeneity of an urban society makes it difficult to arrive at a consensus on what the limits of public morality might be. We might also add the complicating factor of our society's somewhat uneven libertarian tradition that affirms the theoretical existence of the right to subscribe to minority versions of morality. These obviously touch upon important issues of constitutional freedoms. As important as the implicit issues may be, however, the explicit issue is public nuisance, a misdemeanor, usually bringing only a fine or, at most, up to a year in the county jail. Talk of offense to public morality or public taste is relatively remote from the old fears of serious damage to the community or its members.

The second dimension—effects upon persons exposed to pornographic productions—generates more intense emotions. Claims are made that exposure to pornography results in infantile and regressive approaches to sexuality that can feed an individual's neuroses or, at the other extreme, that exposure tends to fundamentally and irreversibly corrupt and deprave. The latter argument asserts that exposure to pornography either awakens or creates sexual appetites that can only be satisfied through conduct that is dangerous to society. More simply stated: Pornography is a trigger mechanism that has a high probability of initiating dangerous, antisocial behavior. There also exists what can be called a major counterargument to these, but one that shares with them a belief in the effectiveness of pornography. This argument is that pornography serves as an alternative sexual outlet, one that releases sexual tensions that might otherwise find expression in dangerous, antisocial behavior. For the proponents of this view, pornography is seen as a safety valve or a psychological lightning rod.

The very act of labeling some item as pornographic or obscene creates a social response very close to that brought on by pornography itself. The act of labeling often generates sexual anticipation centered on fantasies about the business of pornography and the erotic character of those who produce it. How else could such benign and hardly erotic productions as family-planning pamphlets and pictures of human birth have come under the shadow of the pornography laws? As with other unconventional sexual expressions, in public consideration of pornography even the dreary details of production, distribution, and sale are matters for erotic speculation. This simplification—defining as totally sexual that which is only marginally connected with sexuality—is perhaps one of the major sources of the public concern over pornography.

Labeling can also be done by individuals, who can thus make pornographic the widest range of materials—*Studs Lonigan, Fanny Hill, Play-*

boy, the Sears Roebuck catalog. This ability leads to the assumption that sexual fantasy and its agent, pornography, have a magical capacity to commit men to overt sexual action. In this view the sexual impulse lies like the beast in every man, restrained only by the slight fetters of social repression. This assumption, founded on the Enlightenment's notion of a social contract, underpins most of our discussions of sex and its sideshow, pornography.

These serious views of pornography can lead directly to the formulation of an empirically testable question. Unfortunately, no one has provided an answer acceptable as the outcome of reliable and systematic research procedures.

WHAT EFFECT—IF ANY?

Of the data that are available on the effects of pornography, the best remain those provided by the investigations of the Institute for Sex Research. Kinsey and his associates indicate that the majority of males in our society are exposed, at one time or another, to "portrayals of sexual action." So are a smaller proportion of females. Further, 77 percent of males who had exposure to "portrayals of sexual action" reported being erotically aroused, while only 32 percent of women reported feelings of arousal. What is significant is that, arousal notwithstanding, no dramatic changes of behavior appeared to follow for those reporting both exposure and arousal. Perhaps even more significant is the fact that Paul H. Gebhard and his colleagues in their book *Sex Offenders* report:

It would appear that the possession of pornography does not differentiate sex offenders from nonsex offenders. Even the combination of ownership plus strong sexual arousal from the material does not segregate the sex offender from other men of a comparable social level.

Summing up their feeling that pornography is far from being a strong determinant of sexual behavior and that the use of pornography tends to be a derivative of already existing sexual commitments, the authors observe: "Men make the collections, collections do not make the men."

However, given the intensity and frequency with which the argument of pornography's corrupting powers is raised, one might wonder whether thinking about pornography has not itself given rise to sexual fantasies, developing an image of men and women as being more essentially sexual than they may in fact be.

The two major dimensions—public offense versus public corruption—result in two different images of the pornographer. Projected through the rhetoric of public corruption we see him as someone self-consciously evil, a representative of the antichrist, the Communist conspiracy, or at the very least, the Mafia. We also tend to see him in terms of the obscenity of ill-gotten wealth as he deals in commodities that are assumed to generate high prices.

Thought of as a public nuisance, he appears in somewhat more realistic hues. Here we find not a sinister villain but a grubby businessman producing a minor commodity for which there is a limited and a marginal profit and which requires that he live in a marginal world. Here our collective displeasure may be derived from his association with a still greater obscenity—economic failure. However, whether the pornographer is Mephistopheles or a Willie Loman, he is one of the few in our society whose public role is overtly sexual, and that is perhaps reason enough to abandon any expectations of rationality in public discussions of the role.

THE FANTASY OF THE STAG FILM

We tend to ignore the social context within which pornography is used and from which a large part of its significance for the individual consumer derives. The stag film is an excellent case in point. Out of context it is rarely more than a simple catalogue of the limited sexual resources of the human body. Stag films are rarely seen by females and most commonly by two kinds of male groups: those living in group housing in colleges or universities and those belonging to upper-lower class and lower-middle class voluntary social groups. The stag film serves both similar and different functions for the two major categories of persons who see them.

For the college male they are a collective representation of mutual heterosexual concerns and—to a lesser degree—they instruct in sexual technique. For this group the exposure is either concurrent with, or prior to, extensive sociosexual experience. Exposure comes later in life for the second group: after marriage or, at the very least, after the development of sociosexual patterns. For this audience the group experience itself provides validation of sexual appetites in social milieus where other forms of validation, such as extramarital activity, are severely sanctioned. The films primarily reinforce masculinity and only indirectly reinforce heterosexuality. This reinforcement of heterosexuality is reflected in the way the films portray the obsessive myths of masculine sexual fantasy. They emphasize, for example, that sexual encounters can happen at any moment, to anyone, around almost any corner—a belief that is a close parallel to the romantic love fantasy so very characteristic of female arousal. In the case of the male, however, sex replaces love as the central element. These films also reaffirm the myth of a breed of women who are lusty and free in both surrender and enjoyment. Last, given the kind of social context within which the films are shown, there is little reason to assume that their sexual arousal is not expressed through appropriate sexual or social actions.

Pictorial representations of sexual activity lend themselves to the same approach. Unlike films and more like written materials, their use is essentially private. Nonetheless, patterns of use remain congruent with other patterns of social life and process; they represent anything but the triggering mechanisms through which the social contract is nullified and raging, unsocial lust (whatever that might be) is unleashed. The major users of pictorial erotica are adolescent males. If these materials have any use, it is as an aid to masturbation. There is no evidence, however, that the availability of dirty pictures increases masturbatory rates among adolescents. This is a period in life when masturbatory rates are already extremely high, particularly for middle class adolescents. Indeed, in the absence of hard-core pornography, the boys create their own stimulation from mail-order catalogues, magazine ads, and so on. In middle class circles, many young men and the majority of females may grow up without ever having seen hard-core pornography.

If exposure to this kind of pornography, while facilitating masturbation, does not substantially affect masturbatory rates, it is still possible that such materials may shape the content of the masturbatory fantasy in ways that create or reinforce commitments to sexual practices that are harmful to the individual or to others. In this area little is known. It may be observed that most pornographic materials share with the masturbatory fantasy a sense of omnipotence, but the acts represented are rarely homosexual, nor are they sadistic beyond the general levels of violence common in contemporary kitsch. Once again, one suspects a reinforcing or facilitating function rather than one of initiation or creation.

The pornographic book, in contrast to photographs and films, represents a very different social situation. Few books are read aloud in our society, and it is very unlikely that this would occur with a book of descriptions of overt sexual activity. In fact, prosecutors take advantage of this by reading allegedly obscene books aloud in court with the aim of embarrassing the jury into a guilty verdict. The privately consumed erotic book merely provides fantasy content or reinforcement of fantasy that is already established. Few books lead to overt action of any kind, and the erotic book is unlikely to be an exception.

PORNOGRAPHIC FRINGELAND

The most difficult problem in considering pornography is the fringeland found on newsstands: the pulp books, national tabloids, men's magazines, and pinup collections which line the racks in drugstores, bus stations, and rail and air terminals. The girlie magazines are often under attack for nude pictures. The current magic line of censorship is pubic hair, though recently it was the bare breast or exposed nipple. Not so very long ago, navels were ruthlessly airbrushed away and Jane Russell's cleavage was an issue in gaining the censor's approval of the movie "Outlaw." The Gay Nineties were made gayer with pinups of strapping beauties clad in tights revealing only the bare flesh of face and hands.

In our era the pulp book freely describes most sexual activity with some degree of accuracy, although less explicitly and more metaphorically than hard-core pornographic pulp books. Such books are clearly published for their capacity to elicit sexual arousal, and they are purchased by an audience that knows what it is buying.

To view these examples of fringe pornography exclusively in terms of a sexual function might well be misleading. Since we tend to overestimate the significance of sexual activity, we see the trends of representation in these works as indicators of sexual behavior in the community. An increase in works about homosexual love is taken as an indication of an incipient homosexual revolution or even as the cause of a homosexual revolution. If we find more books about adultery, sadomasochism, or fast-living teenagers, we believe that there must be more adulterers, sado-masochists, and fast-living teenagers in our midst. With a dubious logic reminiscent of primitive magic, many believe that if the number of such representations increases, so will the frequency of such acts, and conversely that the way to cut down on this antisocial behavior is to suppress the pornographic representations.

In the fringeland there is a greater attempt to place sexual activity in the context of a social script, with a greater concern for nonsexual social relations and social roles, and a more direct treatment of appropriate social norms. Some part of this, particularly its common trait of compulsive moralizing, is an attempt to establish a spurious—but defensible under the Roth decision—"redeeming context." This may also represent the producer's awareness that more than simple lust is involved, that the reader may bring to the work a complex of motives, many of which are nonsexual.

For example, the psychiatrist Lionel Ovesey links some of the fantasies of his homosexual patients not to their sexual commitments, but to their problems of managing other personal relations, particularly in their jobs. The management of dominance or aggression in nonsexual spheres of life or the management of ideologies and moralities of social mobility may be the organizing mechanisms of such fantasies while sexuality provides an accessible and powerful imagery through which these other social tensions may be vicariously acted upon. Possibly it is overly simplistic to view this marginal pornography merely as something exclusively sexual.

These items at the fringeland are of most concern in the formulation of community standards. The girlie magazine and the pulp book are visible and priced within the range of the mass market. The hardcover book available at a high price in a bookstore may well cause no comment until it goes on the drugstore racks in paperback. Because such items are sold at breaks in transportation or in locations that tap neighborhood markets, they are the most visible portion of the problem and are the source of the discontent among those who are committed to censorship.

ELUSIVE STANDARDS

The dilemma, then, becomes the formulation of community standards, and this has been the dilemma of the courts themselves. One interesting attempt to strengthen enforcement of conservative standards is the interpretation of federal law to allow prosecution of a seller in the jurisdiction in which materials are received rather than in the ones from which they are mailed. Thus in the rather liberal jurisdiction of New York, where the sale of obscene materials must be compared in the mind of the judge with all the other kinds of crimes that come before him, the seller may well be seen as a small-timer, his crime a misdemeanor. However, in a rural jurisdiction where religious standards are more conservative and a pornography offense is viewed more seriously—especially when compared with the strayed cows and traffic violations that make up the most of the court docket —the seller is a heinous criminal.

The Supreme Court may wish to establish a national standard, allowing some jurisdictions to be more liberal but none to be more conservative. Thus the Supreme Court may build a floor under the right of materials to be protected under the First Amendment, at the same time constraining, through the use of the Ginzburg decision, the importation of materials through wide mailing campaigns into conservative communities. In its more recent decision, the court indicated—somewhat Delphically—that its concern in the future would be with three areas, none of them directly concerned with the content of any works charged as pornographic. These were sales of smut to minors, obtrusive presentation, and "pandering" *a la* Ginzburg. The court's decisions, however, may well be too conservative in a period when a national society is being created through penetration by the mass media of larger and larger elements of the society. Indeed, it is likely that most legal revolutions have been imposed from above and that communities will fall back to the set floor, if allowed to do so. To trust to local innovation is to trust to nothing.

Pornography is as elusive as mercury. That of the past often no longer fills the bill. The use and users of contemporary pornography vary. Indeed, it might be said that sex itself would not change if there were no more pornography. Pornography is only a minor symptom of sexuality and of very little prominence in people's minds most of the time. Even among those who might think about it most, it results either in masturbation or in the "collector" instinct.

What is most important about pornography is not that it is particularly relevant to sexuality, but that it elicits very special treatment when it confronts the law. In this confrontation the agencies of criminal justice, and especially the courts, behave in a very curious manner that is quite dangerous for the freedom of ideas as they might be expressed in other zones of activity such as politics, religion, or the family. Our best protection in this regard has been the very contradictory character of the courts which carefully excludes the consideration of sexual ideas from the general test of the expression of ideas: Do they give rise to a clear and present danger? Our problem is not that pornography represents such a danger —it is far too minor a phenomenon for that—but that the kind of thinking prevalent in dealing with pornography will come to be prevalent in controlling the advocacy of other ideas as well.

GINSBERG v. NEW YORK

Obscenity and the Young

MR. JUSTICE BRENNAN delivered the opinion of the Court.

This case presents the question of the constitutionality on its face of a New York criminal obscenity statute which prohibits the sale to minors under 17 years of age of material defined to be obscene on the basis of its appeal to them whether or not it would be obscene to adults.

. . . Appellant was prosecuted under . . . two counts, which charged that he personally sold a 16-year-old boy two "girlie" magazines on each of two dates in October 1965, in violation of § 484-h of the New York Penal Law. . . . The judge found (1) that the magazines contained pictures which depicted female "nudity" in a manner defined in subsection 1 (b), that is "the showing of . . . female . . . buttocks with less than a full opaque covering, or the showing of the female breast with less than a fully opaque covering of any portion thereof below the top of the nipple . . . ," and

Reprinted from *The United States Law Week*, 36 (April 23, 1968). Footnotes have been omitted. Editors' title.

(2) that the pictures were "harmful to minors" in that they had, within the meaning of subsection 1 (f) ". . . that quality of . . . representation . . . of nudity . . . [which]. . . (i) predominantly appeals to the prurient, shameful or morbid interest of minors, and (ii) is patently offensive to prevailing standards in the adult community as a whole with respect to what is suitable material for minors, and (iii) is utterly without redeeming social importance for minors." He held that both sales to the 16-year-old boy therefore constituted the violation under § 484-h of "knowingly to sell . . . to a minor" under 17 of "(a) any picture . . . which depicts nudity . . . and which is harmful to minors," and "(b) any . . . magazine . . . which contains . . . [such pictures] . . . and which, taken as a whole, is harmful to minors." . . .

The "girlie" picture magazines involved in the sales here are not obscene for adults. . . . But § 484-h does not bar the appellant from stocking the magazines and selling them to persons 17 years of age or older, and therefore the conviction is not invalid . . . .

*   *   *   *

The New York Court of Appeals "upheld the Legislature's power to employ variable concepts of obscenity" . . . [stating:]

". . . material which is protected for distribution to adults is not necessarily constitutionally protected from restriction upon its dissemination to children. In other words, the concept of obscenity or of unprotected matter may vary according to the group to whom the questionable material is directed or from whom it is quarantined. . . . "

Appellant's attack is not that New York was without power to draw the line at age 17. Rather, his contention is the broad proposition that the scope of the constitutional freedom of expression secured to a citizen to read or see material concerned with sex cannot be made to depend upon whether the citizen is an adult or a minor. . . .

*   *   *   *

Appellant argues that there is an invasion of protected rights under § 484-h constitutionally indistinguishable from the invasions under the Nebraska statute forbidding children to study German, which was struck down in *Meyer* v. *Nebraska* . . . , the Oregon statute interfering with children's attendance at private and parochial schools, which was struck down in *Pierce* v. *Society of Sisters* . . . , and the statute compelling children against their religious scruples to give the flag salute, which was struck down in *West Virginia State Board of Education* v. *Barnette* . . . . Rather § 484-h simply adjusts the definition of obscenity ". . . to social realities by permitting the appeal of this type of material to be assessed in terms of the sexual interest . . ." of such minors. . . . That the State has power to make that adjustment seems clear, for we have recognized that even where there is an invasion of protected freedoms ". . . the power of the state to control the conduct of children reaches beyond the scope of its authority over adults . . . ." . . .

The well-being of its children is of course a subject within the State's constitutional power to regulate, and, in our view, two interests justify the limitations in § 484-h . . . . First of all, constitutional interpretation has consistently recognized that parents' claims to authority in their own households to direct the rearing of their children is basic in the structure of our society. "It is cardinal with us that the custody, care and nurture of the child reside first in the parents, whose primary function and freedom include preparation for obligations the state can neither supply nor hinder." . . . The legislature could properly conclude that parents and others, teachers for example, who have this primary responsibility for children's well-being are entitled to the support of laws designed to aid discharge of that responsibility. . . .

The State also has an independent interest in the well-being of its youth. The New York Court of Appeals . . . Chief Judge Fuld . . . emphasized its significance in [an] earlier case . . . . In his concurring opinion . . . , he said:

"While the supervision of children's reading may best be left to their parents, the knowledge that parental control or guidance cannot always be provided and society's transcendent interest in protecting the welfare of children justify reasonable regulation of the sale of material to them. . . ."

. . . The only question remaining, therefore, is whether the New York Legislature might rationally conclude, as it has, that exposure to the materials proscribed by § 484-h constitutes such an "abuse."

Section 484-e of the law states a legislative finding that the material condemned by § 484-h is "a basic factor in impairing the ethical and moral development of our youth and a clear and present danger to the people of the state." It is very doubtful that this finding expresses an accepted scientific fact. But obscenity is not protected expression and may be suppressed without a showing of the circumstances which lie behind the phrase "clear and present danger" in its application to protected speech. . . . To be sure, there is no lack of "studies" which purport to demonstrate that obscenity is or is not "a basic factor in impairing the ethical and moral development of . . . youth and a clear and present danger to the people of the state." But the growing consensus of commentators is that "[w]hile these studies all agree that a causal link has not been demonstrated, they are equally agreed that a causal link has not been disproved either." We do not demand of legislatures a "scientifically certain criteria of legislation." . . . We therefore cannot say that § 484-h, in defining the obscenity of material on the basis of its appeal to minors under 17, has no rational relation to the objective of safeguarding such minors from harm.

[*Editors' Note:* The Court then examined and rejected the challenge to the law of vagueness.]

MR. JUSTICE FORTAS, dissenting.

This is a criminal prosecution. Sam Ginsberg and his wife operate a luncheonette at which magazines are offered for sale. A 16-year-old boy was enlisted by his mother to go to the luncheonette and buy some "girlie" magazines so that Ginsberg could be prosecuted. He went there, picked two magazines from a display case, paid for them, and walked out. The offense of the Ginsbergs was duly reported to the authorities. The power of the State of New York was invoked. Ginsberg was prosecuted and convicted. The court imposed only a suspended sentence. But as the majority here points out, under New York law this conviction may mean that Ginsberg will lose the license necessary to operate his luncheonette.

The two magazines that the 16-year-old boy selected are vulgar "girlie" periodicals. However tasteless and tawdry they may be, we have ruled (as the Court acknowledges) that magazines indistinguishable from them in content and offensiveness are not "obscene" within the constitutional standards heretofore applied. . . . These rulings have been in cases involving adults.

The Court avoids facing the problem whether the magazines in the present case are "obscene" when viewed by a 16-year-old boy, although not "obscene" when viewed by someone 17 years of age or older. It says that Ginsberg's lawyer did not choose to challenge the conviction on the ground that the magazines are not "obscene." He chose only to attack the statute on its face. Therefore, the Court reasons, we need not look at the magazines and determine whether they may be excluded from the ambit of the First Amendment as "obscene" for purposes of this case. But this Court has made strong and comprehensive statements about its duty in First Amendment cases—statements with which I agree. . . .

In my judgment, the Court cannot properly avoid its fundamental duty to define "obscenity" for purposes of censorship of material sold to youths, merely because of counsel's position. By so doing the Court avoids the essence of the problem; for if the State's power to censor freed from the prohibitions of the First Amendment depends upon obscenity, and if obscenity turns on the specific content of the publication, how can we sustain the conviction here without deciding whether the particular magazines in question are obscene?

The Court certainly cannot mean that the States and cities and counties and villages have unlimited power to withhold anything and everything that is written or pictorial from younger people. But it here justifies the conviction of Sam Ginsberg because the impact of the Constitution, it says, is variable, and what is not obscene for an adult may be obscene for a child. This it calls "variable obscenity." I do not disagree with this, but I insist that to assess the principle—certainly to apply it—the Court must define it. We must know the extent to which literature or pictures may be less offensive than *Roth* requires in order to be "obscene" for purposes of a statute confined to youth. . . .

I agree that the State in the exercise of its police power—even in the First Amendment domain—may make proper and careful differentiation between adults and children. But I do not agree that this power may be used on an arbitrary, free-wheeling basis. This is not a case where, on any standard enunciated by the Court, the magazines are obscene, nor one where the seller is at fault. Petitioner is being prosecuted for the sale of magazines which he had a right under the decisions of this Court to offer for sale, and he is being prosecuted without proof of "fault"—without even a claim that he deliberately, calculatedly sought to induce children to buy "obscene" material. Bookselling should not be a hazardous profession.

The conviction of Ginsberg on the present facts is a serious invasion of freedom. To sustain the conviction without inquiry as to whether the material is "obscene" and without any evidence of pushing or pandering, in face of this Court's asserted solicitude for First Amendment values, is to give the State a role in the rearing of children which is contrary to our traditions and to our conception of family responsibility. . . . It begs the question to present this undefined, unlimited censorship as an aid to parents in the rearing of their children. This decision does not merely protect children from activities which all sensible parents would condemn. Rather, its undefined and unlimited approval of state censorship in this area denies to children free access to books and works of art to which many parents may wish their children to have uninhibited access. For denial of access to these magazines, without any standard or definition of their allegedly distinguishing characteristics, is also denial of access to great works of art and literature.

If this statute were confined to the punishment of pushers or panderers of vulgar literature I would not be so concerned by the Court's failure to circumscribe state power by defining its limits in terms of the meaning of "obscenity" in this field. The State's police power may, within very broad limits, protect the parents and their children from public aggression of panderers and pushers. This is defensible on the theory that they cannot protect themselves from such assaults. But it does not follow that the State may convict a passive luncheonette operator of a crime because a 16-year-old boy maliciously and designedly picks up and pays for two girlie magazines which are presumably *not* obscene.

HARVARD LAW REVIEW

The Legitimacy of Demonstrations and Some Limits on Free Expression

I. INTRODUCTION

Whatever distinctions may be drawn between demonstrations and other forms of self expression, it is generally recognized that demonstrations are within first amendment protection. Often a demonstration has significant publicity advantages over more conventional media of expression, since it can attract extensive news coverage and widespread public interest; and for persons unpopular with or unknown to the general public, or without financial resources, a demonstration may be the only effective means to publicize a message or reach a desired audience. Also, a demonstration may provide an opportunity to mobilize supporters and to strengthen the demonstrators' bargaining position. If the demonstrators represent a significant voting bloc or if they gain the sympathy of other citizens, political leaders cannot afford to turn a deaf ear, especially when the demonstration creates a condition of unrest in the community. Whenever the demonstrators are complaining of a bona fide wrong, society's interests will be advanced if their grievance is brought to public attention and relief is granted; and the danger that demonstrating minorities may possess disproportionate political power would seem to be outweighed by the desirability of keeping the majority informed of minority complaints.

Demonstrations are nevertheless subject to greater state regulation than "pure speech." Mr. Justice Goldberg, writing for the Court in *Cox v. Louisiana*, said:

Reprinted by permission of the publisher from "Regulation of Demonstrations," *Harvard Law Review*, 80 (June, 1967), pp. 1773-1782, 1788. Copyright ©1967 by The Harvard Law Review Association. Footnotes have been omitted.

We emphatically reject the notion urged by appellant that the First and Fourteenth Amendments afford the same kind of freedom to those who would communicate ideas by conduct such as patrolling, marching, and picketing on streets and highways, as these amendments afford to those who communicate ideas by pure speech.

Demonstrations will sometimes conflict with the state's interest in preventing violence or abuse of property, and the state should be permitted to maintain the free flow of traffic and to insure that public facilities serve the needs and convenience of other citizens. Demonstrations may also interfere with governmental operations or financially burden the state whenever additional police officers are required to maintain order. Although Mr. Justice Black apparently feels that the state may impose blanket prohibitions on demonstrations, the prevailing view seems to be that the state may impose only "reasonable" restrictions on time, place, duration, or manner. The "reasonableness" of a regulatory measure must necessarily be viewed in terms of the competing interests of the demonstrators and the state. This Note will set forth some of the restrictions which a state may impose on demonstrations, and then proceed to the more important question of what techniques the state may use to enforce otherwise legitimate restrictions.

II. PROTECTION OF STATE AND PRIVATE INTERESTS
A. Prevention of Violence and Disorderly Behavior

The courts have declared without hesitation that demonstrations lose their constitutional protection if the participants engage in violence. The Supreme Court has also upheld an injunction against labor picketing when a background of prior violence by the picketers "tainted" their present activities, and presumably the same relief would be available against demonstrators. Some kinds of conduct short of violence may also subject demonstrators to arrest or dispersal. The Court has held that a speaker may be arrested when he "passes the bounds of argument or persuasion and undertakes incitement to riot" or when his words would cause an average man to fight. However, the Court has also noted that speech "may indeed best serve its high purpose when it induces a condition of unrest, creates dissatisfaction with conditions as they are, or even stirs people to anger," and on occasion it has invoked the "clear and present danger" test to determine when provocative conduct or language exceeds constitutional protection. The application of such a test would depend on circumstances independent of the demonstrators' conduct or message, since a demonstration which would arouse no response from a cosmopolitan audience may still induce violence by its very presence in the Watts section of Los Angeles during a period of unrest. If the unvarying nature of audiences can be taken into account, very slight taunting may be enough to withdraw constitutional protection under some circumstances.

Sometimes noisy conduct alone may justify restrictions on demonstrations in the interest of preserving peace and quiet. Although in *Edwards v. South Carolina* the Court granted protection to "boisterous," "loud," and "flamboyant" conduct in the form of singing, cheering, clapping, and stomping, in that case the demonstration occurred during the day on a statehouse driveway. Demonstrations held in such places as hospital zones, public libraries, or residential neighborhoods during sleeping hours would not seem to be entitled to the same protection.

When violence or disorder arises solely as a result of audience hostility, the police must ordinarily seek to control the crowd rather than to disperse the demonstration. In principle, a hostile audience should not be permitted to suppress a peaceful demonstration by acts of violence which necessitate police intervention, but the Court has left much to be desired in explaining the boundaries and application of the "hostile audience" doctrine. The doctrine would not seem to apply when the audience, though hostile to other persons, is in support of the demonstrators, for the doctrine is designed only to prevent suppression of unpopular views by opponents. Moreover, the doctrine apparently does not reach more subtle types of suppression, such as heckling and jeering, since ordinarily members of the crowd would have an equal right to be heard, particularly when the heckling does not substantially interfere with communication of a message or when the purpose of the demonstration is to provoke a hostile response for enhanced publicity.

The hostile audience doctrine proceeds on the assumption that the police will be able to control the crowd, and the Court has not decided whether the police may suppress a demonstration when crowd hostility is uncontrollable. Conceivably the demonstrators could argue that they have an interest in the publicity value of their own bloodshed or in any event that they have a right to determine their own risks. Nevertheless, the ensuing violence may endanger not only the demonstrators, but also innocent bystanders and the police as well; moreover, under these circumstances, it is not possible to protect the right to demonstrate, since the crowd would soon suppress the demonstration if the police did not. Nevertheless, it may be undesirable for the continuation of a demonstration to depend on a police determination of whether a crowd is uncontrollable. The police are likely to ignore the rights of the demonstrators or underestimate their ability to control the crowd, particularly when prompt action is necessary. This factor makes it probable that the Court will continue to avoid the "uncontrollable crowd" question by always finding that the police failed to devote their best efforts.

B. Traffic Facilitation and Safety

The Court has expressed willingness to uphold reasonable regulatory measures designed to facilitate the flow of traffic, and lower courts have uniformly upheld convictions of demonstrators for obstructing traffic without permission. The "reasonableness" of traffic regulations which restrict demonstrations depends on such factors as the time of day, the size of the demonstration, the physical characteristics and regular use of the property, and the ease with which normal traffic can be diverted. Whenever possible, the state should seek to accommodate demonstrations within the framework of traffic regulation. At certain times of day, some streets and sidewalks may be too congested to accommodate large gatherings; but smaller demonstrations which do not substantially interfere with traffic should be permitted, since the demonstrators have an interest in access to large rush hour audiences. The convenience of other pedestrians may require the demonstrators to march in single file on narrow sidewalks, or to space themselves properly and restrict their numbers before business premises. Similarly, safety requirements may justify greater restrictions on roads with fast moving traffic than on ordinary streets. Finally, if the same or an equally desirable audience can be reached at an alternative location, the demonstrators could not insist on remaining at the more congested location.

Some lower courts have apparently found a special state interest in curtailing night demonstrations. The prevention of crime and the maintenance of safety are more difficult at night . . . .

C. Interference with Government Operations and Other Public Uses

Ordinarily the state may prohibit or restrict demonstrations which substantially interfere with governmental operations or the regular use of public property. The most obvious example of interference is physical obstruction, as in the case of demonstrators in a rowboat who blocked a submarine launching. Similarly, the very presence of demonstrators in public buildings may upset normal operations. Mr. Justice Black stated that "libraries, schoolhouses, fire departments, courthouses, and executive mansions are maintained to perform certain specific and vital functions. Order and tranquillity of a sort entirely unknown to the public streets are essential to their normal operation." While some demonstrating in public buildings would seem permissible, the governmental interest in orderly operations should always be entitled to priority.

Restrictions on demonstrations may also be necessary to prevent more subtle types of interferences. The Court in *Cox v. Louisiana* upheld a statute which prohibited groups from attempting to influence judges by demonstrating "near a courthouse," and the District of Columbia Circuit upheld a restriction on demonstrations against foreign embassies, noting a strong federal interest in protecting foreign officials from embarrassing disturbances which might jeopardize foreign relations. More recently, in *Adderley v. Florida*, the Court upheld trespass convictions of demonstrators who gathered on the driveway and grounds of a jailhouse to protest the earlier arrest and confinement of some fellow demonstrators. The Court appeared to rely on the security demands around jailhouses and the necessity of prompt ingress and egress. The dissent, however, urged that the jailhouse was an "obvious center of protest" and a proper forum to petition for redress of the earlier arrests. . . . [It] would seem undesirable to prohibit such demonstrations, since often police abuse, unlike judicial abuse, may only be remedied by public pressure, and furthermore, because the decisions of the police more directly affect the everyday lives of citizens than judicial decisions. . . .

D. Residential Demonstration

The Court has not decided whether a state, in protecting privacy and quiet of the home, may prohibit or restrict demonstrations on public property in residential neighborhoods. Although the Court held unconstitutional a prohibition of door-to-door distribution of religious matter, in many instances a demonstration can be a greater inconvenience to the homeowner than the religious evangelist. Despite the annoyance of answering the door bell and occasional altercations, the homeowner has the power to avoid the message of the evangelist without state assistance simply by expelling him from the residence. A demonstration, however, can reach the homeowner with a message from nearby streets and sidewalks in which the homeowner has no proprietary rights, and if the homeowner wishes to escape the message, he may often be forced to forego the comforts of home or the enjoyment of his yard. Even a small, quiet demonstration may attract large crowds and newsmen, which may further expose the homeowner to noise and the scrutiny of outsiders. A demonstration could also have more subtle effects on the homeowner's relationships with his family, neighbors, or friends, who might be annoyed by the demonstration or ask embarrassing questions. Also, whenever the demonstrators can reach the desired audience at another location, they would seem to have no special interest in demonstrating in a residential neighborhood. State courts have generally viewed residential picketing of a public official with disfavor; and particularly when the crowd is complaining of his "official acts," there is often no need to expose the official's private life to the "pressing attention of outside affairs."

Nevertheless, in many cases the demonstrators' interest in reaching a residential audience will outweigh the interests of privacy. In the case of a protest against housing discrimination in neighborhoods closed by mutual consent of owners, the residential neighborhood will be a focal point of dispute, and the demonstration may not be effective if held elsewhere. . . .

Since a factual analysis will be required in each case to determine which interests are entitled to priority, a blanket prohibition of residential demonstrations would not seem permissible. . . . The first amendment would seem to give demonstrations a presumption of legality, even in residential neighborhoods, and when an injunction is sought, the homeowner should be required to show that the demonstration will be an unreasonable interference.

E. Private Property

Ordinarily the state can protect private property owners by forcible expulsion or trespass convictions of demonstrators who refuse an owner's request to leave. Some property which is technically "private," however, must be open for demonstration if it serves governmental functions, or has governmental sponsorship and other official connections. Also, when private property has sufficient "public characteristics," the demonstrators can sometimes present a compelling case for use of the property. Some business establishments open to the general public, such as supermarkets, are surrounded by spacious privately owned parking lots, and particularly when nearby public streets and sidewalks are congested, inconvenient, or otherwise unavailable, the demonstrators could argue that use of the property should be allowed so long as interference with customers is kept at a minimum. It would seem, however, that the demonstrators would have to show a special relationship with the proprietor which necessitates use of the property for effective communication of a message.

A common form of demonstration on private property is the sit-in in protest of discrimination in services by business proprietors. In such a case the main issue is not whether free speech interests are entitled to priority, but whether the state may enforce a private decision to discriminate through physical expulsion or trespass convictions of demonstrators. In *Hamm v. City of Rock Hill*, where the Court struck down trespass convictions, the Civil Rights Act of 1964 was construed to grant demonstrators a federal right to sit in and demand equal services in "public accommodations" when services are refused for reasons of racial discrimination. Nevertheless, the Act would not seem to protect demonstrators who are protesting matters unrelated to racial discrimination, who continue to sit in after receiving equal services, or who sit in to protest discriminatory hiring practices, even when the hiring practices are in violation of the Act. In such cases, trespass convictions would seem permissible since the demonstrators have no legitimate business purpose for staying on the premises and their complaint does not relate to a denial of services which they could rightfully demand by staying on the premises until served.

When a sit-in demonstration is not protected by the Act, the validity of trespass convictions under current law would seem to depend on whether the proprietor's decision to discriminate was influenced by "state action." In cases which arose before the Act the Court always managed to find "state action" either in statutory law, local custom, or declarations by local officials; it has never faced the issue of whether a purely private decision to discriminate is enough to defeat trespass convictions. . . . Even the Court's most liberal advocates of expanding the meaning of state action, however, have indicated that the state should be permitted to enforce trespass convictions when the decision to discriminate is "essentially private." . . .

F. Regulation of Message and Purpose

When the signs displayed by demonstrators are obscene or maliciously defamatory, civil damages or criminal penalties may be imposed. Also, injunctive relief has been granted against "patently false" picketing signs, although courts have been reluctant to enjoin when the issue of falsehood is open to doubt. The doctrine of prior restraint would not be an obstacle to an injunction because the specific defamatory or obscene matter can be offered in evidence, and the injunction can be phrased to avoid inhibition of otherwise legitimate future conduct. . . .

The state may also prohibit demonstration picketing which exerts an unjustifiable degree of coercion on private individuals. As in the labor area, a demonstration picket which seeks to induce a business proprietor to commit a crime may be prohibited or enjoined on petition of an injured party. . . .

When the picketers have an "adequate legal remedy," a business proprietor could argue that the picketers should be required to pursue their legal remedy instead, on the ground that the demonstrators' interest in picketing is outweighed by the general policy in favor of settling disputes on the legal merits without the interference of demonstration pressures. . . . [In] *Hamm v. City of Rock Hill,* the Supreme Court was unsympathetic to the argument that the legal remedies available under the Civil Rights Act of 1964 should preclude sit-in demonstrations in demand of equal services. . . .

Picketing of a storeowner by a disgruntled purchaser would seem to present the strongest case for requiring recourse on a claim which he knows is without legal merit, and good business judgment may dictate the payment of even a false claim to halt the picket. . . .

[Section III has been omitted.]

IV. CONCLUSION

In regulating demonstrations the state should be careful to identify a substantial interest worthy of protection, since the Court has always had misgivings about restrictions on first amendment rights. Furthermore, the state should consider the possible effects of a regulation on favored groups which it might otherwise wish to leave unembarrassed by regulatory impositions. Even a regulation which protects a legitimate state interest may still be vulnerable on equal protection grounds if it treats less favored groups differently than other groups, like the Rotary Club or the American Legion. Finally, the regulatory system taken as a whole should not be so formidably elaborate and complex that it inflicts "death by a thousand cuts" on the right to demonstrate, or discourages expression by minority groups through fear of a regulatory imbroglio.

JOHN COGLEY, LEWIS S. FEUER, PAUL GOODMAN,
IRVING KRISTOL, and BAYARD RUSTIN

Limits on Civil
Disobedience: A Symposium

DISSENT IS NOT ENOUGH

JOHN COGLEY, *Editor of* THE CENTER MAGAZINE, *The Center for the Stud of Democratic Institutions*

The logic of those opposed to civil disobedience lock, stock and barrel is the best case I know *for* it. That logic at its crudest, and perhaps most forthright, holds "My country right or wrong, but right or wrong my country." The final value, then, is obedience to the law of the land, just or unjust; obedience takes precedence over religion, morality and personal conscience.

From "On Civil Disobedience, 1967," *The New York Times Magazine* (November 26, 1967), pp. 27ff. ©1967 by The New York Times Company. Reprinted by permission of the authors and the publisher.

For the believing Jew or Christian, such a view is nothing short of idolatry. It puts the law, or the democratic process if you will, above everything else, on earth or in heaven. Yaweh's commandment, the first, was: "You shall have no other gods before me." Peter, the leader of Jesus's apostles, said without reservation: "We must obey God rather than men."

But civil disobedience is not only a problem for the religious-minded. The atheist and agnostic have claims on their conscience no less demanding. Obeying God rather than men, or putting conscience above consensus, is not merely a matter of dissent, or of protesting by legal means when one is actually involved in doing evil. For many, it is a matter of simply refusing to be implicated, of drawing the line and saying: "Hereon I stand . . . I can do no other."

In practice, this may mean refusing military service, whether or not the refusal falls within the legal limits of conscientious objection. It may mean illegally encouraging and abetting others to resist the draft. It may mean withholding the taxes that buy instruments of human destruction. It may mean refusing to observe civil-defense regulations. It may take any number of forms, all of them requiring that man-made laws be broken in order that a higher law be upheld.

Some Germans, a pitiful few, practiced civil disobedience during the Nazi period. Today we honor their memory. Two decades ago, at Nuremberg, we established the principle that under some circumstances such disobedience is a moral duty. During the war-crimes trials some were sentenced to death for not practicing it and others were given prison terms. We took these drastic steps not because the prisoners were patriotic Germans but because they obeyed inhumane, immoral and reprehensible orders.

In their own defense a number of Germans argued that their obedience was unwilling. They had dissented as much as they could, they claimed, until the final showdown, when it was obey or else. But we knew then how to distinguish between dissent and disobedience. Dissent, we decided, was not enough. Is it enough in the U.S. today for the growing number who feel that the nation is embarked on an immoral course in Vietnam?

More and more Americans are becoming convinced it is not. They feel an obligation to go beyond the "good Germans" of a quarter century ago who went along with whatever the Nazis did.

When, for example, these Americans learn that *both* sides in Vietnam have tortured prisoners, they do not want to be implicated in the excesses of "our side." When they learn that our forces are killing civilians, turning villages into a wasteland, and destroying crops, they want no part of the brutal business. They are as horrified by the scorched-earth policy in 1967 as they were in 1942. When they read in The Saturday Evening Post that one million children have been injured in Vietnam and a quarter of a million youngsters have been killed, they feel the time has come to withdraw all support, military, political, and financial, whatever the law demands.

The Nuremberg judiciary determined what constitutes a war crime: "ill-treatment of civilian populations, murder or ill-treatment of prisoners of war, wanton destruction of cities, towns or villages, inhuman acts committed against any civilian population."

Dissent, it has been made painfully clear, is not enough to put an end to such outrages; as the dissent has escalated so has the war. The man who takes religion, morality and conscience seriously has no choice then, it seems to many, but to respond with a resounding, unequivocal, unqualified Luther-like "No" whenever he is either asked for his support or it is legally demanded from him.

There are, to be sure, limits on justifiable civil disobedience. Those opposed to the Vietnam war have no right to destroy law and order at home or to practice sedition or sabotage. To say they did would be to turn the case for civil disobedience into a charter of anarchism. Their moral, not legal, right to disobey extends only as far as their moral duty: to resist evil, to refuse to cooperate with evil-doing, to do all in their power to persuade others that the evil they see *is* evil, and to encourage others to have no part in it.

We asked this much of the Germans caught in an infinitely more restrictive straitjacket than we find ourselves in. We can ask no less of ourselves, whatever the cost.

WE SHOULD DISTINGUISH BETWEEN DISOBEDIENCE AND RESISTANCE

LEWIS S. FEUER; *Professor of Sociology, University of Toronto*

We should distinguish between civil disobedience and civil resistance. The first is limited to dramatizing a particular issue; it retains a faith in representative democracy, and takes for granted that once the facts are known, and the people's sense of responsibility awakened, the necessary reforms will be made. Civil disobedience is justified when an oppressed group finds itself deprived of lawful channels for remedying its condition because of an arbitrary obstruction in the democratic workings.

Civil resistance, on the other hand, is total and unlimited, for it claims that the entire society is corrupt, that representative democracy is a failure, and that the resisters' weapon must be revolutionary. It regards each episode as part of a "guerrilla warfare" against society. It twists the vocabulary of civil disobedience to this purpose. The Student Nonviolent Coordinating Committee says it uses "nonviolent" in quotation marks, that is, meaninglessly, or deceptively. Civil resistance is advocated in the United States by two groups—the Ku Klux Klan (as in Meridian, Miss.) and the New Left, most recently in its demonstrations against the Vietnam war.

In the last analysis, we judge acts of civil disobedience and resistance in terms of what we think of the motives and rationality of their practitioners. The director of the Washington Pentagon demonstrators announced: "We are now in the business of wholesale and widespread resistance and dislocation of the American society." The New Resisters have an apocalyptic image of themselves as the successors to the abolitionists.

The wisest American of his time, Justice Holmes, knew the abolitionists well, and as a youth, shared their madness. They "taught me a lesson," however, he said, as he recognized the basis of fanaticism. The abolitionists were often more intent on killing white men than on bettering the lot of the slaves. John Brown's favorite text was: "Without the shedding of blood, there is no remission of sins," and 20 years before the Civil War he was insisting that slavery could be ended only through a blood atonement. The New Resisters, as the Chicago Conference for New Politics last September [1967] made evident, are driven by a similar fanaticism; their resolutions reeked more of venom against Americans than of a desire for Asians' freedom.

To justify their civil resistance to the Vietnam war, the New Left claims that the American democracy has denied them a hearing. They fail to mention that their well-financed candidates in the last Congressional elections and primaries were rejected by the voters. The New Left, defeated by representative democracy, wants therefore to destroy and replace it with a "participatory democracy"—that is, the rule of its "guerrilla warriors" and activists.

Thus its civil disobedience has evolved into civil resistance, an anti-democratic ideology of rule by a dictatorial elite. No wonder that at the Chicago conference, some of its adherents began to awaken and to speak openly of its "fascism" and "totalitarianism." Benito Mussolini's march on Rome was also an act of massive civil resistance.

The New Resistance has tried to borrow the aura of the European resistance movements. The latter, however, were fighting the Nazis who had abrogated all constitutional processes, banned the opposition parties, and imprisoned their leaders. It makes no sense to describe the American democracy in such terms, and the efforts of the resisters to do so only accentuate their irrationality. At the same time, they remain strangely benign to the call of Lin Piao, Mao's defense minister in September, 1965, for a "people's war" of Asia, Africa and Latin America against North America and Western Europe.

Our entry into World War II was largely the outcome of our refusal to condone the expansion of the Japanese empire into Indochina and Southeast Asia. Our presence in Vietnam today is due to our similar refusal to condone a Chinese expansionism. An American departure, as Southeast Asians themselves generally recognize, would probably uproot such fragile growths of democracy as now exist. Draft evaders in World War II used much the same arguments as the draft-card burners today. The New Left is using all the worn arguments that the Old Left used against American involvement during 1939 to 1941. The draft-card burners and the New Left have just as little moral justification. This "prophetic minority" is one of false prophets.

THE RESISTERS SUPPORT U.S. TRADITIONS AND INTERESTS

PAUL GOODMAN, *Educator, Social Critic, Author of* GROWING UP ABSURD and PEOPLE OR PERSONNEL

The great majority of resisters do not consider themselves as lawless, whether they impede the draft, refuse war taxes, or try to bar recruiters and war contracts from the campuses. We hold that it is the Vietnam policy that is illegitimate. It has been created by a hidden government of military-industrial lobbyists and the C.I.A.; the Executive has gone beyond his mandate; there has been no genuine debate and voting in Congress; the public has been lied to and brainwashed. The Government is a usurper, so sovereignty reverts to the people more directly. It is the resisters who support American traditions and interests, and our behavior is itself traditional, not unlike the civil-rights movement, the labor movement, populism, abolitionism (and nullification), and the American Revolution itself. As in the previous cases, most action has been nonviolent though often disobedient to authorities, and there has also been sporadic violence, usually started by authorities.

Rather than "defying" the law, most resisters welcome a test of legitimacy in the courts, believing that, when everything is duly aired, we will be found lawful, just as recently the civil-rights trespassers were found (or became) lawful. In American tradition, the meaning of law is always emerging. The Government has been loath to accept the challenge, choosing instead to pick off individuals, hoping to deter. Now, however, the draft-card burners are being subpoenaed and there may be a massive showdown.

The aim of testing the law and nonviolent confrontation, trying to persuade by putting oneself on the line, is to get the Americans to make up their minds and change their minds; it is not to frighten or compel. Unfortunately, since the populace has been sluggish and complacent, occasional violence seems to be advantageous to wake people up; certainly it is mainly violent incidents that the TV and press want to notice. And naturally, resisters are frustrated by their powerlessness when, even now as I write this,

our Government is killing those people. Yet I cannot accept the *putschist* use
of violence, for instance, to "take over" a draft board or burn it down by
a physical power play. This is unacceptable not because it is a fantasy—in a
complex technology a few clever people can make a shambles—but because
out of the shambles can come only the same bad world.

Nonviolent confrontation asks, "What is your real will, when you
confront our resistance and have to think, feel and decide? Do you mean,
in order to continue your routine, to jail so many, beat so many, investigate so many, bring police on the campus, pass panicky unconstitutional
laws, invoke martial law, poison the community further?" By and
large, except as an awakener, violence prevents confrontation. Attacked
physically, a policeman or soldier responds routinely as a professional,
with tear gas or bayonet, but the aim is to get him to think and feel as man
and citizen. Confronted, he may respond routinely anyway, but hopefully
he cannot continue to do so.

It is possible that the Americans do really intend the Vietnam war or
don't care at all. They may be truly complacent with their standard of
living, arrogant about American power, indifferent to the lapse of democracy and the militarizing of society, deaf to world outrage, callous about
gooks. If this were so, we resisters would have to think in other terms, of
exile or "underground." But there is evidence that we are succeeding, that
we represent the general will of the body politic.

I here lay all my stress on the legitimacy of resistance. It does not follow,
however, that our movement is not radical or even revolutionary, perhaps
beyond what many moral resisters think. The Vietnam war is not something isolated that can just be written off. Really to get out of it—and especially the young want really to get out of it and will continue to fight
for that—will require a major reconstruction of the American economy, the
use of technology, the system of education, foreign relations, the structure
of authority and the whole quality of American life. This year the military budget is $84-billion. More significantly, 86 per cent of the money
for research and development is for military purposes. Is that the future
we intend?

CIVIL DISOBEDIENCE IS NOT JUSTIFIED BY VIETNAM

IRVING KRISTOL, *Essayist, Co-editor of* THE PUBLIC INTEREST

Has there ever been, in this country, a movement of protest so unreflec-
tive about its principles of action as the present anti-Vietnam "crusade"?
I cannot offhand think of one. The kinds of discrimination and judgment
that have long been the staple of moral and political philosophy seem

utterly incomprehensible to it. One even encounters young people—and not-so-young people, too—who appear to think that dodging the draft is actually a form of conscientious objection! So one is perforce compelled to insist on some elementary distinctions:

(1) Civil disobedience is not a right—though it may, under certain circumstances, be an obligation. A right is a particular freedom you may exercise without penalty. An obligation is something that, in principle, you are not free to evade, regardless of penalty.

(2) Civil disobedience is always defensible—if not always practicable—when one is confronted by the unjust action of an unjust political regime. It *may* be defensible, in certain extreme cases, when one is confronted by the unjust action of a regime that is, on the whole, just and legitimate (i.e., deserving of our loyalty).

(3) Those who are morally committed to civil disobedience can properly claim that the government which arrests them, or the law that punishes them, is so perverse as to be without due authority. What they may *not* do in good conscience is to practice civil disobedience—and then hire a clever lawyer to argue that it wasn't in violation of the law at all, but rather the exercise of some kind of "right."

(4) Civil disobedience is to be distinguished from "dissent" at the one extreme and "resistance" at the other. Dissent assumes that lawful agitation and argument and demonstration can achieve the desired change in government policy. Civil disobedience openly breaches the law and scornfully accepts the penalty; it aims to mobilize opinion through self-sacrificial, exemplary action. Resistance may include all sorts of covert and illegal actions, and will almost certainly include the provocation and perpetration of violence where this is possible.

(5) Those who believe in "resistance" inevitably regard civil disobedience merely as a tactic, to be employed under conditions where more militant action would be futile. In this case, civil disobedience ceases to have any moral dimension at all and is nothing but a highly organized and artfully contrived species of riot.

(6) Even were I opposed to the Administration's policy in Vietnam, which I am not, I would not regard this case as one in which civil disobedience is justified. The opportunities for dissent are obviously abundant, and even Ho Chi Minh seems to think they can be effectual. But I realize that there are some good people who feel strongly that civil disobedience is the only honorable course open to them. I would only ask of these individuals that they distinguish themselves from those who, talking bombastically of "resistance," mindlessly flirt with revolution-making. You can emulate Thoreau when confronted with the Mexican war, or Lenin when con-

fronted with World War I. But the idea of a Leninist Thoreau is an
intellectual and moral absurdity.

THE POLITICAL RESPONSE MUST BE WEIGHED

BAYARD RUSTIN, *Chief Organizer of the 1966 March on Washington and
Executive Director of the A. Philip Randolph Institute in Harlem*

Since the dawn of civilization there has been an ongoing conflict between
man and organized society; in modern times, between man and state.
Antigone, Socrates and the early Christians accepted death rather than submit to laws they considered morally wrong. Thoreau was jailed for refusing to pay taxes because he opposed both slavery and the "unjust war with
Mexico." And the abolitionist faced slander, brutality, loss of property
and imprisonment in defiance of the Fugitive Slave Law and the Dred
Scott decision.

In all these cases, those who broke the law felt not only a personal moral
imperative but also what George Fox called "the secure faith" that their
open and nonviolent opposition would ultimately bring others to see the
truth and thus help improve society. Traditionally, two compelling ideas
underlay the disobedient's secure faith. First, he had affection for, and
faith in, his country, and sought by his action to improve or change a
particular law or condition which he sincerely believed injurious to himself, to others, and to the state itself.

During his trial, Socrates sought to clarify this point when he calmly
turned to his accuser, Anytus, and said, "Men of Athens, I honor and love
you . . . but I shall never cease from the practice and teaching of philosophy, exhorting anyone whom I meet and saying to him . . . from virtue
comes every other good, *public* and private. This is my teaching."

In other words, Socrates argued that his teaching, far from corrupting
Athens or its youth, would improve both.

Secondly, practitioners of civil disobedience have defended their action
not as "a right" but rather as "a duty" to themselves, to others and ultimately to their society. Their allegiance has been to a "higher law" which
they felt the state ignored to its detriment.

In the apology, Socrates also made this point when he told the court,
"I shall never alter my ways, not even if I have to die many times. . . . for
I will obey God rather than you . . . and so I bid you farewell."

In addition to these two principles, most resisters have seriously strug-
gled with the following questions:

(1) Have I exhausted the available constitutional methods of bringing
about the desired change?

(2) Do the people I urge to join me sincerely seek to improve the society or do they wish to excite passions that would destroy society itself?

(3) What is likely to be the effect of the resistance on me, on others, and in the community?

(4) Are my own motives and objectives clear to myself and to others; is my aim genuine social change or mere self-gratification?

(5) Given that I oppose specific laws, am I prepared, out of my deep respect for law itself, to suffer the consequences of my disobedience?

Adherence to the standards embodied in these questions can result in morally defensible acts of disobedience. But morally defensible acts are not always or necessarily relevant in political terms. And it is precisely in political terms that peace in Vietnam, like civil rights at home, finally will be determined.

No eternal algebraic formula can guarantee that a given act of disobedience will stimulate the necessary political response. What disturbs me, however, about much of the recent antiwar resistance is that it does not seek a political response at all; it therefore becomes self-corrupting.

Today we are not faced, like Antigone, Socrates or the early Christians, with surrender or death. Political alternatives remain open. They must, therefore, be considered along with moral concern if progress is to be achieved.

III.

Freedom of Religion

Among the first phrases in the First Amendment is the provision that "Congress shall make no law respecting an establishment of religion, or prohibiting the free exercise thereof . . . ." What these few words mean for the relationship between church and state in America has been a matter of considerable controversy, especially during the past two or three decades.

Despite the urgings of Roger Williams, Thomas Jefferson, and others that there be a "wall of separation" between church and state, religion (and Christianity especially) has received substantial encouragement from government. As Alexis de Tocqueville observed, ". . . from the earliest settlement of the emigrants, politics and religion contracted an alliance which has never been dissolved."[1]

In 1962, almost 130 years later, two political scientists surveyed the nature of the church-state relationship and concluded:

. . . through the years, government at all levels has officially encouraged religious practices and has offered special concessions to churches. By act of Congress, the pledge of allegiance to the United States is made to "this nation under God." The currency of the country carries the national motto, "In God We Trust." The Supreme Court of the United States opens each session with the intonement, "God save the United States and this Honorable Court." Each house of Congress appoints a Chaplain who invokes blessings and prays for God's guidance in the daily proceedings. Chaplains are attached to all the armed forces of the United States; Sunday attendance at chapel exercises is compulsory at West Point, the Air Academy, and Annapolis. Church property and income are generally exempt from federal and state taxes. Sunday is legally recognized as a day of rest in every State; vestiges of Sunday "blue laws"—which prohibit the operation of non-essential businesses on the Sabbath—are still to be found in every community in the country. The Bible is commonly used in taking court oaths, "So help me God"; and it is read in many public schools

---

as part of the daily exercises. In some states, custody and adoption laws are tailored to religious beliefs.[2]

As the preceding listing suggests, much of the governmental encouragement of religion takes place at the state and local level. Historically, such encouragement was more extensive than it is today. In the early nineteenth century, all of the New England states except Rhode Island afforded the Congregationalist Church special status. A number of other states required that public-office holders be Christians, and in some cases that they be Protestants.[3] Not until the 1930's, did the United States Supreme Court hold that the provisions of the First Amendment applied to the states as well as to the federal government.

However, despite the active support given by government to churches in a number of states, church membership in the first half of the nineteenth century did not exceed 20 per cent of the population.[4] In response to the low level of church membership, many faiths launched evangelical crusades to bring the nation "into the fold." The number of persons affiliated with specific faiths rose rapidly in the last part of the nineteenth century, and today more than 90 per cent of the nation claim some particular religious preference.[5]

Accompanying this growth in church membership has been an increasing religious tolerance, although it has been slower in coming to Catholics and Jews, especially the latter. We continue to confront contemporary counterparts of the nineteenth-century Know-Nothings, the American Protective Association, and the American Protestant Union in the far less widespread but nonetheless vehement anti-Catholicism and anti-Semitism of the Ku Klux Klan, the American Council of Churches (not to be confused with the *National* Council of Churches), and numerous groups of the "Radical Right." Moreover, Christians from larger denominations sometimes have been reluctant to accept the advocates of some smaller and more "deviant" religious sects.

Even though almost all Americans consider themselves members

---

[2]Marian Irish and James W. Prothro, *The Politics of American Democracy* (Englewood Cliffs, N.J.: Prentice-Hall, 1962), p. 202.

[3]For a comprehensive history of government sponsorship of religion, see Anson Phelps Stokes, *Church and State in the United States* (New York: Harper, 1950), 3 vols.

[4]Franklin H. Littell, "The Churches and the Body Politic," *Daedalus*, 96 (Winter, 1967), 33-36.

[5]According to a Gallup Poll published in the *Los Angeles Times*, December 31, 1967. This poll indicated that church attendance was on the rise as compared with a similar poll two years before. In addition, 97 per cent of the carefully selected representative sample of adult Americans professed a belief in God. On the other hand, there is some reason to believe that religious commitment, if not church attendance, may be declining. See Rodney Stark and Charles Y. Glock, "Will Ethics Be the Death of Christianity?" *Trans-action*, V (June, 1968), 714.

of a specific religious denomination, many church leaders believe that the influence of religion in our lives has declined and that all aspects of society have become increasingly secular. Yet there can be little doubt that belief in God is almost universal in America and that this faith plays a central role in politics, both domestic and international.[6] Those who do not share this norm continue to experience sanctions.

In the face of seemingly contradictory trends of secularization and growing numbers who identify with some religious faith, the Supreme Court appears to be establishing an increasingly high wall of separation between church and state. But the construction of this wall has been hesitant and often uneven. Moreover, it is paradoxical that the Court, in seeking to establish a wall of separation, runs the risk of favoring nonbelief, thus "establishing" secularism as the civil religion of the nation. Two examples of the way the Court presently draws the line on those practices which it believes breaches that wall by "establishing" religion may help to illustrate the difficult path it has chosen in order to avoid hostility to religion.

First, the Court has held that no tax may be levied to support any religious activity or institution. Yet public funds may be expended for textbooks, school lunches, and transportation for parochial-school children—on the theory that such expenditures benefit the child and not the religion (although some state courts, for example, in Wisconsin and Oregon, have held such "child benefits" unconstitutional).

Second, the Court has prohibited prayers and Bible reading for religious purposes in public schools while allowing school districts to release some students earlier than others so that they may go off campus to obtain religious instruction.

As in their interpretation of the Constitution's prohibition on the establishment of religion, so also in guaranteeing the free exercise of religion the courts have sought to draw some fine lines. They have attempted to guarantee freedom of religious worship but have drawn the line on religious practices which were believed inimical to the public interest, such as those which (1) are considered potentially injurious to public health and safety, (2) pose a "clear and present danger" to public peace and order, (3) contravene accepted standards of public morality, or (4) enable one to avoid such civic responsibilities as the payment of taxes or military service. In the case of military service, the exemption from combat duty or the provision for alternative public service is allowed under specific and narrowly (but not clearly) defined circumstances.[7]

---

[6] For a discussion of this point, see Robert N. Bellah, "Civil Religion in America," *Daedalus*, 96 (Winter, 1967), 1-21.

[7] These general rules are drawn from Donald A. Gianella, "Religious Liberty, Nonestablishment, and Doctrinal Development, Part I: The Religious Liberty Guarantee," *Harvard Law Review*, 80 (May, 1967), 1387-1431.

Obviously, these four general rules do not solve the problem of determining when religious worship is subject to state restrictions. The difficulty of this problem is suggested by a number of the Supreme Court decisions on this question. The Court has ruled that people cannot be declared ineligible for unemployment compensation because they refused to accept jobs which would require them to work on their day of worship. But the Court has also sustained state laws which prohibit those whose day of worship is *other than* Sunday from operating their businesses on Sunday.[8] In guaranteeing the right of religious belief, the Court has gone so far as to strike down trespassing and soliciting laws which work hardship on those who advocate their beliefs door-to-door or on street corners. At the same time, the Court has held that religious *practices*, such as polygamy and snake handling, may be prohibited and that public-health measures, such as smallpox vaccination for all school children and blood tests for marriage licenses, may be required.

If all this seems confusing, if not contradictory, the fault may not lie with the members of our highest court. The First Amendment provision on religious freedom says two things: (1) "Congress shall make no law respecting an establishment of religion"; and (2) Congress shall not legislate "prohibiting the free exercise thereof." Each of these phrases can contradict the other, and understanding that the problem lies initially in our Constitution may help clarify the dilemmas the Supreme Court confronts.

For example, if Congress—or a state—does not provide funds to help some aspects of education in a parochial school, it places the children in that school at a disadvantage vis-à-vis their counterparts in public schools; the faithful of that religion (Roman Catholicism is not the only religion with parochial schools) are, in a sense, impeded in the "free exercise" of their worship. But if government does decide to aid such a school, and thereby aid its adherents in their worship, is it not legislating "respecting an establishment of religion"?

A moment's reflection on many of the specific issues in this general area will show how the inherent conflict was built into the original Constitution. Even a Court attitude of "A plague on [all] your houses [churches]!" by which no religion is allowed state aid, is a blind alley. Under this notion should a fire department be prevented from doing its work on a burning church because that would constitute aid to religion? If letting a church burn down seems an absurd extension of the "no aid" position, at what other specific point can the wall of separation between church and state be erected?

---

[8] Almost every state has one or more "never-on-Sunday" laws, prohibiting specific activities (such as boxing or haircutting) in some states and most types of industry and commerce in some other states.

The Court's refusal to adopt an all-or-nothing stance on defining the proper relationship between government and religion is an uneasy approach, for it is uncertain what values are so significant they can warrant a breach in the wall of separation. Yet, in long-run terms, one clear result visible from the Court's seemingly ambivalent position is that it has permitted—if indeed it has not spawned—religious pluralism in this country. This theme is made explicit by Wilber G. Katz and Harold P. Southerland in the first article of this chapter. These legal scholars place in perspective a number of recent Supreme Court decisions dealing with religion. Of special interest is their argument that certain kinds of state support of parochial schools are consistent with the concept of government neutrality in public affairs.

In *United States* v. *Seeger* (1965), the Supreme Court noted two trends in modern theology which tend to erode the distinction between the sacred and the secular and which highlight the ethical content of religion. The first trend is the shift from transcendental and supernatural perspectives to a greater emphasis on the immanence of meaning in nature and in human existence. The second of these developments is the movement among some theologians and faiths from God-centered dogma to a focus on man and his relationship to the universe. An increasing number of legal scholars have been urging that it will be necessary for the Court to take such notions of religion into account in interpreting the religion clauses of the Constitution. Some have argued that this requires a new definition of "religion" for legal purposes. William Carroll formulates such a definition in the second article of this chapter. His position is that religion should be defined as "the search for answers to ultimate questions." He illustrates how this definition might be applied to the resolution of some of the most difficult constitutional issues dealing with religion which continue to confront the courts.

But, as we stressed in the introduction to this book, there are important limits on the capacity of the courts to assure liberty. A good example of these limits is provided by the aftermath of the Supreme Court's decisions prohibiting both prayers in the public schools (*Engel* v. *Vitale*, 1962) and religious readings from the Bible (*Murray* v. *Curlett* and *Abington School District* v. *Schempp*, 1963). Despite the Court's unequivocal declaration that such required practices were unconstitutional, they continue to be part of the regular schedule in many schools. In 1964-1965, Frank Way, Jr., conducted a nationwide survey of public elementary-school teachers to determine the degree of compliance with the Court's decisions; 1,712 teachers responded to his questionnaire. He found that before 1962, 61 per cent of his respondents had said morning prayers in their classrooms, while in 1964-1965, only 28 per cent took part in such observances. Almost half of his respondents conducted Bible readings before 1962, but 21 per cent held

Bible readings in 1964-1965. The greatest degree of noncompliance was found in Southern states.[9]
Thus, while the Court's decisions appear to have resulted in the elimination of religious observances in many public schools, a large number of children still recite prayers or read the Bible in their class-rooms. The questions arise: Why is there compliance in some schools and not in others? What factors distinguish those local officials who comply from those who don't? Just such concerns are at the center of the selection by the political scientist Robert Birkby, who finds that there are no easy answers. Birkby examines the reactions in Tennes-see to the Court's prohibition of Bible reading in the Schempp case. Unlike Way's study, this article focuses on school boards and administ-rators, the "officials under the gun" of responsibility to obey the law.

As we have suggested is true for other aspects of liberty, so also full religious freedom depends ultimately on a citizenry willing to accept, and perhaps even value, diversity. Thus it is appropriate for those who seek to expand liberty to understand the sources of religious bigotry. Like other forms of intolerance, religious prejudice is traceable in large part to the intellectual rigidity which characterizes what has come to be called the "authoritarian personality." Among the social and demographic factors which are associated with religious bigotry are rural upbringing, lower occupational status, regional origin (big-otry is most common in the South and least in the West), lower edu-cational attainment, social isolation, and political conservatism.[10]

Another source of religious intolerance appears to be religion itself. In a recent extensive study of anti-Jewish prejudice, sociologists Charles Glock and Rodney Stark concluded: ". . . religious outlooks and images of the modern Jew seem to lie at the root of anti-Semitism of millions of American adults. . . . Indeed only 5 per cent of Americans with anti-Semitic views lack all rudiments of a religious basis for their prejudice."[11]
This does not mean that religious teachings and practices are the most important determinants of religious intolerance, but it is a seeming paradox that they are related at all. The final article in this chapter, by psychologist Milton Rokeach, examines the "paradoxes of

---

[9] H. Frank Way, Jr., *Liberty in the Balance* (2nd ed.; New York: McGraw-Hill, 1967), pp. 83-84. Way's survey did not deal with all types of religious observance. For example, in some schools which have eliminated morning prayers or Bible readings, prayers of grace are recited at snack time.

[10] See Don Stewart and Thomas Hoult, "A Social-Psychological Theory of the Authoritarian Personality," *American Journal of Sociology*, 65 (November, 1959), 277; and Herbert Greenberg and Don Fare, "An Investigation of Several Variables as Determinants of Authoritarianism," *Journal of Social Psychology* (February, 1959), pp. 105-111.

[11] *Christian Beliefs and Anti-Semitism* (New York: Harper, 1966), p. 205.

religious belief." Rokeach finds that nonbelievers, compared to those
with formal church affiliations, are often less anxious, less bigoted, and
more humanitarian, and he suggests some reasons why this is so.
These reasons provide some clues as to how we might move closer to
our professed ideal of freedom of belief.

It may be that whatever contributions religious dogma and practice
make to religious bigotry and other intolerance will be at least miti-
gated by the new teachings on religious freedom formulated by
Roman Catholic bishops at Vatican II, by the Christian ecumenical
movement, and by the increased social awareness of many clergy. [12]
But even if the adherents of different faiths become more tolerant of
one another, it is not likely that they will equally lessen their hostility toward those few whose conscience dictates that there is no God.
It is anomalous indeed, as Professor Rokeach points out, that atheists
are more tolerant of those who believe in God than believers are of
atheists.

But, whatever the gap between what Americans publicly say and
what they privately think and do, an important corrective to any quick
cynicism about our people is to realize how far we have come historically in closing that gap. As Professor John Roche noted in the first
chapter of this book, there is far more protection of those exercising
freedom today than in any alleged "Golden Age." For those who doubt
this, a brief survey of Gustavus Meyer's study of American bigotry will
demonstrate the point. [13] It has been a very long time since
Americans burned Roman Catholic nunneries or bombarded their
churches with cannon. Aside from a few who scuttle in the dark corners of America, no one now believes that Jews use the blood of Christians in their rituals. Some measure of the progress made even in the
past thirty years is the changing proportion of Americans who indicated they would vote for a Catholic for President—a proportion which
rose from 64 per cent to 84 per cent. Even more striking, only 46 per
cent of Americans in 1937 said they would vote for a Jew for President,
while in 1967, 82 per cent indicated they would do so. [14] All this has
meant an immense gain in the chance men have to exercise their
religion without fear of reprisal or social ostracism.

---

[12]On this last point, see Harvey G. Cox, "The 'New Breed' in American Churches:
Sources of Social Activism in American Religion," *Daedalus* 96 (Winter, 1967), 135-150.
[13]*The History of Bigotry in the United States* (New York: Random House,
1943).
[14]Data from a Gallup Poll and commentary published in the *San Francisco
Chronicle*, June 5, 1967.

WILBER G. KATZ and HAROLD P. SOUTHERLAND

Religious Pluralism and the Supreme Court

I

This essay examines the pattern of religious pluralism in the United States and the role that the Supreme Court has played in its development. . . . Pluralism . . . describes a society in which there prevails an attitude toward differences that reinforces and contributes to social cohesiveness.

A religiously pluralistic society, then, is one in which the principal religious groups not only claim freedom for themselves, but affirm equal freedom for others, whatever their beliefs may be. In such a society, these groups have also an internal freedom which is reflected in tolerance of criticism and openness to new insights. Individuals are free to doubt and to believe. This freedom is affirmed because of a realization of the need for dialogue, because groups and individuals have a stake—a religious stake—in the freedom of others. The model pluralism is also one in which there is a sensitivity to the differing needs of various groups and a disposition to accommodate these needs. Such a society need not embody perfection; it may contain groups that do not believe in or practice religious freedom. But a society can approximate the model pluralism if such groups are no great threat to freedom, if a trust in the common commitment to religious freedom prevails among the principal groups.

In this essay, the recent work of the Supreme Court will be interpreted as expanding religious freedom and thus creating a legal structure favorable to the maturing of this kind of religious pluralism. This interpretation may be debatable, legally and historically; but however the Court's work is interpreted, the influence of its decisions on American religious culture can be neither ignored nor minimized.

Controversy in church-state matters centers on the First Amendment's cryptic injunction that "Congress shall make no law respecting an establishment of religion, or prohibiting the free exercise thereof." This provision is now held to bind also the state legislatures by virtue of the due-process clause of the Fourteenth Amendment. The historical meaning of the quoted words is at best obscure. But there is general agreement that they

Reprinted from "Religious Pluralism and the Supreme Court," *Daedalus* (Winter, 1967), pp. 180-192, with permission of *Daedalus*, Journal of the American Academy of Arts and Sciences, Boston, Mass. Winter 1967, "Religion in America." Some footnotes have been omitted, and the remainder renumbered to run in sequence.

were designed to accomplish some kind of separation of church and state. When inquiry is made, however, as to the degree and kind of separation required, agreement disappears—with respect both to historical meaning and to policy objectives. It is here submitted that the Court has made it clear that the church-state separation required by the Constitution is not one that insulates government from contacts with religion, but rather one that maximizes religious freedom through a policy of government neutrality. The Constitution does not limit religious freedom to the freedom compatible with strict separation; it requires only the separation compatible with maximum freedom. (Religious freedom has, of course, its limits, as the courts have made clear in cases dealing with polygamy, blood transfusion, snake handling, and compulsory education.)

The Supreme Court has expanded freedom in two principal ways. It has insisted upon a policy of neutrality that forbids government promotion or sponsorship of religious beliefs. By this insistence, the Court has not merely protected the freedom of those who hold different beliefs; it has protected the freedom of commitment to favored beliefs from being compromised by government sponsorship. In the second place, the Court has also expanded religious freedom by permitting, and sometimes requiring, special provisions to be made for religion where this is necessary to neutralize the otherwise restrictive effects of government's expanding activities.

These actions have not always been viewed as actions expanding religious freedom, nor have the Court's opinions always been couched in these terms. But for the study of religion and American culture, the prime significance of the Court's recent work has been its creation of broadly libertarian structures for the religious pluralism of the future.

II

The outlines of neutrality, the dominant theme in the Court's church-state decisions, began to emerge in 1947 in *Everson v. Board of Education*, the first of the Court's controversial decisions in this area. In this case, New Jersey's provision for bus transportation for parochial-school students was attacked as a "law respecting an establishment of religion" prohibited by the First Amendment. Although the opinion sustaining the statute was primarily a discussion of the limits of separation, it included a statement that the First Amendment requires the state to be neutral—not only neutral toward sects but also neutral toward "groups of religious believers and non-believers."

The meaning of neutrality became much clearer in 1961 when the Court unanimously struck down a historic provision of the Maryland constitution requiring a declaration of belief in the existence of God as a prerequisite to holding public office. The plaintiff was a member of the American Humanist Association who had precipitated the test by applying for a commission as a notary public. In holding that the test oath requirement violated his "freedom of belief and religion," the Court declared, in effect, that the state may not discriminate on grounds of religion, regardless of whether the discrimination favors a particular belief or favors all who believe in God at the expense of non-theists. In this case, the Court departed for the first time from traditional usage of the word *religion*, referring to "religions . . . which do not teach what would generally be considered a belief in the existence of God" and citing "Ethical Culture and Secular Humanism."

In the 1962 and the 1963 cases on public-school devotions, the plaintiffs included both sectarians who objected to the particular kind of worship that was sponsored and secularists who objected to any religious devotions. In all of the cases, the Court held that public-school authorities may not sponsor practices which imply the taking of sides in relation to religion. In the *Regents' Prayer* case,[1] the emphasis was on the impropriety of the Regents' action in promulgating an official prayer, notwithstanding its nonsectarian character and the broad approval given it by Jewish and Christian spokesmen.

In the *Schempp* case,[2] the neutrality doctrine received repeated emphasis. The Court stated a test: To avoid violating the "no-establishment" clause, an action of a public agency must not be designed to promote (or inhibit) religious beliefs or practices. In the words of one of the justices, neutrality requires "the extension of evenhanded treatment to all who believe, doubt, or disbelieve—a refusal on the part of the State to weight the scales of private choice." All but one of the justices considered official sponsorship of daily devotions to be inconsistent with neutrality.

Some of the Court's critics have argued that toleration is all that a religious minority (including those who profess no religion) can reasonably expect. Erwin N. Griswold, for example, wrote in his criticism of the *Regents' Prayer* case:

The child of a nonconforming or minority group is, to be sure, different in his beliefs. That is what it means to be a member of a minority. Is it not desirable, and educational, for him to learn and observe this, in the atmosphere of the school—not so much that he is different, as that other children are different from him? And is it not desirable that, at the same time, he experience and learn the fact that his difference is tolerated and accepted? No compulsion is put upon him. He need not participate. But he, too, has the opportunity to be tolerant. He allows

---

[1] *Engel v. Vitale*, 370 U.S. 421 (1962).
[2] *Abington School Dist. v. Schempp*, 374 U.S. 203 (1963).

the majority of the group to follow their own tradition, perhaps coming to understand and to respect what they feel is significant to them.[3]

This view is incompatible with the kind of pluralism envisaged by the Court, a pluralism based not on tolerance but on equal freedom. As Mark DeWolfe Howe has said, leaders in the formative period of our government aimed at "converting the liberal principle of tolerance into the radical principle of liberty" and "believed that it might be achieved by prohibiting the governmental establishment of religion and guaranteeing religious freedom to all persons."[4]

The case of the humanist notary made it clear that the protection of the neutrality principle extends to those who do not believe in God. The 1965 conscientious-objector decisions had, therefore, been foreshadowed. Exemption from military service for conscientious objectors has traditionally been predicated on opposition to war stemming from religious training and belief. In 1948, Congress added the qualification that religious belief for this purpose means "belief in relation to a Supreme Being," to the exclusion of moral, philosophical, or other views. But, in *United States v. Seeger*, the Supreme Court held that the exemption covers an agnostic whose opposition to war is based on "belief in the devotion to goodness and virtue for their own sakes, and a religious faith in a purely ethical creed." The Court refused to attribute to Congress any narrow or parochial concept of religious belief, although it seems quite likely that a narrow concept had been intended. The test, the Court said, was "whether a given belief that is sincere and meaningful occupies a place in the life of its possessor parallel to that filled by the orthodox belief in God of one who clearly qualifies for the exemption." Citing an impressive array of theological authorities, the Court stated that its interpretation embraced "the ever broadening understanding of the modern religious community."

Thus far, this section has dealt with the way in which the neutrality doctrine protects the freedom of those who hold a particular belief from governmental action penalizing them or promoting other beliefs. But the promoting of religious beliefs or practices by government would impair also the freedom of those who hold the favored beliefs. The neutrality rule protects the freedom of religious commitment from the devitalizing effects of government sponsorship.

Recent observers of American religious culture have seen that "establishment" can be a threat to free religion even where there is no established

[3] Erwin N. Griswold, "Absolute Is in the Dark," *Utah Law Review*, Vol. 8 (Summer, 1963), pp. 167, 177.
[4] Mark DeWolfe Howe, review of Stokes, *Church and State in the United States*, *Harvard Law Review*, Vol. 64 (November, 1950), pp. 170-72.

church. Peter L. Berger has written of "the religious establishment in America" as the principal threat to the vitality of Christian commitment.[5] The danger is that churches may become captive institutions submerged in a culture religion identified with the American Way of Life. Berger called the public schools "the principal agency representing the politically established culture religion." From this point of view, one can readily see at least symbolic importance in what the Court has done in checking the use of the public schools to propagate this faith.

* * * *

Varying reactions of "believers" to the public-school prayer decisions give clues to varying attitudes toward this internal religious freedom. Initial comments of religious spokesmen were largely critical of the decisions. They often interpreted them as restrictions of the religious freedom of the majority and rejected the Court's assertion that free exercise of religion "has never meant that a majority could use the machinery of the State to practice its beliefs." Second thoughts brought many religious leaders to defend the Court and to oppose efforts to nullify its decision by amendment of the constitution. Some of the second thoughts were induced by concern over the peculiar religiosity of many of the demands for Constitutional amendment. They had an almost hysterical quality that seemed to reflect a fear of genuine religious freedom that was masked behind an insistence that religious belief have the support of agencies of government. Church leaders came to see the dangers of civic religion as a substitute for other religious commitment. They came to see government sponsorship of religion as a threat to the prophetic witness of the churches and a threat to religious freedom. According to one witness at the Congressional hearings, "the threat is not the secularization of our schools but the secularization of our religion." The Court's insistence on neutrality came to be seen as a protection against this threat.

Critics of the Court often claim that the prayer and Bible reading decisions are hostile to traditional religion and amount to an establishment of secularism. These claims ignore not only the point just developed, but also the Court's careful assurances that neutrality toward religion does not mean the elimination from public education of all study of religious beliefs and practices. On the contrary, the Court warned:

It might well be said that one's education is not complete without a study of comparative religion or the history of religion and its relationship to the advancement of civilization. It certainly may be said that the Bible is worthy of study for its literary and historic qualities. Nothing we have said here indicates

---

[5] Peter L. Berger, *The Noise of Solemn Assemblies,* (Garden City, N. Y., 1961).

that such study of the Bible or of religion, when presented objectively as part of a secular program of education, may not be effected consistent with the First Amendment.

Educators are beginning to struggle with the practical problems inherent in such "objective" study of religion. The difficulties in maintaining neutrality are formidable. There must be no "teaching for commitment"; the teaching must be "about" religion and not "of" religion. Furthermore, even in a community with a large Protestant majority, it would not be neutral to limit the instruction to beliefs of Protestant churches. There may be even greater difficulty in maintaining neutrality toward traditional religious beliefs and other views of man and his relationships. There is always a danger that teaching about representative faiths (Protestant, Catholic, and Jewish) will carry the implication that this tri-faith pluralism is the American religion, that all good Americans are at least nominally committed to one of these faiths.

Perfect neutrality, however, is not required. In one area, at least, the Court has tolerated what Mark DeWolfe Howe has called "de-facto establishment."[6] The Court has refused to upset traditional Sunday-closing laws. Notwithstanding the admittedly religious roots of these laws and the religious language in which some of them are still cast, the Court found that Sunday laws are now designed to serve the secular purpose of providing a uniform day of rest and recreation.

III

The Court has also protected religious freedom by holding that the establishment clause does not forbid special provisions for religion of a type that may be called "neutralizing" aids. These are provisions made to neutralize the restrictions of religious freedom that would otherwise result from government's secular activities. The classic example of such provisions is the chaplaincy program in the armed services. This program is designed not to promote religion, but to promote religious freedom. When the government separates men from ordinary opportunities for worship and pastoral care, it may properly provide substitute opportunities. Such action accords with a policy of neutrality and is therefore not forbidden by the establishment clause. This assertion may be made with confidence although the chaplaincy program has never been before the Court.

Religious exemptions furnish other examples of neutralizing aids. A familiar case is that of the draft exemption of religious conscientious objectors. In the 1918 *Selective Draft Law Cases*, the Court brushed aside a

---

[6]Mark DeWolfe Howe, *The Garden and the Wilderness*, p. 11.

contention that the exemptions were invalid under the "no-establishment" clause, and the recent cases reaffirm this view. This does not mean that Congress might not constitutionally abolish all exemptions for conscientious objectors. The result is that conscription is an area where the effective scope of religious freedom depends upon action by Congress, subject only to a constitutional duty to avoid discrimination.

In certain other areas, however, religious exemptions may be mandatory. This has recently been the Court's ruling with respect to unemployment-compensation laws. These laws provide compensation only for persons willing to accept employment, and for most workers this means willingness to take a job requiring work on Saturday. In 1963, the Supreme Court held that the Constitution requires that a Seventh Day Adventist be exempted from this requirement. This result, the Court said, "reflects nothing more than the governmental obligation of neutrality in the face of religious differences, and does not represent that involvement of religious with secular institutions which it is the object of the Establishment Clause to forestall."

Even more striking is the decision of the California Supreme Court that the First Amendment requires exempting from narcotics laws the traditional use of peyote in religious ceremonies. The court assumed that non-religious use of peyote might be proscribed. The dominant consideration in requiring the exemption was apparently the court's view of the value of cultural pluralism:

In a mass society, which presses at every point toward conformity, the protection of a self-expression, however unique, of the individual and the group becomes ever more important. The varying currents of the subcultures that flow into the mainstream of our national life give it depth and beauty. We preserve a greater value than an ancient tradition when we protect the rights of the Indians who honestly practiced an old religion in using peyote one night at a meeting in a desert hogan near Needles, California.[7]

Exemptions for Sabbatarians are often written into Sunday-closing laws. While these exemptions are not mandatory, they have been upheld by the Court as not involving "establishment." Special exemptions for other religious groups are increasingly common. For example, the recent amendments to the Social Security Act exempt from social-security taxes the members of religious groups that are conscientiously opposed to insurance and that make adequate provision for their own dependent members. These are examples of what Justice Harlan called the "many areas in which the pervasive activities of the State justify some special provision for religion to prevent it from being submerged in an all-embracing secularism."[8]

---

[7] *People v. Woody*, 61 Cal. 2d 716, 394 P. 2d 813, 821-22 (1964).
[8] *Sherbert v. Verner*, 374 U.S. 398, 422 (1963).

All of these illustrations show that an insulating type of church-state separation is not required. Avoiding religious controversies is not the prime objective of church-state policy. If all religious exemptions were outlawed, legislative bodies would, to be sure, be protected from troublesome involvement in religious disputes. But this protection would be at the expense of religious freedom. It is for this reason that the Court has held that such insulation is not required by the First Amendment. The Court apparently believes that the health of American religious pluralism is such that issues concerning religious exemptions need not be kept out of the public forum.

Permissible aids for religion are not limited to aids in the form of exemptions, as the case of the chaplaincy program makes clear. But can the use of public funds for education in religious schools be defended as a neutralizing aid, a means of promoting freedom of religious choice? This question is the principal item of unfinished church-state business faced by the Supreme Court. To understand the question one must begin with an impressive fact: the enormous cost of public education. This cost is properly assessed upon all taxpayers, whether or not they patronize the public schools. But the burden of this cost, in the absence of neutralizing aids, greatly reduces the practical freedom to choose a school that combines general education with religious training. The Constitution guarantees the rights to conduct and to patronize religious schools if they meet general standards, but taxes for public education hamper the freedom to enjoy this right. The position taken in this paper is that in a religiously pluralistic society freedom of religious choice is a matter of general sympathetic concern, and that the legal structures for such a society ought, therefore, to permit financial aids to be voted in order to neutralize restraints on such freedom.

Many educational aids have already been provided by both federal and state governments. Among the more important federal statutes are the National Defense Education Act, the Higher Education Facilities Act, and notably the Elementary and Secondary Education Act of 1965. State aids include not only provisions for transportation, standard textbooks, and various auxiliary services, but also appropriations for college scholarships and tuition grants. Aids at the college level raise less controversy than those for elementary and secondary education. Proposals for aid at the lower levels bring out deep-rooted oppositions to private schools in general and Roman Catholic schools in particular.

Even at the elementary-school level, however, there is widening recognition among religious leaders of the strength of the case for government aid as a feature of free pluralism. Dr. F. Ernest Johnson, long an education expert of the National Council of Churches, wrote that he considers opposition to transportation and textbook aid to be unfair and "a conspicuous example of the fact that Americans seem readier to accept the idea of cultural pluralism than to accept its consequences."⁹ Recently, Milton Himmelfarb has challenged the "wall of separation" position from which American Jews have traditionally opposed aids to religious schools. ¹⁰ He developed the case for government aid not only in terms of fairness and of national educational policy, but also as a means of preserving a vigorous pluralism as a safeguard of freedom.

These views have increasing support because of increasing trust in the commitment of American Catholics to religious freedom. The declaration of Vatican II on this subject and the new openness of Roman Catholicism to other religious groups have combined to create a new climate for American religious pluralism.

The Supreme Court has spoken twice on the subject of educational aids. Twenty years ago, the Court upheld in the *Everson* case the constitutionality of a state statute providing reimbursement of the cost of bus transportation to parochial schools. The Court stated the neutrality rule in language already quoted and said also:

> We must be careful, in protecting the citizens of New Jersey from state-established churches, to be sure that we do not inadvertently prohibit New Jersey from extending its general state law benefits to all its citizens without regard to their religious belief. ¹¹

The same opinion, however, included also a general statement against aid to religion which is often cited by advocates of strict separation. The actual decision in *Everson* can be regarded as settled since the Court voted in 1961 in a similar case not to permit reargument of the question.

It is possible, of course, to distinguish between costs of transportation and costs more directly related to education; many other distinctions might conceivably be drawn. The type of aid provided by the federal education act of 1965 furnishes a convenient focus for considering the general problem. This statute provides that projects submitted by local public-school authorities must include arrangements such as dual enrollment in which children in private schools can participate. Dual enrollment (or "shared time") refers to an arrangement by which parochial-school pupils also attend the public school on a part-time basis. Such arrangements have long been in operation for subjects such as industrial arts and home economics; they have been held constitutional in the only case in which a test has been made. The use of dual enrollment has recently been extended to

---

⁹F. Ernest Johnson, "A Problem of Culture," *Religion and the Schools* (Fund for the Republic, 1959), p. 71.

¹⁰Milton Himmelfarb, "Church and State: How High a Wall?" *Commentary*, Vol. 42 (July, 1966), p. 23.

¹¹*Everson v. Board of Education*, 330 U.S. 1, 16 (1947).

instruction in sciences, languages, and other subjects not always available in religious schools.

A second title of the education act authorizes grants for textbooks and school-library resources. State authorities receiving funds under this title must give assurances that such books and resources will be provided on an equitable basis for the use of children and teachers in private schools.

Both of these provisions for private schools are questioned by those who are committed to an insulation type of church-state separation. The American Civil Liberties Union, for example, has declared that dual-enrollment programs "present grave constitutional and civil liberties problems under the Establishment Clause . . . because of the substantial benefit that [they] confer upon sectarian schools and because of the joint involvement by secular and church authorities."

Much of the Congressional debate on the education act centered on the so-called "child-benefit" theory, under which it was contended that the bill granted aid only to children and not to religious schools. On this theory, so the argument runs, these aids furnish no precedent for other, more substantial types of aid, such as grants for purchase of scientific equipment. This child-benefit distinction is highly unsatisfactory since all these aids benefit both the children and their schools. All such aids can be defended, however, as neutralizing aids designed to promote freedom in the choice of school.

While prophecy in constitutional law is foolhardy, we hazard the prediction that the Court will not adopt a broad prohibition of programs that help religious schools meet the costs of standard education. None of the bases on which such a prohibition might conceivably be rested seems likely to appeal to the Court. It is highly unlikely that the Court, after its careful exposition of the neutrality principle, will ever take "absolute separation" as a major premise. Nor does it seem likely that the Court will say that separate school systems are so undesirable in a pluralistic society that the establishment clause should be construed as forbidding neutralizing aids. It is also unlikely that the Court will support the claim of opponents of parochial schools that their religious freedom includes freedom from taxes levied to protect freedom of educational choice. Nor is it likely that the Court will follow the fear-inspired logic of those who believe that Roman Catholic attitudes toward religious freedom are still ambivalent, notwithstanding the declarations of Vatican II.

Finally, one may trust that the Court will not consider questions of educational aids to be so hot that they must at all costs be kept off the agendas of Congress and state legislatures. These are issues that can be left to the democratic process because of the healthy vigor of American religious pluralism: a pluralism that is finding its unity in a spreading trust in the common belief in religious freedom.

IV

Decisions of the Supreme Court have here been interpreted as creating a legal structure within which religious life in the United States can move toward a mature pluralism that reflects an active commitment to religious freedom. Discussion has focused on two applications of a general principle of neutrality. The structure created by the Court is partly permissive. Government may aid religion in ways which protect religious freedom in the context of government's own pervasive activities. But part of the Court's structure is restrictive. Government may not take sides in religious matters; it may not promote religious beliefs—either specific beliefs or religion in general.

It is easy to belittle the practical importance of these restrictions. In the public-school cases, for example, did the Court actually add to the freedom of minorities? Did it actually increase the freedom with which beliefs are held by the majority? It is easy to give a negative answer, and it is easy also to criticize the Court's "absolutist" rhetoric. But such judgments miss an important point. The principal importance of the Court's decisions in this field is symbolic. The Court is commending to citizens of a country with many faiths the ideal of an expanding and deepening religious freedom. In doing so, it is not surprising that the Court uses high-sounding rhetoric. As in the cases on desegregation, if the Court succeeds, it will be through its influence on changing attitudes.

It is not impossible that cultural development in the United States will be toward a pattern in which religious life is sustained more by the vitality of inner freedom than by the pressures of social establishment. It is not impossible that development will be toward a pluralism in which minorities are accorded not the grace of toleration but the right of equal freedom. If these developments do take place, future historians may assign some of the credit to the Supreme Court.

WILLIAM CARROLL

Toward a New Definition of
Religious Belief

* * * *

I . . . propose that for constitutional purposes religion be defined as the search for answers to the ultimate questions—such as: Who made man and the universe? What is the end of man?[1] These are questions which historically have frequently been answered on the basis of religion (in the sense of belief in the supernatural) derived from revelation, tradition, reason, other sources, or from a combination of two or more of these sources. These questions have also been answered on the basis of systems of thought which have nothing to do with religion in the sense of belief in God, gods, or the supernatural—revealed, traditional, or natural. . . .

Obviously, there is no consensus in the United States—or indeed in the world—about the answers to these ultimate questions. . . . [Unless] religion is defined to include both belief and nonbelief in God in regard to both the free exercise and the establishment clauses, the state cannot be wholly neutral, the liberty inherent in the one or the limitation inherent in the other will be applied differently to believers and nonbelievers.

It is possible to conceive of two ways in which the state could be neutral in regard to religion, defined as concerned with these ultimate questions: first, the state could have nothing whatever to do with any matter related to these questions; or, second, it could simply refuse to support any particular set of answers. . . .

---

[1]Such a definition was long ago implied by Justice Frankfurter in a free exercise case, when, speaking for the Court, he said, "Certainly the affirmative pursuit of one's convictions about the ultimate mystery of the universe and man's relation to it is placed beyond the reach of the laws": *Minersville School District* v. *Gobitis,* 310 U.S. 586, 593 (1940).

The third session of Vatican II adopted a "Declaration on the Church's Relations with Non-Christians," the summary of which contained the following Introduction:

"The community of all peoples is one. One is their origin, for God made the entire human race live on all the face of the earth. One, too, is their ultimate end, God. *Men expect from the various religions answers to the riddles of the human condition: What is man? What is the meaning and purpose of our lives? What is moral good and what is sin? What are death, judgment, and retribution after death?":* Council Daybook, *Vatican II,* Session 3. Edited by Floyd Anderson (Washington, D.C.: National Catholic Welfare Conference, 1965), p. 282 (emphasis added).

Reprinted by permission of the author and the publisher from "The Constitution, the Supreme Court, and Religion," *The American Political Science Review,* 61 (September, 1967), 657-674. All footnotes but two have been omitted.

Between these two alternatives . . . only the latter is consistent with our historic practice and with the requirements of the common good in our own day. From the earliest times in America the state has been concerned with education, a concern which has steadily mounted, so that the great bulk of formal education is now conducted by the state, while even private education is subject to state standards and is the recipient of state favor, particularly in the form of tax exemptions. Moreover, the state has long maintained museums, libraries, and concert halls, and encouraged research. And even in the narrow realm of religion, in the sense of belief in God, the state has maintained an attitude of friendly cooperation, admittedly engaging in some practices which would fail to meet the demands of neutrality, but which nevertheless manifest a recognition on the part of the state of the undoubted contribution which matters of the spirit make to the "general welfare."

* * * *

The understanding of the establishment clause suggested here would allow leeway for the operation of the free exercise clause and should always be interpreted with an awareness of the requirements of the free exercise clause. It thus would avoid the tendency of some legal commentators to emphasize the establishment clause to the virtual exclusion of the free exercise clause. For example, it would permit an exemption from Sunday closing laws for persons who observed some day other than Sunday as the Sabbath, as well as the special arrangement required by the Court for Sabbatarians seeking unemployment compensation. In a land where faiths and nonfaiths are so diverse, some provision ought to be made for the nonconformist if the free exercise of religion is to continue to enjoy its honored place in our scheme of things. The controlling issue in an exemption case is the freedom of the person who needs the exemption to follow his conscience and to stay out of jail. To be sure, not every conscience can be accommodated to all the laws of the land, but when general laws conflict with conscientious scruples, exemptions ought to be granted unless some "compelling state interest" intervenes, to employ a test applied by the Court in a recent exemption case. At best, the way of the nonconformist for conscience's sake is hard, our Constitution requires that he not be unnecessarily burdened by general laws, even when these laws seem wise and good to the vast majority of Americans. We can afford to be generous in these matters, and we ought to be as generous as the good order of the country will admit.

* * * *

There . . . [are] a number of problems in regard to the religion clauses of the Constitution which have not yet been settled by the Court, and which can properly be considered in the light of the proposed concept of governmental neutrality and the proposed definition of religion. . . .

[For example, the] problem of the conscientious objector and the religion clauses of the Constitution is made particularly acute by the phraseology of the exemption for conscientious objection found in the Selective Service Act of 1948, which exempts a person "who, by reason of religious training and belief, is conscientiously opposed to participation in war in any form." Then the act goes on to define religion as follows: "Religious training and belief in this connection means any individual's belief in a relation to a Supreme Being involving duties superior to those arising from any human relation, but does not include essentially political, sociological, or philosophical views, or a merely personal moral code." This definition certainly does not embody a governmental position of neutrality between belief and nonbelief in God. The Court recently faced the problem of applying this definition, but because of the facts before it, and by some judicial redrafting of the legislation, the Court was able to dodge the central question which was raised.

. . . The Court . . . went into a lengthy discussion of the problem of the concepts of religion and a Supreme Being, quoting modern theologians and other sources. Throughout this discussion the Court seems to be saying that many persons who do not believe in God in the traditional sense, actually believe in some kind of a Supreme Being, however vague, even if they do not know it. In the light of these considerations the Court in effect then redrafted the legislative definition of religion for conscientious objection[.]

There are two ways of interpreting this redrafted test: first, . . . [c]onscientious objection can be claimed if somehow, in some remote, confused, or even unknowing way, the objector believes in a Supreme Being. This interpretation is almost compelled by a later paragraph in the opinion of the Court which in effect defines a "merely personal" code (which Congress said could not be the basis of exemption) as one "which is not only personal but which is the sole basis for the registrant's belief and *is in no way related to a Supreme Being.*"

The second possible (but doubtful) interpretation of the Court's redraft of the legislative standard of religious belief is that any belief—even a firm belief that God does not exist—meets the test of religious belief, so long as it is as intense and as firmly held as that of an orthodox believer in God. . . .

Thus the Court's attempt to redraft the religious test for conscientious objectors is unsatisfactory under both possible interpretations of the intention of the Court if governmental neutrality in matters of religion is to be preserved, even though the Court's device may have obtained justice for the litigants before it. The definition of religion for constitutional purposes which has been proposed in this paper does, however, suggest a test which would meet the constitutional requirement of neutrality. An applicant for exemption could be asked: Do you, because of your concept of the origin of man and the universe, or because of your concept of the end of man, conscientiously object to participation in war of any kind? This test would place believers and nonbelievers, orthodox and unorthodox believers in a Supreme Being on a plane of equality and thus preserve for government its proper role of neutrality.

* * * *

[Consider, too,] the question of governmental aid to religion in the field of education. . . . Placing federal and state aid to religion in the same category, and speaking only in terms of the Constitution of the United States, it is possible to divide this problem into two questions: Can government aid religion by providing or arranging for courses in religion in public institutions? Can government aid religion by providing financial aid and cooperation to educational institutions operated by religious organizations?

To consider the question of the study of religion in public institutions it is necessary to distinguish between education below the college level and education at or above the college level. Below the college level the rights and duties of parents loom large, the state and the parents in a very real sense share in the task of educating the child. Parents can quite legitimately seek to protect their children from ideas or practices in the religious sphere which they consider unscientific, heretical, or merely absurd. This claim of parents can be met by confining instruction largely to tool subjects and by treating references to the ultimate questions in such subjects as history and literature in a neutral fashion. Such neutrality would become progressively more difficult as the student advanced toward graduation from high school, but perhaps it could be approximated within some tolerable limits. Moreover, this approach would leave wide gaps in the students' education in regard to the ultimate questions, gaps which could be filled only haphazardly and unevenly, by parents, Sunday schools, or other devices. This is not a happy solution to the problem—indeed, it has been argued that such neutrality is impossible—but in communities where arrangements for filling the gaps are not feasible, the training offered would enable children to acquire some skills and information, which might justify the risk of incidental indoctrination regarding the ultimate questions. Neutrality and the rights of parents, as well as education itself, could be better served by some system of released or dismissed time religious education or, even better, by a system of shared time under which students could examine in detail the implications of the ultimate questions for history, literature, and other subjects without exposing themselves to systems of thought or belief from which their parents wished to protect them. . . . The point is that while children should not be required to study religious or non-religious beliefs which their parents do not hold, both the private and the public good are served by a system which both permits children to explore the ultimate questions and protects their tender consciences. While the Constitution does not require that special arrangements be made for study (segregated by belief) of the ultimate questions in elementary and secondary education, the Constitution, in conformity with the proposed rule of neutrality, would permit such study, provided of course that believers and nonbelievers were given equal opportunities to provide the instruction contemplated. For by arranging for such a system, government does not prefer one kind of belief or nonbelief over another, rather it merely permits persons to make their beliefs meaningful . . . and thus promotes the free exercise of religion.

At the college and university level, the principle of neutrality in matters of religion requires that we recognize and accept the practices which the principle of academic freedom and other factors have already established, and that we extend the application of these practices. That is to say, the answers to the ultimate questions are already being explored in philosophy, literature, political science, and many other disciplines, each instructor, and indeed each student, being free to answer these questions according to his own insight. Moreover, state colleges and universities offer courses frankly labeled "religion" (as do many private institutions), which study the tenets of various recognized religions, often based on revelation as understood in the religion studied. If the principle of neutrality is to be fully implemented, so-called courses in religion, narrowly defined, must be given the same place in the curricula of state universities which is now given to other disciplines, which explore the ultimate questions. If the state is to be neutral in matters of religion, defined to include both belief and nonbelief, it is forbidden not only to prescribe devotional readings, but also to exclude revelation or other spiritual sources from the curriculum.

. . . Not every state college could be expected to offer courses in every religion, just as not every college offers courses on Mongolian poets. Normal academic standards, such as the availability of competent instructors and student interest, would operate in the establishment of courses in the traditional religions as they do in other disciplines. . . .

The more widely publicized problem is whether government may, under the proposed concept of neutrality in matters of religion, give aid to schools operated by churches. Assuming that government may give aid to private organizations in the pursuit of some public purpose, and assuming that the aid is not confined to church schools, the answer is affirmative. For the state, if it is religiously neutral, may not establish any religious tests— neither those that condition aid on a corporate commitment to God nor those based on no corporate commitment to God. Just as the original Constitution requires that "no religious test shall ever be required as a qualification to any office or public trust under the United States," so the First and Fourteenth Amendments require under the rule of neutrality that "no religious test shall ever be required as a qualification" for the receipt of governmental aid by any person or organization. For purposes of determining eligibility for governmental aid, the creeds, acknowledged or unacknowledged, of those who operate the organizations applying for aid are as irrelevant as their color or race.

The state may, of course, elect not to give aid to private schools, or to any other category of private institutions. To distinguish between a public institution and a private one is reasonable and does not disrupt the neutral role which the establishment clause imposes upon government. To be sure, it has been argued that justice requires that government aid schools operated by religious organizations, but, without examining this claim, it is safe to say that, in view of all the practical difficulties which might arise, the validity of the claim in individual circumstances ought to be left to the political branches rather than be erected as an immutable principle of constitutional law. For if every demand for individual treatment arising from religious convictions had to be honored, government might well be led into a bewildering morass of remedial actions; in our pluralistic society many governmental actions and expenditures will inevitably provide services which some of our citizens cannot conscientiously use, and which will be positively offensive to the scruples of many?[2] Nevertheless, if the political branches of the government decide, for whatever reasons, that subsidies be given to private schools, no religious test may be constitutionally applied to determine eligibility for these subsidies, if government is to be neutral in matters of religion.

*   *   *   *

[2]Although Lew Pfeffer holds that the Constitution positively forbids governmental aid to parochial schools, he can be effectively quoted in support of the more limited concept that the Constitution does not require governmental aid for parochial schools. Discussing the argument that to exclude parochial schools from federal aid to education would interfere with freedom of religion, he writes:

"During the past decade there has been a growing movement to fluoridate the water supply in order to protect the teeth of our children. Many municipalities have engaged in the program. But drinking fluoridated water violates the conscience of Christian Scientists. A number of suits have been brought to stop the program, but all have proved unsuccessful and the Supreme Court has refused to interfere with these decisions. It would undoubtedly be a great expense for Christian Scientists living in communities with a fluoridated water supply to purchase unfluoridated water as required by their conscience and the demands of life. Compulsion of life is at least as potent as compulsion of law, yet I have not come across a single report of a demand by Christian Scientists that the government give them money so that they can buy such water and thus be economically able to exercise their freedom of religion. I doubt very much that, if such a demand were made, serious consideration would be given to it by the courts.": "Federal Funds for Parochial Schools? No," *Notre Dame Lawyer*, 37 (March, 1962), 317.

ROBERT H. BIRKBY

To Pray or Not To Pray: Non-Compliance in the School Prayer Cases

I

* * * *

Engel v. *Vitale* had foreshadowed the Supreme Court's decision in the 1963 case of *Abington School District* v. *Schempp*. In *Engel* the Court declared the New York Regents' prayer invalid as an establishment of religion. The narrow holding was "that the constitutional prohibition against laws respecting an establishment of religion must at least mean that in this country it is no part of the business of government to compose official prayers for any group of the American people to recite as a part of a religious program carried on by government." The broader implications of the decision brought an immediate reaction from all parts of the country. Religious groups split over the wisdom of the decision, newspapers praised or damned the Court, and private individuals quickly took sides.

After the initial reaction, church groups began to assess the probable future of all types of devotional exercises in the public schools. Despite differing opinions concerning the desirability of such exercises most conceded that, if challenged, required exercises such as Bible reading and recitation of the Lord's Prayer were doomed. Some churches tried to prepare their members for this eventuality. The relative lack of outcry when the *Schempp* decision confirmed the predictions may be looked upon as an index to the success of the churches' "educational" program.

In its simplest form *Schempp* declared that the required reading of the Bible without comment and the use of the Lord's Prayer as a regular religious exercise in the public schools was constitutionally impermissible as an establishment of religion. The Court was careful to note that "nothing we have said here indicates that . . . study of the Bible or of religion, when presented objectively as part of a secular program of education, may not be

Reprinted from "The Supreme Court and the Bible Belt: Tennessee Reaction to the 'Schempp' Decision," *Midwest Journal of Political Science*, Vol. X, No. 3 (August, 1966), pp. 306-308, 310-319, by Robert H. Birkby by permission of the author and the Wayne State University Press. Copyright 1966, by Wayne State University Press. Some footnotes have been omitted, and the remainder renumbered to run in sequence. Tables have been omitted.

effected consistently with the First Amendment." As a result of this decision there was no doubt about the invalidity of the practices in Pennsylvania and Baltimore where the cases originated. In theory there should be no doubt about the status of similar programs in other states including Tennessee. Yet a cursory reading of the newspaper documents a definite lack of compliance in several states. One school superintendent in Tennessee explained why his schools had not changed their practice: "In that the state law has not been voided, I as Superintendent instructed the teachers to proceed as before."

II

If the *Schempp* decision had any effect in Tennessee it should be noticeable in the policies adopted and enforced at the school district level. The State Commissioner of Education was reported as saying that it was permissible to read the Bible in public schools despite *Schempp* but he left the final decision to local school officials. The school boards were left free to continue the practice required by state law or to comply with the Court's ruling. This study was undertaken to determine what the school boards did and, if possible, why. Even though it was expected that, in Gordon Patric's words, the "decision was put into effect in diverse ways and 'obeyed' to varying degrees," board action in response to *Schempp* was classified as changing or not changing policy. All districts reporting a departure from the pre-*Schempp* provisions of state law were considered changing districts. It was believed that one of several factors could be used to explain the differences between changing and non-changing districts. These were degree of urbanization, extent of religious pluralism, articulate opposition within the district to devotional exercises, or differences in the socio-economic composition of the school boards.

To test these suppositions three questionnaires were prepared and sent out in late 1964 and early 1965. One was mailed to each of the 152 superintendents of schools in the state. The second was mailed to the chairman and two other randomly selected members of each school board. The third was sent to the remaining school board members in those districts from which responses were obtained to either or both of the first two questionnaires. The superintendents were asked what the policy on Bible reading and devotional exercises had been in their district before June, 1963, and what it currently was. They were asked to identify any factors inducing change and to describe, in each time period, the policy-making role of the board, superintendent, principals, teachers, parents, religious groups, and any other participants. The first group of board members was asked about current (post 1963) policy, how it differed from that of the past, what groups or persons made policy suggestions to the board, and what groups or persons were con-

134 ROBERT H. BIRKBY

sulted by the board. The second group of board members was simply asked to supply information on age, occupation, education, income, religious affiliation, length of service on the board, and length of residence in the school district of its members. Response to the first and third questionnaires was good. Ninety-two (60.5%) of the superintendents responded; ninety-seven (21.2%) of the first group of board members representing eighty-four of 152 districts replied; and 237 (56.1%) of the second group of board members from 109 out of a possible 121 districts returned the questionnaire. By combining the reports of the superintendents and the first group of board members (cross-checking where possible) the policy currently in effect in 121 of the state's 152 school districts was determined.

Of the 121 districts, 70 were reported to be still following the requirements of state law. The other 51 districts were reported to have made some changes in their policy but only one of these completely eliminated all Bible reading and devotional exercises. The other fifty merely made student participation voluntary and left the decision whether to have devotional exercises to the discretion of the classroom teacher. Thus 42 percent of the reporting school districts no longer adhere strictly to the provisions of state law even though all but one could have some form of classroom devotional exercise.

* * * *

. . . Partial compliance with *Schempp* is not explained by degree of urbanization. There are no significant differences in the socio-economic characteristics of changing and non-changing board members. In the changing districts the board members did not report any overt pressure for compliance. And, by a rough test, the extent of religious pluralism in the district had no effect. These findings are significant and justify reporting. It may well be that the population of the State of Tennessee is too homogeneous—socially, religiously, and economically—for any of these tests to be significant.[1] In some other state with greater diversity, urbanization and religious pluralism might be more important. Even so, Tennessee reaction would remain unexplained.

III

The reported response by Tennessee school districts to *Schempp* might be explained by one other hypothesis. There is in the questionnaires some support for it but not enough to make it possible to assert that it is correct. What follows then is largely speculative. The line of reasoning starts with a distinction between procedural and substantive change in policy. Policy change in any situation may take the form of (1) altering procedure without

---

[1] A semi-humorous comment of one of my senior colleagues is relevant: "In Tennessee the cities are made up of rural people who just happen to live close together."

altering the policy goal, (2) changing procedure to reach a new policy goal without, however, making the new goal explicit, or (3) changing the policy goal with or without a change in procedure. Although we cannot be sure, it seems fairly safe to say that in the fifty school districts which overtly changed their policy on Bible reading and delegated the decision to the teachers there has been little change in fact. That is, it is suspected that the classroom teachers are "voluntarily" conducting Bible reading and devotional exercises just as they did before *Schempp.*[2] One might go a step further and assert, without being able to prove it, that the school boards were aware that this would probably happen. I am suggesting that the board members acted consciously either to save the substance of the program or to avoid upsetting the community status quo by making slight procedural changes. In the language of Sayre and Kaufman, the contestants who had the prizes of the game were able to keep them by responding to a rules change with a rules change of their own. A comment by a lawyer on the board of a changing district indicates the compromise nature of the policy adopted:

My personal conviction is that the Supreme Court decisions are correct, and I so told the Board and Superintendent; but I saw no reason to create controversy. If the Board had made public a decision abolishing devotional exercises, there would have been public outcry. I believe all staff members understand that the continuance of devotional exercises in their schools and in their rooms is entirely voluntary and subject to discontinuance upon objection of any individual or minority group.

There are other reasons that a board might adopt this strategy of procedural change. It could be used to reduce disagreement within the board itself. It could be suggested by an individual as a means of reducing his own tensions between a desire to comply with the Court's decision and a desire to retain perceived advantages of devotional exercises. Finally, change in procedure without change in substance might be made to forestall demands for even greater change. There is nothing in the questionnaire responses to indicate which of these alternatives is correct and it is possible that all were present to some extent. If any or all of these suppositions are correct, a desire to retain the program rather than religious pluralism and urbanization would be responsible for the formal change. To this point the hypothesis does not provide an answer to the question of why the form was changed in some districts and not in others. It does emphasize that the answer must be sought in psychological rather than in demographic or socio-economic factors.

---

[2]This suspicion is based on unsystematic conversations with classroom teachers from two or three districts which made this formal change and on the questionnaire responses of a few superintendents who indicated doubt that any actual change had occurred.

The question being asked in any impact study is why the Court's decision is not self-executing. In a different context Richard Neustadt has concluded that a self-executing order must have five characteristics: (1) the issuer of the order must be unambiguously involved in making the decision, (2) the order must be unambiguously worded, (3) the order must receive wide publicity, (4) those receiving the order must have control of the means of implementation, and (5) there must be no doubt of the individual's authority to issue the order. Neustadt was speaking of orders issued by the President but there is no reason that the same analysis cannot be applied to Court decisions. In this instance, there was no doubt that the Court did in fact make the decision though one school board member suggested that the Court was "controlled by small pressure groups." When applied to the Tennessee statute the wording of the order, although negative in content, was clear enough. There was wide publicity. The members of the boards of education had control of the means of implementation. However, the fifth factor was not so obviously present.

There was some confusion about the Court's decision. It was clear enough that required devotional exercises were forbidden but the Court did not commit itself on the status of voluntary programs such as those adopted by the fifty changing districts in Tennessee. This ambiguity caused one superintendent to assert confidently "we believe our policy [voluntary participation] is in accordance with the ruling of the Supreme Court and in accord with the desires of the people in this community."

More important is the question of the Court's authority to issue the order. The policy maker's reaction to a judicial decision will be conditioned by his perception of the Court's role in general, his beliefs concerning the importance of the challenged activity or program, his perception of the attitudes of his reference groups and constituents on the issue, and his perception of his role. The differences in policy position may be the result of a general attitude toward the Court and its role in the American system of government.[3] The following comments are typical in content and intensity.

---

[3] Speaking to the American Philosophical Society in 1952, Justice Felix Frankfurter observed that "broadly speaking, the chief reliance of law in a democracy is the habit of popular respect for law. Especially true is it that law as promulgated by the Supreme Court ultimately depends upon confidence of the people in the Supreme Court as an institution." Frankfurter, *Of Law and Men*, Elman, ed. (New York: Harcourt, Brace & Co., 1956), p. 31. Brehm and Cohen report an experiment demonstrating that the more credible the source of a communication the greater the change in the recipient's attitude even when there was wide discrepancy between the recipient's initial attitude and the content of the communication. Jack W. Brehm and Arthur R. Cohen, *Explorations in Cognitive Dissonance* (New York: John Wiley and Sons, 1962), pp. 247-48.

Changing Districts

* * * *

A Superintendent: I think the Supreme Court is correct. Very few people understand the religious issue, less seem to understand what is meant by religious freedom, and relatively few seem to understand the Supreme Court's role in our government.

* * * *

Non-Changing Districts

* * * *

A Superintendent: I am at a loss to understand the necessity for this survey. I am of the opinion that 99% of the people in the United States feel as I do about the Supreme Court's decision—that it was an outrage and that Congress should have it amended. The remaining 1% do not belong in this free world.

* * * *

The Court-attitude is only one of the variables affecting the impact of a judicial decision. The other major variable is the policy maker's assessment of and commitment to the challenged program or activity. Comments on the benefits and value of Bible reading and devotional exercises came only from the school board members and superintendents from the non-changing districts. These are typical:

A Farmer: I believe that if the Bible is removed from our schools and is not read that would be the first step toward removing the Holy Bible from our free society. Then we would eventually drift into heathenism.

A Merchant: This nation was founded and has grown under the firm belief in God. For those who do not believe it, there are places where they do not believe. Let them go there if they choose.

* * * *

In some of these instances the belief in the importance of the program was sufficiently intense to override any desire to comply with the decision. In other instances, respondents combined attacks on the Court with a defense of the program. It seems reasonable to assume that the relative intensities of the Court-attitude and the program-attitude determined in large part the policy position taken by the school board.[4] In changing districts the board must have felt a greater obligation to follow the Court ruling than to continue to enforce their beliefs in the value of devotional exercises. In the non-changing districts *Schempp* was repudiated either because of a pre-existing negative attitude toward the Court or because of a strong belief in the value of the program, or both.

---

[4]The Court-attitude and the program-attitude may be either complementary or divergent. If complementary, one attitude would be positive and the other negative; they would reinforce each other and make reaching a decision relatively easy. If the two atti-

Perceptions of the attitudes of constituents or clientele are important but seem to be secondary. They play the role of reinforcing or modifying the Court-attitude and/or the program-attitude. . . .

On the basis of the information available, it is impossible to weigh the value of the perceptions that went into the making of the policies. But one might hazard a guess that in the changing districts a perception of the Court as an authoritative body exercising legitimate power was strong enough to override any commitment to devotional exercises. The reverse, of course, would hold true in non-changing districts. The weight given to reference group attitudes and the direction of those attitudes probably, though not necessarily, varied in the same direction as the final policy decision and served to reinforce attitudes toward the Court or beliefs in the value of devotionals. That is, public opinion in changing districts probably was perceived by the board as favoring or at least not opposing compliance with *Schempp* and strengthened the board's desire to comply.[5]

One warning is in order. It is not asserted that procedural change to save substance and intensity of attitude explains what took place in Tennessee. All that is claimed here is that with the failure of the initial hypotheses in this study this additional explanation is possible and is supported to some extent by the response to the questionnaires.

IV

*   *   *   *

One must conclude with Robert A. Dahl that "by itself, the Court is almost powerless to affect the course of national policy."[6] It may delay or

---

tudes were divergent they would carry the same sign and the policy position would be unpredictable if no more were known. The possibilities and results can be diagrammed:

Court-attitude Direction	Program-attitude Direction	Policy-Position Expected
+	—	compliance
—	+	non-compliance
+	+	variable
—	—	variable

In the last two instances shown the intensity of the basic attitudes and the effect of secondary perceptions will determine the final policy position adopted.

Of those responding to this survey from changing districts only one indicated a negative Court-attitude as compared to twenty-six who expressed a favorable attitude. In non-changing districts the ratio was two favorable to thirteen negative expressions. No respondent expressed a negative program-attitude but only two from changing districts as contrasted to twenty-one from non-changing districts made positive statements. Both groups indicated a belief that their course of action had the approval of their constituents.

[5] One board chairman reported that he and the superintendent made the decision to leave devotional exercises to the teacher's discretion "since no one else seemed to be interested."

[6] R. A. Dahl, "Decision-Making in a Democracy: The Supreme Court as a National Policy-Maker," 6 *Journal of Public Law* 279, 293 (1958).

accelerate adoption of policy but cannot impose or reverse policy. Court decisions, therefore, will increase in effectiveness as those who have to implement them are either in accord with the Court's position or are sufficiently convinced of the legitimacy of the Court's exercise of power that this conviction overrides any prior commitment to an alternative policy. A limit is thus placed on the ability of the Court to make policy and this impales the justices on the horns of a strategic dilemma. Their decisions have the greatest effectiveness when the policy laid down is non-controversial and the Court's prestige is high. But in a period of massive social (and therefore legal) change the justices' policy choices will be controversial and as a result the Court's prestige will be lower than in quieter periods. The options available are to deal with one problem area at a time in an attempt to maximize effectiveness by minimizing controversy or to take the problems as they come since any decision will have some, even if not total, effect. Unless we are to counsel judicial abdication the only way to resolve this dilemma is for the Court to utilize every legitimate means at its disposal to convince other policy-makers and the general public that its policy choice is the best of the possible alternatives.

MILTON ROKEACH

Religion as a Source of Religious Intolerance

All organized western religious groups teach their adherents, and those they try to convert, contradictory sets of beliefs. On the one hand, they teach mutual love and respect, the golden rule, the love of justice and mercy, and to regard all men as equal in the eyes of God. On the other hand, they teach (implicitly if not openly) that only *certain* people can be saved—those who believe as they do; that only *certain* people are chosen people; that there is only one real truth—theirs.

Throughout history man, inspired by religious motives, has indeed espoused noble and humanitarian ideals and often behaved accordingly.

Reprinted by permission of the author and the publisher from "Paradoxes of Religious Belief," *Trans-action* Magazine (January-February, 1965), pp. 9-12. Copyright © 1965 by Washington University, St. Louis, Mo.

But he has also committed some of the most horrible crimes and wars in the holy name of religion—the massacre of St. Bartholomew, the Crusades, the Inquisition, the pogroms, and the burnings of witches and heretics.

This is the fundamental paradox of religious belief. It is not confined to history. In milder but even more personal forms it exists in our daily lives.

In 1949 Clifford Kirkpatrick, professor of sociology at Indiana University, published some findings on the relationship between religious sentiments and humanitarian attitudes. Professor Kirkpatrick investigated the oft-heard contention that religious feeling fosters humanitarianism; and, conversely, that those without religious training should therefore be less humanitarian. His conclusions were surprising—at least to the followers of organized religion. In group after group—Catholic, Jewish, and the Protestant denominations—he found little correlation at all; but what there was was negative. That is, the devout tended to be *slightly less* humanitarian and had more punitive attitudes toward criminals, delinquents, prostitutes, homosexuals, and those who might seem in need of psychological counseling or psychiatric treatment.

In my own research I have found that, on the average, those who identify themselves as belonging to a religious organization express more intolerance toward racial and ethnic groups (other than their own) than do non-believers—or even Communists. These results have been found at Michigan State University, at several New York colleges, and in England (where the Communist results were obtained). Gordon Allport in his book, *The Nature of Prejudice*, describes many of the studies that have come up with similar findings. In a recent paper he read at the Crane Theological School of Tufts University, he said:

On the average, church goers and professedly religious people have considerably more prejudice than do non-church goers and non-believers.

Actually, this conclusion is not quite accurate. While non-believers are in fact generally less prejudiced than believers toward racial and ethnic groups, it does not follow that they are more tolerant in every respect. Non-believers often betray a bigotry and intellectual arrogance of another kind— intolerance toward those who disagree with them. Allport's conclusion is valid if by "prejudice" we only mean ethnic and religious prejudice.

Organized religion also contends that the religious have greater "peace of mind" and mental balance. We have found in our research at Michigan State University—described in my book, *The Open and Closed Mind*— that people with formal religious affiliation are more anxious. . . .

* * * *

In a study in Lansing, Michigan, we found that when you ask a group of Catholics to rank the major Christian denominations in order of their similarity to Catholicism, you generally get the following order: Catholic first, then Episcopalian, Lutheran, Presbyterian, Methodist, and finally Baptist. Ask a group of Baptists to rank the same denominations for similarity, and you get exactly the reverse order: Baptist, Methodist, Presbyterian, Lutheran, Episcopalian, and finally Catholic. When we look at the listings of similarities they seem to make up a kind of color wheel, with each one of the six major Christian groups judging all other positions from its own standpoint along the continuum. But actually it turns out that all these continua are basically variations of the same theme, with Catholics at one end and Baptists at the other.

Apparently people build up mental maps of which religions are similar to their own, and these mental maps have an important influence on everyday behavior. If a Catholic decides to leave his church and join another, the probability is greatest that he will join the Episcopalian church —next the Lutheran church—and so on down the line. Conversely, a defecting Baptist will more probably join the Methodist church, after that the Presbyterian church, and so on. The other denominations follow the same pattern.

The probability of inter-faith marriage increases with the similarity between denominations. When a Catholic marries someone outside his faith, it is more likely to be an Episcopalian, next most likely a Lutheran, and so on.

What of the relation between marital conflicts and inter-faith marriages? In general we find that the greater the dissimilarity, the greater likelihood of conflict both before and after marriage.

We determined this by restricting our analysis to couples of whom at least one partner was always Methodist. We interviewed seven or eight all Methodist couples; then another group in which Methodists had married Presbyterians; then Methodists and Lutherans; and on around. We not only questioned them about their marital conflicts, but also about their pre-marital conflicts. How long did they "go steady"? (The assumption is that the longer you go steady beyond a certain point, the more likely the conflict.) Did parents object to the marriage? Had they themselves had doubts about it beforehand? Had they ever broken off their engagement? For marital conflict, we asked questions about how often they quarreled, whether they had ever separated (if so, how many times), and whether they had ever contemplated divorce. From the answers we constructed an index of pre-marital and post-marital conflict.

These findings raise an issue of interest to us all. From the standpoint of mental health, it can be argued that inter-faith marriages are undesirable. From the standpoint of democracy, is it desirable to have a society in which everyone marries only within his own sect or denomination? This is a complicated matter and cannot be pursued here. But these findings do suggest that somehow the average person has gotten the idea that religious differences—even minor denominational distinctions within the Christian fold—*do* make a difference; so much difference in fact that inter-faith marriages must result in mental unhappiness.

To pull together the various findings: I have mentioned that empirical results show that religious people are on the average less humanitarian, more bigoted, more anxious; also that the greater the religious differences, the greater the likelihood of conflict in marriage. Does a common thread run through these diverse results? What lessons can we learn from them?

It seems to me that these results cannot be accounted for by assuming, as the anti-religionists do, that religion is an unqualified force for evil; nor by assuming, as the pro-religionists do, that religion is a force only for good. Instead, as indicated at the beginning, I believe that these results become more understandable if we assume that there exist simultaneously, within the organized religions of the West, psychologically conflicting moral forces for good *and* evil—teaching brotherhood with the right hand and bigotry with left, facilitating mental health in some and mental conflict, anxiety, and psychosis in others. I realize that this seems an extreme interpretation; but the research bears it out.

Gordon Allport makes a similar point:

Brotherhood and bigotry are intertwined in all religion. Plenty of pious persons are saturated with racial, ethnic, and other prejudice. But at the same time many of the most ardent advocates of racial justice are religiously motivated.

We are taught to make definite distinctions between "we" and "they," between believer and non-believer; and sometimes we are urged to act on the basis of these distinctions, for instance in marriage. The category of man that comes to mind when we hear the word "infidel" or "heretic" is essentially a religious one. It is part of our religious heritage. But it is pretty difficult psychologically to love infidels and heretics to the same extent that we love believers. The psychological strain must be very great; and a major result must be guilt and anxiety.

This kind of dichotomy is not confined to religion. Gunnar Myrdal, in *The American Dilemma*, described the conflict between American ideals of democracy and practice of discrimination against minority groups, and the guilt, anxiety, and disorder it spawned. We are familiar in international affairs with the enormous psychological discrepancy between the humanitarian ideals of a classless society advocated by the Marxists and the anti-humanitarian methods employed by them for its achievement. No wonder there have been so many defections from the Communist cause in America and Europe! When the strain between one set of beliefs and another set of beliefs—or between belief and practice—becomes too great, one natural response is to turn away from the whole system.

I suspect that such contradictions lead often to defection from religion also. Most of the time, however, the result is psychological conflict, anxiety, and chronic discomfort arising from feelings of guilt. The contradictions in religious teachings are more subtle than those in politics and would, for the most part, be denied consciously. A conflict between ideological content and ideological structure—between *what* is taught and *how* it is taught— must be very subtle. A particular religious institution not only must disseminate a particular religious ideology; it must also perpetuate itself and defend against outside attack. It is this dual purpose of religious institutions, I hypothesize, which leads to the contradiction between the *what* and the *how*. It leads to the paradox of a church disseminating truly religious values to the extent possible, while unwittingly communicating anti-religious values to the extent necessary.

RESOLVING CONTRADICTIONS

Gordon Allport, writing on the relation between religion and bigotry, has suggested two types of religious orientation. He calls them the *extrinsic* and the *intrinsic*. The extrinsic outlook on religion is utilitarian, self-centered, opportunistic, and other-directed. The intrinsic, in contrast, includes basic trust, a compassionate understanding of others so that "dogma is tempered with humility" and, with increasing maturity, "is no longer limited to single segments of self interest." Allport does not imply that everyone is purely either intrinsic or extrinsic; rather, all range somewhere along the continuum from one pole to the other.

The extent to which a particular person has an intrinsic or extrinsic outlook depends largely on the way he is able to resolve the contradictory teachings of his religious group. This in turn depends on the particular quality of his experiences with others, especially with parents in early childhood. A person is more apt to be extrinsically-oriented if his early experiences included threat, anxiety, and punishment or if religion was used punitively, as a club to discipline and control him.

Good empirical evidence exists which supports Allport's distinctions. W. Cody Wilson has succeeded in isolating and measuring the extrinsic religious sentiment and in showing that it is closely related to anti-Semitism. Also, one of my collaborators, Dr. G. Gratton Kemp, has isolated two kinds of religiously-minded students, all enrolled in one denominational college. One group was open-minded and tolerant. The other group was closed-minded and highly prejudiced. Dr. Kemp studied their value orientations over a six-year period. He found that while they expressed similar values when in college, they diverged sharply six years later. Both groups ranked their religious values highest but then parted abruptly. The open-minded group put social values next and theoretical values third. The closed-minded group also ranked religious values highest, but political values were second in importance for them and economic values third. It is obvious that the total cluster of values is quite different between the open-minded and the closed-minded groups. These findings clearly suggest that religious people do indeed differ strongly in their orientations toward life to the extent that their religious outlook is, as Allport claims, extrinsic or intrinsic.

AN ANTI-HUMANITARIAN VICTORY?

All the preceding leads to the following tentative conclusions: the fact that religious people are more likely to express anti-humanitarian attitudes, bigotry, and anxiety and the fact that religious similarity and dissimilarity play an important role in marital conflict may both be interpreted as the end result of the emergence of the extrinsic rather than the intrinsic orientation toward religion. They also suggest that, in most people, the extrinsic orientation predominates. This greater prominence of extrinsic attitudes in turn seems to arise out of the contradictory beliefs transmitted through organized religion: humanitarian on one side, anti-humanitarian on the other. One constructive suggestion that might be advanced is that ministers, rabbis, and priests should better understand the differences between the *what* and the *how* of belief, and the fact that contradictions between the *what* and the *how* can lead to excessive anxiety, pervasive guilt, and psychic conflict and, therefore, to all sorts of defensive behavior capable of alleviating guilt and conflict. Representatives of organized religion should consequently become more sophisticated about the unwitting contradictions introduced into religious teachings, and try to eliminate them—as the Catholics are doing now with belief in Jewish guilt for the crucifixion.

Parents are really the middlemen between the forces of organized religion and the child. What factors in rearing, in parental attitudes, in discipline techniques, in the quality of reward and punishment are likely to lead to what Allport has called the intrinsic orientation toward religion? What factors lead to the extrinsic? The data suggest that the more the parent encourages the formation and development of extrinsic attitudes toward religion, the more he hinders the growth of the child into a mature and healthy human being. The more he strengthens the intrinsic religious orientation, the more he helps his child grow healthy, mature, tolerant, and happy.

The conflict between the ideal and what seems to be the practical is widespread. But the current readjustment in racial relations, in which clergymen have taken so large a part, for all its upset and pain indicates that these dichotomies are neither eternal nor inevitable. Nor is the extrinsic orientation necessarily the "practical" one. Research and practice in race relations, criminology, and child-rearing have consistently shown that the nonpunitive and accepting approach brings better results.

Change is underway, in the church and in the home, and brings with it, hopefully, greater emphasis on resolving the paradox between the what and the how of religious belief.

IV.

Racial Equality and the Law

Everyone makes choices about objects he prefers as against those he does not. When translated into actions, such choices constitute discrimination. Further, objects are selectively preferred, producing for each person a distribution of preferences and discriminating behavior. In this, some preferences and behaviors are highly rewarded or approved while others are penalized or ignored. Against this obvious fact of social and personal life, democratic theory has set the value of equality, denying that some kinds of preferential behavior and belief should be rewarded. The important word here is *some*; for it is clear that not *all* preferential behavior and belief are regarded as inimical to the value of equality. The question is: Which manifestations of inequality are to be supported by law, and which are to be opposed?

Consider the operation of laws, in particular and general. A traffic law forbids speeds over 20 mph in a school zone. Persons driving under that speed are treated differently than those driving over it: in one case, noninterference with behavior; and in the other, punishment of behavior. Even a simple law such as this discriminates—for a purpose that is socially approved, that is, the protection of school children.

But to this aspect of law found in all societies, democratic theory adds another, namely, equal protection of the law, which requires that when the law discriminates between approved and punishable behavior, it must apply equally to all persons who fall into one category or the other. Irish speedsters are not to be exempt while Italians are arrested, because the police chief is Irish. Yet some exemptions, some denials of equal protection of the law, are regarded as reasonable by law and court. Doctors or firemen on emergency runs may speed without fear of prosecution, because the value of their work outweighs the value of having the law apply to all equally.

This series of simple examples illustrates two points: (1) The act of discrimination is widespread among men. (2) Law always discriminates, like men, to achieve some valued end. These points are necessary as a background for seeing that the democratic insistence upon equality does not mean to deny all inequality or all discrimination—

only that which hinders the achievement of important goals of the society.

People often disagree over which goals are most valued (or which have priority), and hence controversy is inevitable over what types of discrimination will be denied by law. For much of our history we believed that discrimination against women, supported by law, was not hostile to our societal welfare. The feminist movement struck against this condition, not by focusing first on the discriminatory devices, but by criticizing the socially accepted view that women were inferior. Once beliefs that women should be discriminated against socially and politically were undermined, support for eliminating the discriminatory laws was more easily mobilized. The case of women's rights also illustrates a number of points. Obviously, there is a generational (or longer) difference in definitions of discrimination. More important, the act of defining is partly a moral and philosophical problem and partly a political struggle between those seeking to bar discrimination and those who wish to continue it.

If we accept this relationship between equality and the law, we can then raise some interesting questions:

—What social goals are in controversy? What values are being served by discrimination, and what values are threatened?

—What groups cluster around conflicting goals, and what strategies and arguments do they employ?

—To what degree is this clash subject to resolution by an analysis of facts, and what does the available evidence tell us?

—What are the conditions under which one group prevails and another gives way?

—What leadership role is played by the courts, administrative bodies, the schools, the mass media, and so on, in convincing a majority to accept new definitions of equality?

—What formulas for achieving the contested view of equality are offered, and which are successful?

Questions such as these help us to put analytic handles on the often abstract notion of equality. They enable us to conceive of equality as something far more than a quotation from Lincoln or a decision by the Supreme Court.

In our time, while other minorities are involved, the main contest for equality involves the Negro. Bursting into national view in the past fifteen years, this contest has come to dominate the American domestic scene. From muted murmurs of dissent in civil-libertarian circles, "the issue" has been amplified to reach all levels of society, all institutions of government, and all elements of public and private life. The Supreme Court's 1954 decision in *Brown* v. *Board of Education*, which struck down the "separate but equal doctrine," provided the initial stimulus which has caused Americans to confront, once again, the meaning of equality. [1] With what many whites seem to believe is presumption, the Negro has insisted with increasing impatience that the democratic creed is his heritage, too.

The impact of this demand is felt in ever-widening aspects of the way we live. Equal treatment, and in some cases special (compensatory) treatment, is being demanded in voting, housing, jobs, education, restaurants, hotels, recreation, transportation, and other areas as well. While the jolt of this demand first struck the South, it is felt now in all regions. Legal attacks on official discrimination below the Mason-Dixon line were followed by an outcry against the socially and economically sanctioned circle of poverty associated with discrimination in other parts of the nation. Legal attacks have yielded to, or merged with, mass-action techniques—sit-ins, swim-ins, pray-ins, marches, and riots—to protest both *de jure* (legal) and *de facto* segregation. These attacks have not always been pleasant in the eyes of many whites. But it is clear that such demands for equality will be with us until skin color no longer determines one's share of "the good life." And, unfortunately, that state of affairs appears to be a long way off.

As the readings in this chapter strive to show, all citizens have been compelled to confront their own basic feelings about the one-eighth of our nation that is black. We have been forced to ask whether we believe in equality and on what terms, and to determine what can be done to help alleviate the sources of prejudice and discrimination. As will become readily clear in the pages that follow, good will is not enough. Even it we all come to agree that racial inequality must be eliminated, we still face rather considerable problems in finding ways to achieve that goal.

The magnitude of the problems of assuring racial equality has been dramatically underlined by the riots which have torn America's cities in recent years. In its 1968 report, the President's Commission on Civil Disorders laid the fundamental cause of the riots, and of inequality in general, at the feet of racist attitudes among the white population. In the Commission's words,

. . . the most fundamental cause of the riots was the racial attitude and behavior of white Americans toward black Americans. Race prejudice has shaped our history decisively in the past; it now threatens to do so again. White racism is essentially responsible for the explosive mixture which has accumulated in our cities since the end of World War II. [2]

---

[1] An excellent study of events involved in this single case is Daniel M. Berman, *It Is So Ordered* (New York: Norton, 1966).

[2] Report of the National Advisory Commission on Civil Disorders (New York: Bantam Books, 1968), p. 203.

While there is, in our view, much validity to the charge that racism, as this commission defines it, is the root of much racial inequality, one should not lose sight of the fact that white attitudes toward Negroes have improved enormously in recent decades both in the North and in the South.[3] It is important, however, to note that the proportion of the white population which expresses sentiments of racial equality depends on the context of the equal relationship. In December, 1963, the National Opinion Research Center conducted a survey of white attitudes toward Negroes which illustrates this point clearly, and the results are depicted in the table below.

PRO-INTEGRATION SENTIMENTS[4]

Item	Per Cent Giving Pro-Integration Response (December 1963)
1. "Do you think Negroes should have as good a chance as white people to get any kind of job, or do you think white people should have the first chance at any kind of job?" ("As good a chance.")	82
2. "Generally speaking, do you think there should be separate sections for Negroes in street cars and buses?" ("No.")	77
3. "Do you think Negroes should have the right to use the same parks, restaurants and hotels as white people?" ("Yes.")	71
4. "Do you think white students and Negro students should go to the same schools, or to separate schools?" ("Same schools.")	63
5. "How strongly would you object if a member of your family wanted to bring a Negro friend home to dinner?" ("Not at all.")	49
6. "White people have a right to keep Negroes out of their neighborhoods if they want to, and Negroes should respect that right." ("Disagree slightly" or "Disagree strongly.")	44
7. "Do you think there should be laws against marriages between Negroes and whites?" ("No.")	36
8. "Negroes shouldn't push themselves where they're not wanted." ("Disagree slightly" or "Disagree strongly.")	27

[3]See, for example, Paul B. Sheatsley, "White Attitudes Toward Negroes," *Daedalus* (Winter, 1967), pp. 217-238. See also William Brink and Louis Harris, *Black and*

In other words, whites discriminate in their discrimination, judging some Negro integration concerns more favorably than others. Similarly, different degrees of white acceptance of Negro demands can be seen in the topics covered by other articles in this section.

The first article in this chapter, by sociologists Earl Raab and Seymour Martin Lipset, seeks to explain some of the reasons for the development of prejudiced attitudes. Raab and Lipset stress the importance of the social context of prejudice. Others have sought to explain intolerance in terms of psychological factors. Among the tremendous number of studies published since World War II which deal with the psychological aspects of intolerance and prejudice, perhaps the most influential was conducted by a group of California social scientists and resulted in the 1950 publication of *The Authoritarian Personality*.[5] The concept of authoritarianism is useful in understanding the relationship between personality traits and freedom. A not uncommon definition of an authoritarian personality is the following:

. . . one who is rigidly ethnocentric, anti-democratic, compulsively conventional, punitive and condescending toward those regarded as inferiors, and submissive to authority.[6]

Not everyone who manifests prejudice has an authoritarian personality, and some of those who fit the definition above may not behave in an overtly intolerant way. But it is useful, we think, to bear in mind that intolerance and prejudice may well be symptoms of psychological maladjustment. This perspective helps one to realize that those who would deny freedom to others often deny it to themselves by narrowing their own self-expression. Their personal rigidity may make them

---

White: A Study of U.S. Racial Attitudes Today (New York: Simon and Schuster, 1967). For a study of the attitudes of black and white citizens of Los Angeles after the Watts riot, see Raymond J. Murphy and James M. Watson, *The Structure of Discontent*, and Richard T. Morris and Vincent Jeffries, *The White Reaction Study* (Institute of Government and Public Affairs, University of California at Los Angeles), Reports MR-92 and MR-84, respectively.

[4]This table appeared in Sheatsley, *op. cit.*, p. 224. It is reprinted with permission of the publisher. The table represents what Gunnar Myrdal and others have described as the "Rank Order of Discrimination," in *The American Dilemma* (New York: Harper, 1944). For a current review of Myrdal's thesis, see J. Allen Williams, Jr., and Paul L. Wiener, "A Reexamination of Myrdal's Rank Order of Discrimination," *Social Problems* (Spring, 1967), pp. 443-454, and the literature cited therein; and R. W. Friedricks, "The American Dilemma: An Empirical Test," *American Sociological Review* (August, 1965), 507-538.

[5]T. W. Adorno, Else Frenkel-Brunswik, Daniel J. Levinson, and R. Nevitt Sanford, *The Authoritarian Personality* (New York: Harper, 1950). Six years later, Sanford summarized the factors which help to explain authoritarianism, and students will find his article a good introduction to the subject: "The Genesis of Authoritarianism," in J. L. McCarey, ed., *Psychology of Personality* (Chicago: Henry Regnery, 1956); reprinted in Marie Jahoda and Neil Warren, eds., *Attitudes* (Baltimore: Penguin Books, 1966).

[6]Don Stewart and Thomas Hoult, "A Social-Psychological Theory of the Authoritarian Personality," *American Journal of Sociology*, 65 (November, 1959), 274-279.

incapable of relating openly with others and of perceiving the alternatives that they are offered for personal self-fulfillment.[7] In short, those who are prejudiced and intolerant make life hard for others *and* for themselves.

One of the most disturbing conclusions of the President's Commission on Civil Disorders is this: "Our nation is moving toward two societies, one black, one white—separate and unequal." One indication is that black and white have different views of the worlds in which they live, and each can look at the same phenomenon and see something very different. The second selection in this chapter provides empirical evidence of the existence of these two worlds.

A few months after the urban riots of 1966, Brandeis University's Lemberg Center for the Study of Violence conducted a study of the attitudes of 500 whites and 500 Negroes in three pairs of similar cities. One city in each pair had experienced a riot that summer, and the Lemberg researchers sought to determine why a riot had occurred in one city but not in the other. A summary of the findings of this study comprises the second article in this chapter. The findings hold a number of lessons, three of which are:

1. While there is much dissatisfaction among Negroes with their environment, it is most difficult to understand why riots occur in only some cities and not in others.

2. There are rather wide differences in the attitudes of whites and Negroes on race-related issues.

3. These differences—which no doubt exist in the population as a whole—are an important barrier to securing relevant action to lessen racial inequality.

One of the most significant areas of inequality among races is education. The drive for racial equality in the field of education has two aspects: the *de jure* (legally enforced) segregation in the South; and the *de facto* variety in the North. In the South, under the Civil Rights Act of 1964 and the implementing guidelines of the United States Office of Education, the *de jure* segregation of public schools has been directly attacked. While most children in the South go to segregated schools, in the words of Judge Minor Wisdom of the Fifth Circuit Court of Appeals (which includes Alabama and Mississippi), "The clock has ticked the last tick for tokenism and delay in the name of 'deliberate speed.'" Problems remain, however, despite the court's final-sounding tones. In the next selection, sociologists Michael Aiken and N. J. Demerath lay out clearly the operations and problems at different levels of integration in Southern schools by focusing on the microcosm of two Mississippi school systems. The immense task of

---

[7] For a full discussion of this point, see Christian Bay, *The Structure of Freedom* (Stanford, Calif.: Stanford University Press, 1957), especially Chap. 4.

upgrading educational quality which remains there will tax local resources for at least a generation.

As is now well known, the South is not alone when it comes to racial problems in education. Increasing residential segregation in the North is producing increased school segregation. As of late 1968, the Supreme Court had not yet faced squarely the question of whether such *de facto* segregation is also violative of the values the Court has protected in a series of decisions since *Brown* v. *Board of Education* in 1954. Social commentator Fred Powledge in the next selection discusses Northern cities' efforts at eliminating such segregation. Particularly important for the future is his conclusion that the least has been done where the Negro population is the largest; even New York City's earnest efforts have run into critical problems.[8]

A report on the problems of school segregation which became a classic as soon as it was published in mid-1966 was James S. Coleman's *Equality of Educational Opportunity*, a 737-page study of 600,000 students and 60,000 teachers in 4,000 schools from every state in the nation. This massive effort to measure the quality of modern education and the factors that affect it was too elaborate to catch the public eye. But it reached many professional educators' attention immediately, although its impact has yet to be fully felt even among them. Coleman's findings, which challenge some common notions about *de facto* segregation, is an excellent example of the uses of social science in rethinking, and perhaps reformulating, important public policy. We present Coleman's own reflections on the nature of the findings and his suggestions about policies for overcoming the poor quality of education associated with present segregated school systems.[9]

Yet another field where the fight for equality under law takes place is that of housing. The Lemberg Center's six-city study cited above shows that in riot areas the lack of better housing was regarded as a major source of dissatisfaction and the cause of riots by about 75 per cent of ghetto dwellers. The desire of Negroes to escape the ghetto runs squarely against one of the many fears of whites, namely, that Negroes in the neighborhood reduce housing values. This fear, and all it implies, as well as a general apprehension about close contact with Negroes, appears to be deep-seated. In almost every case where

---

[8] For a survey of major problems, see Meg Greenfield, "What Is Racial Balance in the Schools?" *The Reporter* (March 23, 1967), pp. 20-26. For a series of case studies in Northern school segregation, see T. Bentley Edwards and Frederick M. Wirt, *School Desegregation in the North.* (San Francisco: Chandler Publishing Company, 1968); Robert Crain *et al., The Politics of School Desegregation* (Chicago: Aldine Press, 1967); and Raymond W. Mack *et al., Desegregation and Education* (New York: Random House, forthcoming).

[9] For a résumé and analysis of the Coleman report, see Christopher Jencks, "Education: The Racial Gap," *New Republic* (October 1, 1966).

voters have expressed their opinions on fair-housing laws, such laws have been defeated or repealed. In the next selection, George and Eunice Grier examine what housing segregation and discrimination have produced and analyze the role of law in this regard. Their discussion of a careful study by Luigi Laurenti shows how his data strongly attack the belief that property values decline when Negroes move in next door. [10]

The final selection in this chapter treats some of the implications of voting equality. The Civil Rights Act of 1965 climaxed the drive to open the polls to Southern Negroes, a drive which had engaged the full battery of federal actions—even a Constitutional amendment. As a result of this massive effort, Southern Negro registration has increased immensely in recent years. But, as political scientists Donald R. Matthews and James W. Prothro conclude in an excerpt from their book, *Negroes and the New Southern Politics*, the Negroes' gains through the ballot may be less than liberal enthusiasm had anticipated.

Before and after reading the material in this chapter, the student may wish to return to the questions raised at the outset of this introduction. These queries provide a way of looking at the struggle for equal protection under the law as one aspect of the continuing political process by which Americans settle policy questions. But beyond these interpretive schemes, it is well to remember that what is basically involved here is a sizable minority of Americans appealing to the common conscience of us all and demanding that they be granted their full measure of individual dignity. Note also that because minorities comprise a disproportionate element of the poor, they experience severe problems with regard to obtaining due process of law. These matters will be dealt with in Chapter V. It is clear that demands for equality cannot be met without a massive commitment to redress wrongs and to deal with the world *as it is*, not as our fears lead us to believe it is. So far, that commitment has been slow in coming.

---

[10] For a review of research in this field, see Bernard Meer and Edward Freedman, "The Impact of Negro Neighbors on White Home Owners," *Social Forces* (September, 1966), pp. 11-19. For a survey of the controversy, see John W. Berry, "Open Housing," *Editorial Research Reports* (August 16, 1967), pp. 599-616. For a classic study of this field dealing with favorable changes in racial attitudes resulting from interracial housing, see Morton Deutsch and Mary Evan Collins, "Interracial Housing," in William Petersen, ed., *American Social Patterns* (Garden City, N.Y.: Doubleday, 1956), pp. 3-57.

EARL RAAB and SEYMOUR M. LIPSET

The Social Context of Intolerance

FRAME OF REFERENCE—THE SITUATIONAL FACTOR

Not only do prejudiced attitudes differ widely from one individual to another, but they tend to differ from one situation to another for any given individual. For an attitude is not a thing, it is a process; it is an interaction. It is an interaction involving not only the person and the object, but all other factors that are present in any situation. . . .

Sherif and Cantril have called this situational factor "frame of reference." . . .

*   *   *   *

There are a number of different ways in which this "situational" character of prejudice may be described:

—A general attitude, about Negroes, for example, does not predetermine specific attitudes about Negroes. In other words, if a person has a general stereotype of Negroes, and a general hostility towards Negroes, this does not automatically mean that he will have an unfavorable attitude towards working in the same factory with Negroes.

—One specific attitude towards Negroes, e.g., working with them, may have a quite different texture from another specific attitude, e.g., living next to them.

—The same person may have one attitude about working next to Negroes in one situation, and a different attitude about working next to them in another situation.

—In sum, a prejudiced attitude may shift from one moment and situation to another.

*   *   *   *

THE SITUATION OR THE PERSONALITY

Perhaps then the most effective and workable approach to understanding the phenomenon of prejudice is through an investigation of the kinds of *social situations* which give rise to and sustain prejudiced behavior and attitudes. This is a sharply different approach from that which would investigate what kinds of *people* are prone to prejudice.

Reprinted by permission of the authors and the publisher from *Prejudice and Society*, pp. 14-16, 25-28, 32-35, 38-39, by Earl Raab and Seymour M. Lipset (New York: Anti-Defamation League of B'nai B'rith, 315 Lexington Avenue, New York, N.Y. 10016). Editors' title. Footnotes have been omitted.

This is not to underestimate the special validity of an approach to prejudice from the vantage point of personality and personality differences. There are good reasons for making such a psychological approach. Prejudice serves an emotional function for many people. It helps them to shift blame from themselves to others, to rationalize their aggressions, or otherwise provides an outlet for their special emotional needs. Some people with special emotional needs have a special susceptibility to prejudice. In attempting to understand or remedy the particular virulence or persistence of a given individual's prejudice, it is often necessary to understand his psychological history.

One white factory worker got along very well with his co-worker who happened to be Negro. They were friendly, ate their lunches together, worked together harmoniously. Suddenly the white worker began to have severe marital troubles and seemed headed towards a divorce. He began to make slurring references to the Negro's race and they finally had to be separated. Another man, bitter because he was making no progress in his business firm, blamed the "Jews" in top management and became vocally anti-Semitic, although it turned out that there weren't any Jews in the management of the firm. One study of veterans found that those who were generally frustrated and felt that they had been subject to "bad breaks" in the service were more often prejudiced than those who felt they had experienced "good breaks" in the service. There is evidence that many of those who stigmatize the Negro as hyper-sexual are indeed guilt-ridden by their own sexuality, and are attempting to rid themselves of that guilt by projecting it onto the Negro.

The body of psychological knowledge which throws light on these reactions is extremely helpful in explaining individual differences and in helping to treat individual problems. Since certain emotional needs are universal, in one degree or another, this knowledge even helps to explain the special "attractiveness" that prejudice seems to have for human beings in general.

But it does not explain the specific *social problem* of prejudice with which our society is currently burdened. Presumably the factory worker who was having trouble with his wife would have found *some* scapegoat, even if there were no Negro available. It might have been the thinnest man in the factory, or the fattest, or the one with red hair, or perhaps just the one with whom he was most incompatible. The need to blame other people instead of oneself; to irrelevantly work out on other people one's guilt or aggressiveness or fear is an unhealthy condition in itself. It is a problem in mental health. Those who have this problem are undoubtedly more susceptible to prejudice and to other social aberrations than those who do not have such a problem. But this condition itself does not create the specific social evils attending prejudice as described earlier. It is only when these problems are displaced on groups and help establish a deep-going pattern of denying equal opportunity to specific groups that the social problem of prejudice emerges. In short, the factory worker's psychological reaction does not create the social problem of prejudice, it merely operates within the social framework of a pattern of prejudice which already exists.

Furthermore, the psychological approach, as valuable as it is, does not explain the preponderance of people who engage in prejudiced behavior, but do *not* have special emotional problems. It does not explain the widespread pattern of prejudice. It does not explain why prejudice is more intense in one place and time than in another.

THE LESSONS OF SOCIAL SITUATIONS

These aspects of the social problem of prejudice are explainable only in terms of our *learning* prejudice much as we learn our other basic patterns of social behavior. But people do not typically learn their social values and social behavior in the same way that they learn the arithmetic table. It is not a matter of formal training or mere intellectual acceptance. A child may "learn" the social precept that it is wrong to steal, but may steal nonetheless. He has effectively learned the social value of honesty only to the extent that he has "internalized" that value; i.e., to the extent that this social value has become a natural and unthinking part of his behavior. It is not that he weighs consequences, but that it would "go against his grain" to steal. This is not the kind of learning which basically is effected in the classroom, or even at the mother's knee. It is shaped fundamentally not by lecture or exhortation, but, in a kind of "creeping socialization," by the kinds of social situations in which people live, and, especially, in which they grow up.

It then becomes necessary to define more precisely the nature of "social situation" as it applies to prejudice; and to discover the kinds of social situations which give rise to and sustain prejudice.

*   *   *   *

The pattern of community *practices is the fountainhead of prejudice: of prejudiced behavior and of prejudiced attitudes.*

The growing child learns his social behavior primarily by following the modes and models of behavior around him. Indeed, he has little choice. He learns how to behave towards people of other racial and religious groups by seeing how other people behave, and by automatically participating in the behavior patterns which already exist.

*   *   *   *

SOCIAL INVOLVEMENT REPRODUCES PREJUDICE

In other words, the basic element in the learning of prejudice is involvement in social situations, i.e., behavior patterns which are themselves prejudiced in nature. Such social situations may be prejudicial:

1—Where the individual's own behavior is prejudiced as part and parcel of the community's prejudiced pattern of life, e.g.: segregated schools, buses, waiting rooms, complete social segregation, habits of deference.

2—Where the models of behavior around the child behave in a prejudiced fashion. This may consist of the direct perception of the community's prejudiced pattern of life. It may consist of the direct perception of the symbolic *evidences* of the community's prejudiced pattern of life, as in signs and advertisements. It may consist of an indirect perception of such a pattern through the mass media.

3—Where the unfavorable images of minority groups projected by the social pattern lend themselves to prejudicial behavior. Both the educational and employment status of the Negro, for example, have been artificially depressed. Especially where his contact with minority group members is limited, the child finds it only natural to behave towards Negroes as though they were constitutionally ignorant, and fitted only for menial positions in life. Then, there are the concomitants of low economic and educational status, and of the lower stake which an oppressed minority group may feel that it has in society: a proportionately high level of superstition, for example, or of ostentation, or of crime. These evidences, too, the child will accept as part of the normal state of things, everything else being equal.

In these several ways, then, it is on the level of actual behavior situations that the normal reproduction of prejudice is effected. It is within the framework of these behavior situations that individual differences, except perhaps the most pathological, operate. It is on the base of these behavior situations that the behavior-attitude spiral of prejudice builds. Attitudes and explicit ideologies are most firmly constructed on the foundation of these existing social situations.

Indeed, the attitudes which must develop to accompany human behavior are *implied* in this behavior and it is in this way that such attitudes are primarily learned rather than by direct instruction. By the time a child is told for the first time that "Negroes are inferior," he is already convinced of it. On the other hand, by the time he is told for the first time that "Negroes are *not* inferior" it is already often too late. He will resist the idea. Or, if he is finally intellectually convinced of the fact that Negroes are not inferior, he may evade the consequences. He may find some other reason for behaving towards the Negroes *as though* they were inferior. It is axiomatic in all learning situations that rhetorical exhortations have little chance of success when they are in battle against actual behavior patterns. For example, a child will not tend to be honest because his father tells him to be, if the same father is constantly engaged in dishonest practices himself.

Studies of the development of prejudice in children show that young children who have not yet been involved in prejudiced behavior patterns, may pick up prejudiced talk, but this doesn't affect their unprejudiced behavior. Later, after having become involved in prejudiced behavior patterns, they may pick up democratic language in the schools or elsewhere, but this doesn't affect their prejudiced behavior. By the age of 15, Gordon Allport points out, "considerable skill is shown in imitating the adult pattern."

They are now able to rationalize their prejudiced behavior whenever necessary and resort to the prejudiced ideologies which do not precede but follow prejudiced behavior patterns.

In brief, the pattern of *community practices* serves as the primary source of prejudice in behavior and attitude.

*   *   *   *

INFLUENCES ON THE CHILD

The child learns his prejudiced behavior and attitudes primarily from the modes and models of behavior around him; and the modes and models of behavior which are most influential on the child are normally those of the people or groups with whom he most closely identifies. The most potent influence on the very young child is likely to be at the family level. As a teen-ager, the most potent influence is often likely to come from his circle of peers.

*   *   *   *

Families and other traditional groups are the most effective instruments that a society has for directly transmitting its values and favored modes of behavior.

*   *   *   *

THE FAMILY FOLLOWS THE COMMUNITY

In other words, family and group practices are typically consistent with prevailing community practices. These community practices provide the "frame of reference," the social *situations* which are the key to the genesis and sustenance of prejudice. Such practices can be prejudicial by:

1—Prescribing the modes of behavior by which the individual himself will behave towards minority group members in various settings; i.e., as employees, as fellow-workers, as neighbors, as social acquaintances, as friends.

2—Providing direct or indirect evidence of the modes of behavior which the rest of the community applies to minority group members in these various settings.

In addition, the unfavorable images of minority groups projected by the community pattern, which support these practices, are themselves perpetuated by these practices.

This network of prejudicial situations in a community typically generates prejudice in a child without formal or explicit training. Lillian Smith wrote:

"I do not remember how or when but by the time I had learned that God is love, that Jesus is his Son, and came to give us a more abundant life, that all men are brothers with a common Father, I also knew that I was better than a Negro, that all black folks have their place and must be kept in it, that sex has its place and must be kept in it, that a terrifying disaster would befall the South if I ever treated a Negro as my social equal."

Most people would have difficulty remembering the "how or when" of their prejudice, because in most cases there was no single impact and no single time, but rather the gradual, normal and inexorable press of the Prejudiced Community.

LEMBERG CENTER FOR THE STUDY OF VIOLENCE

A Comparison of Negro and White Attitudes: Two Different Worlds

In trying to learn how to inhibit racial violence, a logical first step is to find out whether or not there are basic differences in community attitudes that could account for—or help account for—riots breaking out in some

Reprinted by permission of the publisher from *Six-City Study—Survey of Racial Attitudes in Six Northern Cities: Preliminary Findings* (mimeo.; Waltham, Mass.: Brandeis University, 1967), pp. 1-21, 23. A footnote and five tables have been omitted. Editors' title.

places and not in others. As part of this objective, the Lemberg Center has contracted with Roper Research Associates to undertake a survey of attitudes of both Negroes and whites in each of the six cities, under a grant from the Ford Foundation.

*   *   *   *

THE SIX CITIES

. . . [Three] of the cities selected for the survey (and for the study) experienced riots during the summer of 1966 and three did not. Moreover, the cities were selected in pairs so that specific inter-city comparisons can be made. With full realization that no two cities in the United States can be completely alike in all or even in most characteristics, each riot city was paired with a non-riot one which had at least *some* similarities or points of interest in common, thus reducing the extraneous environmental factors that could make one city more riot-prone than another.

*   *   *   *

FINDINGS

The preliminary findings of the survey are as follows:

1. Riot Potential

Comparisons of the data obtained in the riot and non-riot cities do not reveal any simple explanation as to why the three *did* riot and the other three did *not.* Factors were uncovered which seem to increase the likelihood of riots. Other factors appear to be riot-inhibiting. But the study uncovered no single factor which makes any of the cities under study foolproof against riots today. While certain of the cities seem more likely to experience a riot than others, a basic finding is that a riot could occur in *any* of the six cities.

Nevertheless, the survey has shown that riots tend to break out as a result of the interaction of two factors—the "grievance level" of people in the ghetto and the inflammatory nature of the event which precipitates the initial disturbance. These two factors are in a reciprocal relation with each other: the higher the grievance level, the slighter the event required to trigger the riot. Low levels of Negro discontent require an event which is highly inflammatory in order that a riot break out. An "inflammatory event" is usually an incident which is initiated by white people and which is perceived by black people in the ghetto as an act of injustice or as an insult to their community. The greater the injustice is perceived to be, the more "inflammatory" is the effect of the incident.

The evidence for this interaction of factors underlying the riot potential of cities emerges from an accumulation of more specific findings brought out by the survey. These findings will be discussed under three main headings: 1) the level of Negro dissatisfaction, 2) the level of white resistance to change, and 3) the size of the gap between Negro and white attitudes about a number of race-related issues.

2. Level of Negro Dissatisfaction

To ascertain the level of Negro dissatisfaction or "grievance level", a number of questions were selected out of the wealth of data on racial attitudes and opinions as key indices of the degree of Negro discontent in each city. . . .

Using these indices, the survey found that Negro dissatisfaction was highest in three crucial areas. 1) A high level of discontent occurs in the job area: an average of 60% of Negroes in the six cities think the growth of job opportunities for Negroes is going too slowly. 2) Impatience with the opening of housing opportunities is even closer to the boiling point; an average of 76% feel that efforts to provide opportunities for Negroes to live where they want to are going too slowly. Frustrations in these two areas are directly perceived by Negroes as being significant causes of riots. 3) Equally as important as these specific job and housing dissatisfactions is the high level of general dissatisfaction—68% on the average—with local government efforts to solve these problems. *Large numbers of Negroes in all the cities are clearly disturbed and angry, and these feelings have in them a strong riot potential.*

Taking the average score on these . . . indices in each city as a rough measure, the cities were then ranked according to the level of Negro dissatisfaction. It was found that two riot cities head the list as highest in Negro dissatisfaction with "grievance levels" of 56% and 49%, but that the third riot city is lowest in Negro dissatisfaction (35%) of all the cities studied. Thus, it is clear that there is no one-to-one relationship between level of Negro dissatisfaction in a city and the occurrence of a riot. It is also clear that if a riot *did* occur in the city with the lowest level of Negro dissatisfaction, a riot obviously *could* occur in any of these cities.

Nor does a pairing of cities on levels of dissatisfaction produce any simple pattern. One riot city shows a considerably higher level of Negro dissatisfaction than its non-riot partner. Yet, another riot city shows no greater dissatisfaction than its non-riot partner, while still another riot city shows *less* racial dissatisfaction on nearly all the indices than its non-riot sister city.

Do any other simple patterns of factors account for the occurrence of riots in some of these cities and not in others? In exploring this question further, two demographic factors were taken into consideration. One was the percentage of southern-born Negroes in each city. The reason for including this data was that the answers to one question in the survey indicated a feeling among both whites and Negroes (though to a lesser extent among

Negroes) that riots are more likely to break out in Negro communities with a large proportion of newly-arrived Southerners. The other factor was the level of full-time Negro employment in each city. The relevance of this point is obvious.

The findings show that the first factor has a definite relation to the occurrence of a riot while the second does not. If the percentage of southern-born Negroes included in the sample of respondents is averaged for riot versus non-riot cities, the result shows that 75% of the Negro respondents in the riot cities were born in the South while only 55% of the Negro respondents in the non-riot cities were southern-born. On the other hand, the difference in the average level of full-time employment for Negroes between riot and non-riot cities is not significant. An average of 51% of Negroes [interviewed] in riot cities report full-time employment versus an average of 49% in the non-riot cities.

Thus, the evidence shows that a high proportion of southern-born Negroes living in the ghetto increases the possibility that a city will have a riot. It must be pointed out, however, that there is no one-to-one, or systematic relationship between the percentage of southern-born Negroes living in a city and the level of dissatisfaction of Negroes in that city. Higher proportions of southern migrants do not necessarily mean that there will be higher grievance levels in a particular city. We shall return to this point again when we discuss a factor that is systematically correlated with high levels of Negro dissatisfaction.

3. Level of White Resistance to Change

It might be thought, on common-sense grounds, that a riot is more likely to occur in cities in which the white population is resistant to any increase in opportunities for a better life for the Negro population. White resistance to change can be measured either by assessing the steps taken within a city to improve the life chances of the Negro population or by assessing the feelings and opinions of a representative sample of the white population. In this report, we confine ourselves to the second kind of evidence; the first will be reported when the data are fully analyzed.

*   *   *   *

. . . The results permit us to make three observations. First, the level of white resistance to change in *all* the cities is relatively low: the highest is 24%, the lowest 15%. Whites are much more likely to say, in answering any of these questions, that the rate of change is "about right" than to say it is "too fast". Of course, an "about right" answer cannot be taken as an absolute measure of approval of change since a city may not have made much of an effort to change the conditions of its Negro population. But, even given this situation, we can assume that a "too fast" answer indicates a rock bottom, hard-core resistance to change. It is therefore significant that the proportion of whites who display hard-core resistance is so low in all the cities.

The second point is that the difference in levels of white resistance between the various cities is so slight that no significance can be attached to any attempt to rank the cities on this measure.

The third observation is the most important. Except for one riot city—the one with the 24% level of white resistance—there is no direct relation between the level of white resistance and the level of Negro dissatisfaction. Nor is there any systematic relation between the level of white resistance and the occurrence of a riot. We are thus forced to conclude that hard-core white resistance has little bearing on a city's riot potential.

4. The Disparity in Attitudes between Whites and Negroes

If the level of absolute white resistance to change makes no significant contribution to the riot potential of cities, then a more revealing measure of the significance of white attitudes may be the size of the gap between Negro and white opinions on a number of race-related issues. The gap is a measure of the disparity of perceptions of the race problems between Negroes and whites.

The survey results reveal two significant findings: 1) The size of the gap on almost all issues is quite large; it is in fact a gulf. 2) Variations in the size of the gap from city to city are not related to the occurrence or non-occurrence of a riot. The gap represents a national problem independent of local variations. This is not to say, however, that answers to particular questions, such as the perception of police brutality, do not show striking variations from city to city.

This disparity in attitudes will be discussed by aggregating answers to a large number of questions under three headings: 1) the pace of integration, 2) the cause of riots, and 3) the prevention of riots.

THE PACE OF INTEGRATION

The gap between Negro and white attitudes concerning the pace of integration can only be described as enormous. By averaging the percentage of Negroes and whites in each city who selected a "two slow" answer . . . , we can obtain a measure of the gap on this issue. The lowest level (per city) of the gap between the large number of Negroes and the small number of whites who answered "too slow" is 39%. The highest average gap (per city) is 62%. To take an extreme example from the city with the highest gap, 85% of the Negroes said the city was doing too little about integration while only 19% of the whites gave this answer. But the discrepancy regarding rate of change in all the cities is of such proportions as to constitute a national problem of catastrophic dimensions.

THE CAUSES OF RIOTS

Negroes and whites are somewhat closer together on answers to questions concerning the major causes of riots. The average Negro-white difference on this issue ranges from 13 percentage points in one city to 21 percentage points in another. In two of the six cities, there is actual agreement that bad living conditions among Negroes are a major cause of riots. However, Negro-white consensus, such as it is, ends there.

In most cities, only a small minority of whites perceive Negro unemployment or lack of equal job opportunities as a major cause of riots while a majority of Negroes perceive a direct connection between riots and employment opportunities. The situation is the same with respect to the raising of Negro hopes and the breaking of promises by the city governments. Twice as many Negroes as whites see broken promises as a cause of riots, and, in most cases, the responsibility for the broken promises is laid squarely on the shoulders of city governments.

On the issue of police brutality, Negroes and whites are even farther apart. Very few whites [an average of 5%] see police brutality as a cause of riots; many Negroes [an average of one-third] see this as a major cause.

The only factor that large percentages of whites are willing to see as a major cause of riots is "outsiders coming into a city and stirring up trouble," which the vast majority of Negroes reject as a major cause. In other words, whites refuse to see riots as engendered by basic forces and real conditions which exist within the Negro community, and blame outside troublemakers instead. [Whites were 2½ to 8 times more likely than Negroes to blame outsiders for riots.]

PREVENTION

In the area of prevention of riots, the disagreement is much wider than on the causes. The average gap separating Negroes and whites ranges from 29 percentage points in one city to 39 percentage points in another. Whites do come out strongly in favor of equal job opportunities for Negroes, but this is such a general statement of basic democratic rights that its significance is doubtful. When it comes to specific measures to enhance Negro job opportunities, such as on-the-job training by industry and special government training programs for Negroes, white enthusiasm falls off sharply.

In the area of housing, the vast majority of Negroes support open housing laws. But only one-third to one-half of whites are willing to see such laws passed as a way to reduce the possibility of future riots. On the average, about two-thirds of Negroes and less than one-half of whites see a solution in the remodeling or replacing of slums with decent housing.

The only riot prevention measure supported by a majority of both races stressed a relatively uncontroversial but nonetheless significant point. Large numbers of Negroes and whites agreed that "the mayor and other city officials should spend more time in areas where riots might break out, and should really get to know more about what Negroes are feeling." This is the only question in the survey which focused directly on the important issue of communication between Negroes and whites, and the consensus on this point is quite encouraging. Evidence gathered in face-to-face interviewing with leaders of Negroes and whites in the six cities reveals that the lack of communication is a crucial issue. Whites have simply not known, or have not fully realized, how much bitterness and frustration exists in the ghetto.

In fact, it is quite possible that the size of the gap in Negro-white attitudes is less a sign of white unwillingness to institute change, more a product of the ignorance among whites of the actual conditions in the ghetto. If this assumption is correct, then the low level of hard-core white resistance to change is placed in better perspective. The problem facing Negroes and whites is not a matter of pure and simple "racism". Rather, it is concerned with the lack of information among whites as to how Negroes feel and with the inability of our social institutions to meet the need for change unless this need is brought home in an acute, dramatic, and essentially painful form.

5. Negro and White Attitudes toward Riots

There is widespread evidence that, although they are reluctant to admit it, Americans are aware of the fact that they do not make painful decisions, even in a just cause, unless driven by even more painful counter-irritants. The expression "It's the squeaky wheel that gets the grease" is a sign of this implicit insight. The survey results show that both Negroes and whites endorse the "squeaky wheel" principle, so far as riots are concerned.

Although the numbers vary from city to city, sizable percentages of both whites and Negroes agree that "riots have brought about some long-delayed action by the city governments to help the Negro community." The benefits perceived by both groups range from such psychological matters as focusing attention on Negroes' needs and problems to the concrete steps of providing more jobs and better housing.

In addition, more than half of the Negroes and about a third of the whites in each city agree that "if it had not been for riots in the past, Congress would not have passed the civil rights laws." Nevertheless, both whites and Negroes tend to agree that riots are undesirable and unpopular methods of bringing about change. An average of 59% of the Negroes and 63% of the whites in all cities agree with the opinion that only a small minority of Negroes are in sympathy with riots. When Negroes were asked how riots make most Negroes feel, the answers were predominantly negative toward actual riot behavior. When Negroes were asked whether riots help or hurt the Negro cause, they expressed intensely mixed feelings. It is possible (but not yet certain) that Negroes are currently shifting to a more positive attitude toward riots while still feeling quite uncomfortable about using violence to achieve social gains.

It would seem possible that though Negroes do not particularly like being the "squeaky wheel", they are coming to the conclusion that only intense forms of social protest can bring relief from social injustice. The survey turned up some indirect evidence that this may well be the predominant feeling in the ghetto. As was mentioned previously, the evidence shows that high levels of Negro dissatisfaction greatly increase the possibility that a city will experience a riot. We left unanswered the question: what factor is most highly correlated with the index of Negro dissatisfaction? The answer to this question is highly significant. If the cities are ranked for level of Negro dissatisfaction, almost an exact duplicate of the ranking is produced by the averages of Negro agreement with the response: the city government is doing too little to encourage racial integration. This is the only one of the questions included in the index which behaves in this fashion.

It is evident that over half the Negroes in all cities think the city government is doing too little. Nevertheless, it is also clear that when Negroes feel that the city government shows a sincere concern for the basic problems of Negroes by making some attempts to encourage integration, their level of dissatisfaction will be lower, and lacking an inflammatory incident of considerable intensity, they will not riot. Contrariwise, if the Negroes believe that the city government is paying practically no attention to their problems and has no real concern for them, then their grievance level will be high and a relatively trivial incident could release a riot.

[CONCLUSIONS]

*   *   *   *

From these findings, two conclusions pertinent to the present situation can be drawn:

(1) If city governments were to take more active steps to increase opportunities for Negroes and to relieve their sense of injustice, the riot potential within the ghetto would be reduced.

(2) If white populations generally had a fuller appreciation of the just grievances and overwhelming problems of Negroes in the ghetto, they would give stronger support to their city governments to promote change and to correct the circumstances which give rise to the strong feelings of resentment now characteristic of ghetto populations.

MICHAEL AIKEN and N. J. DEMERATH III

The Politics of Tokenism in
Southern Education

"The real choice is whether we're going to obey the law with federal aid or obey the law without federal aid. If we sit back and say 'Make us, sue us' we would be faced with real administrative chaos."

White school board president

"Those of you who do not want to send your children to school with niggers, get out and vote against those liberals and cheap politicians who would jeopardize your child's future."

Midnight leaflet from White Voters League

"So far it's been a honest-to-God miracle. There ain't been any real troubles; our kids has been treated pretty well. It can be did, but it's just beginning and the real trouble ain't even begun yet."

Parent of Negro child in a white school

*   *   *   *

This report is based on two different districts in the Mississippi Delta. One is a growing town of about 40,000, with a cosmopolitan elite tradition. The other is a rural county containing a host of small towns, still encapsulated within the "closed society." We have called the one "River City," the other "Bayou County." However different from each other, they represent neither all of Mississippi nor even all of the Delta itself. The study's data consist of interviews. . . .

Throughout we have changed the names of places and people to protect the guilty as well as the innocent. This is itself a commentary on the open wounds of the Deep South. Our intention was not to act as Feds, finks, or pettifoggers. Yet even the results of anonymous research can be harsh.

*   *   *   *

. . . River City is relatively prosperous and progressive, with a tradition of cultural sophistication and even racial moderation. There is a social distinction here between the white elite and the "redneck" or "peckerwood" families. By contrast, there is little such distinction in Bayou County where the rednecks *are* the elite. The county is tied more firmly to the crumbling cotton economy and has more Negroes and more poverty.

The distinction is reflected in the schools of the two areas. River City has always been proud of its schools. A local historian wrote in 1912, "The River City schools have always been second to none in the state, and the graduates are admitted without examination into the universities of the different states." But in 1912 there were only a few public schools for whites in Bayou County, and those for Negroes developed later and at random. These are hardly a source of pride by any pedagogic standard.

COMPLIANCE IN RIVER CITY

            *   *   *   *

[There has been] increased pressure from the federal courts to speed Mississippi school desegregation. This pressure has been crucial. Without it, there would not even be token desegregation in the state today. . . . [Some] districts are still waiting for compulsion, but most, like Bayou County, have fallen victim to a court order late and unprepared.

River City was an exception. Along with a few other school systems, it decided to stay a jump ahead of the Feds, mainly to guard its federal educational funds. Although the first River City voluntary segregation plan of February 1965 fell far short of US Office of Education requirements, it was nonetheless hailed locally as a bold move. "This is no time," trumpeted a local paper, "for the faint of heart to sit on any Deep Southern school board." And in May 1965 registration of grades one and two only was held for the following September, on a "freedom of choice basis" whereby any student could register for any school, Negro or white.

The registration went smoothly, but two grades were not enough to satisfy federal standards. In June, the courts upset the strategy of "under-integration" by ordering the Jackson, Mississippi, schools to observe the full Office of Education requirement and desegregate four specified grades in September. Flustered but game, the River City bureaucrats fell in line with the decision, knowing it would reach them soon anyway. They added the seventh and twelfth grades to their plan, thus bringing it in line with federal requirements, except that the already registered second grade was substituted, by permission, for the specified tenth.

As in May, August registration was virtually uneventful, though only 147 Negroes out of a possible 1,500 chose white schools. By the following January the number of Negroes still attending those schools had dropped to 121. Note, however, that this was not due to official pressure to switch back to Negro schools, common in some "desegregated" districts. According to the River City superintendent:

We just put our foot down and said, "Brother, you chose to go to a white school and now you're going to." I don't care what color a student's skin is, white, black, purple, or orange—I'm not going to run an educational cafeteria on a short order basis.

No, indeed. Negroes unhappy in the white schools simply dropped out altogether, like an estimated 22,000 other school-age children in Mississippi. The state's compulsory attendance law was never enforced, and it was formally revoked on the heels of the Supreme Court schools decision.

The Negroes that remained in the white River City schools confronted no acute problems. Even the reputed local leader of the United Klans of America admitted, perhaps disappointedly, that everyone behaved nicely. Little was made of the few mild incidents that did occur, such as a little white first-grade girl being kissed by a Negro classmate. Although Negro students were sometimes shoved in the halls amid audible mutterings of "Nigger," their parents had expected far worse.

But desegregation, however uneventful, is a far cry from real integration. Only the smaller children were friendly across the racial barrier. At the high school, even the one cherished example of student acceptance turned out to have its less acknowledged seamy side. The nomination of a Negro student as vice president of the dramatics club was later cancelled by the high school principal, "to save the boy from intended embarrassment," as the principal explained at awkward length. Since the boy was one of the most popular Negro students in the school, it is just possible that the election was on the level and the concern for embarrassment was more projected than altruistic.

Still, even militant civil rights leaders admitted that the teachers did not discriminate socially or in their grading. Unhappily, this fairness did not save the Negro students from academic failure. They did poorly all around, worse in the upper grades than the lower, and worst of all in examinations. At the junior high level, the Negroes made up 15 percent of the student body but 47 percent of the failures. The situation was worse in the high schools where the Negroes opted out of pride and despite counselling for the stiff college preparatory curriculum. In all of this, poor home environment was a factor, but even more important was the poor quality of the Negro schools the students came from. The older students fared worse because they had longer exposure to the crippling Negro schools. Indeed, even the River City school administrators now admit that the notion of "separate but equal" schools is a guilt-allaying myth. But the most important factor in the poor performance of the Negro students, particularly in the high school, was that the brightest Negroes did not opt for white schools. As we shall see later, they had too much to lose by switching.

*   *   *   *

RESISTANCE IN BAYOU COUNTY
                    *   *   *   *

On August 24, 1965, barely a week before school opened, the US district judge ordered the schools of Bayou County to desegregate at least four grades, including the first, by the 1965-1966 school year. There had been no last ditch efforts to ward off the blow, nor, as in River City, to prepare for it. In the absence of a county plan, individual school systems made their own choices as to which three grades, in addition to the first, would be desegregated. Most opted for the last three years of high school, because, as we shall explain, they could be sure of few takers. One nearby county in a similar fix opened all 12 grades to Negroes in a gesture of total resignation, but this was unique.

Bayou County's "freedom of choice" registrations occurred only a few days after the court directive. Phalanxes of special policemen were on duty to ward off incidents and perhaps symbolically to ward off Negroes as well. Negro applicants for white schools were rigorously screened. . . .

Naturally enough there were few applicants—only 48 or about 2 percent of those eligible, although nearly 75 percent of the county's schoolchildren are Negro. The Negro community was not only scared, but it was even less prepared than the whites. One civil rights leader hinted that the court order might have been issued late on purpose, to give them no time to organize. Certainly the decision fell short of the original suit that had asked for more desegregation than four grades and the desegregation of the faculty as well. Many Negroes felt that an elephant had labored to deliver a white mouse. Several schools in the county managed to "escape" Negro students altogether.

Those Negro students who did attend white schools were received with noticeable lack of enthusiasm, though without violence. White teachers were uncomfortable, and a few threatened to quit—no light matter in Mississippi where the startlingly low salaries make recruitment and replacement difficult. Administrators were in a barely controlled panic. One principal gathered his seven Negro students, all girls, and lectured them on how to avoid trouble—by acting like Jackie Robinson! The general assumption was that the Negroes were the potential troublemakers. As one official said, "We haven't had trouble between the races in this area. Our leaders of the Negro people have controlled this thing." Within the schools, Negro students were given a collective cold shoulder. . . . Originally, a few white students were friendly to the Negroes, but they were soon taught better by their peers and parents.

In high school, the girls were better received than the boys. This is no surprise since Mississippi whites have always regarded the young Negro male as a potential troublemaker and a fabled threat to white virginity.

In any case, few boys even made the switch to white schools. In this state, Negro boys who stay in high school are often pursuing either academic or athletic scholarships. Both would be imperiled in a white school, because of higher academic standards and nonintegrated sports.

As to actual "trouble" in the more rural Bayou County, it varied from town to town. In "Bayou City," the largest and most civilized town in the county, "incidents" were fairly rare. In "Raeford," a civil rights hot spot since 1964, they were too numerous to list. We heard complaints about unfair grading by teachers (an unusual charge) as well as about wage cuts, firings, evictions, and other reprisals against Negro parents. "But," said a Raeford school principal smugly, "there's been no knifings or violence or that sort of thing." Apparently it would take a lynching to count as a reprisal in Raeford. It was here, incidentally, that a school official told us, "We don't have many Negroes in Raeford. Most of ours are niggers." . . .

One unmourned casualty of school desegregation in Raeford was the local PTA. In River City, Negro parents went to PTA meetings, but in Bayou City they prudently stayed away. In Raeford, however, the organization was simply disbanded. A white official made the surprising comment that it was no loss—it was run by John Birch types anyway.

As in River City, the Bayou County Negro students made poor grades in the white schools. Again, however, these were not the "best" Negro students. There is probably a good deal of truth in the allegation that the Negroes in the white high schools were more interested in civil rights than education. . . .

MAKING THE OMELETTE

*   *   *   *

Successful desegregation is like making a good omelette. Both require the breaking of "eggs" and delicacy in the midst of heat. Both court disaster as ingredients separate. In this section we shall suggest some reasons why the first course in River City was somewhat more palatable than that in Bayou County. There will be no pointless talk about "good guys" and "bad guys." Instead we shall explore such conditioning circumstances as Delta politics, bureaucracy in the schools, and the civil rights movement within the Negro community. There will be no attempt to explain events through a single monolithic and malevolent "power structure." Instead, we will seek out structural variables that make for differences in the amount of power and the way it is exercised.

Mississippi has never been accused of leading the nation in such newfangled administrative gimmicks as centralization. County rights are as revered as states' rights, especially in education. That state's education system is controlled, by and large, by rural district supervisors who run their bailiwicks like satraps. They and the local and county school boards are responsible only to a highly select electorate. One Negro civil rights activist and registered voter in Bayou County had no idea when school elections were held, let alone how.

Again, however, River City offers an important exception. Here the school board is appointed by the city fathers rather than elected "at large." In affording protection from local constituencies, it provides the board with crucial autonomy and anonymity in running the school system on its own terms. It also allows the board to follow the predilections of the elite it represents. River City's economic elite have both assumed and been pushed into behind-the-scenes political leadership during the civil rights crisis. . . .

To moderates—perhaps even liberals— . . . federal civil rights legislation offered relief to sore consciences. Guilt over segregation had been festering for years, but they were unable to take integrating initiative by themselves. Now they had only to urge compliance with the law, a more temperate counsel. Soon after the civil rights bill of 1964 was passed, 15 such men began to meet regularly but covertly to smooth the transition. Negro leaders were not included, but they knew and called the group "the Friday evening tea club." Once considered radicals by the rest of the white community, the tea club had undergone a recent change in status. By contrast with the Northern civil rights workers who began to flood the town, they became voices of reason, persons to be trusted with planning the changes that were necessary. The middle class Negro leadership also gained by comparison with the outside civil rights workers, and slowly the local high-status whites and Negroes began to coordinate their efforts.

In Bayou County, by contrast, the civil rights movement disrupted the community instead of unifying it. Its small towns had neither a white nor a Negro elite that might cooperate. Lacking moderate leadership the two sides drew back into their separate corners, like boxers waiting for the bell. Even the once typical residential mingling of Negroes and rednecks has declined since it now carries the name of "integration." Moderates, if any, are locked away from one another in a general conspiracy of silence. Indeed, silence is crucial in maintaining the "closed society." One could wildly imagine a town in which every white citizen is a private integrationist but convinced that he is the only one and cowed by the prospects of going against the traditional tide. The image is far-fetched but provocative.

THE BLESSINGS OF BUREAUCRACY

One important difference between the River City schools and those in Bayou County is that the former are more bureaucratized and run by professionals on the way up, while the latter are less bureaucratized and run by men now stripped of professional ambition. Like many school super-intendents in Mississippi, the River City superintendent is a former football coach. But he regards his job as a plum won after many thumb thrusts. He is anxious to succeed to greater heights, and success, in his field, can be reflected from advantages gained by the money pried out of Washington. The River City school headquarters is a factory for the manufac-ture of federal grant proposals—over a million dollars worth for one school year. As the assistant superintendent put it, "We are out to get every dime Washington has to offer, and we're not going to let segrega-tion stand in the way."

Unlike larger school systems, both Northern and Southern, the River City school people are new to the federal game and play it straight. They do not take money and at the same time seek to circumvent the spirit of civil rights legislation. They know they are being watched, and a detected mistake could be disastrous. Moreover, the bureaucracy is small enough to maintain control in the interests of efficiency. Thus, the superintendent and his assistant are inclined to favor faculty integration, because of the shortage of white teachers; they are also privately willing to replace the inefficient "freedom of choice" system with neighborhood schools, even though this means sending white students to formerly all-Negro schools —a recognized danger point.

All this is in sharp contrast with Bayou County. Meet Mr. Sullivan, a high school principal in Raeford who has been in his job 11 years. He says this is "too damn long," but then why hasn't he moved on and up? It seems he has grown used to his comfortable salary and free house and to appeasing the town's resident ideologists, a course which has sealed him off from more sophisticated school districts, such as River City. . . .

All this suggests the plight of the Southern moderate under duress. But we learned that Sullivan is the single most despised white among Raeford Negroes and that he rules the Negro schools with an iron hand while of-fering rationalized clichés about the inferiority of Negro genes. This is a man for whom the "path of least resistance" has become a superhighway, one who fans local prejudices instead of dissipating them. Unlike River City's administrators, he is an impediment, rather than a lubricant, in the desegregation process. But also unlike the protected bureaucrats in the larger towns, he stands naked before a whirlwind of conflicting forces. Unhappily, his position is typical in this region. River City may point the way to the future. But most Delta communities are firmly mired in the past.

So far, however, we have neglected the Negro school administrators. Perhaps they belong in the consideration of the Negro community. But no. These men are cogs in the white machine, picked for docility. The "dual" system of education is a misnomer. There is only one, run by the whites, and Negro principals owe their very jobs to segregation. If faculties are desegregated, they will be the first to go. Not wishing to antagonize whites or Negroes, they opt out altogether. . . .

THE NEGRO COMMUNITY

It is a measure of the Negroes' tragedy that so much of this analysis should concern whites and thus indicate that the Negroes themselves have had relatively little voice in their ultimate destiny. But this is less true in River City than in Bayou County. What is there about the River City Negro community that has allowed it to play a more decisive role in determining its educational fate?

One crucial factor is the River City *black bourgeoisie*. True, the stereotype pictures the Negro middle class as the traditional lair of the "Uncle Tom," but, like all stereotypes, this one is dangerous. Some are "Toms," some are not. It depends on a complex set of factors such as vulnerability to reprisals, age, and relative position on the local political spectrum. River City has several middle class Negroes who are young, who are not vulnerable to white pressure in their occupation, whose images have become "whitened" in comparison to more radical civil rights workers. Such Negroes are hardly radicals themselves but neither have they turned their backs on the "movement." Taking advantage of their image as moderates, they push harder behind the scenes than the whites suspect. Not only do they provide examples by actually sending their own children to white schools (unlike middle class Negroes in most areas), but they also maintain a constant pressure on the white community that is felt despite its quiet subtlety. Using the need for federal funds as leverage, they have kept an eye peeled for violations of the desegregation requirements which might interest Washington. . . .

The present strategy of the River City Negro leaders is to engineer such an influx of Negro students into the white schools that, to relieve overcrowding, "freedom of choice" will have to be abandoned in favor of desegregation by neighborhoods. They reason that when white children are sent to a currently all Negro school, greater attention will be given to facilities and educational standards.

*   *   *   *

The point is not that the River City Negro *bourgeoisie* will move at an optimum pace or even that they would have begun at all without the outside civil rights workers forging the way and providing meaningful comparison. The point is rather that local Negro leaders and outside workers have provided a crucial alliance that may be as salutary in its results as it is uneasy in its day-to-day relations.

In Bayou County, however, the outside workers have had the reverse effect. There local whites and Negroes are farther apart than ever, since there are few middle class Negroes either informed or aggressive enough to take advantage of the situation and consolidate gains by coping with the whites from "inside." One or two urged poorer parents to send their children to white schools, but then failed to provide promised transportation or protection and, more importantly, failed to send their own children. Little wonder that only 2 percent of the Bayou County Negroes made the switch. Little wonder too that Bayou County whites are less impeded in planning for the future and are able to use subservient Negroes as window dressing. . . .

To sum up, serious trouble has not yet occurred in Bayou County, but neither has serious integration. In so unpromising an atmosphere, violence is an ever looming threat, and the local Negroes lack the leadership to either curb the threat or act in spite of it. Again, this is less a failure of nerve than an artifact of community structure.

BEYOND TOKENISM

. . . [As] yet there is no indication that pressure will be applied to force a shift from a "freedom of choice" system to a geographical basis of school attendance. Such a shift is too crucial to be left to local initiative. While it may occur in River City, it is unlikely in the near future of Bayou County.

And yet even geographical desegregation is no educational panacea. It may go beyond tokenism in racial matters since the "rednecks" who now live close to Negroes cannot afford to simply pack up their children and move to middle class white enclaves. But desegregation of this sort courts violence and ultimately differential education on the basis of social class if not race itself. The Negroes may find that a school in a poor neighborhood is never the greatest, whether black, white, or mixed.

This points again to the pervasive problem of poverty. On purely racial grounds, it may be that River City, Mississippi, will be more desegregated in 15 years than New York, Chicago, or Los Angeles—the impacted ghettos to which so many Mississippi Negroes have fled. But desegregation, educational or otherwise, can become a mockery to people so hopelessly poor. In the Delta, and throughout Mississippi, equal opportunity in any field means increasingly the opportunity to share *problems* rather than *benefits*. Equal schooling will continue to be poor schooling. Equal employment may become equal vulnerability to unemployment, and equal voting only the chance to make decisions of little impact.

There are immediate problems that can and must be solved quickly with massive federal funds and stubbornly executed federal legislation. But the tragedies of Mississippi have yet to reach their climax.

POSTSCRIPT

The data and observations in this study go back more than a year, but we have obtained more recent data on River City and its school integration as of February 1967.

Little has changed in qualitative terms. Although a great deal of flak was raised over the Office of Education guidelines for the 1966-1967 academic year, the pattern of quiet compliance has remained as before. Because the number of classes to be integrated through freedom of choice has doubled, so the number of Negro students attending formerly all-white schools has also doubled—but little more. Although the system has yet to integrate the teaching staff, it is not alone in failing to comply in this respect, and it has made a token response by bringing the Negro administrator in charge of the Negro schools into the offices of the white school administration.

But one ironic twist merits special attention. The River City school system was successful in applying for federal free lunch funds for schools with a high proportion of lower class children, funds provided under the terms of the Elementary and Secondary Education Act. It now happens that these "liberal" monies have unintentionally "conservative" consequences; only the Negro schools had sufficient proportions of lower class students to qualify. So if a Negro student moves to a white school he loses his free lunch, sometimes his only decent meal of the day. Here is yet another respect in which integration involves a sacrifice rather than an unmixed blessing. For many the hunger for food is understandably more salient than the thirst for knowledge. Once again freedom of choice in the Delta offers a poor choice at best.

FRED POWLEDGE

Segregation, Northern Style

De facto school segregation exists wherever segregation is a matter of fact, rather than law. To many Americans, it is every bit as awful as the mobs in Little Rock, the bombs in New Orleans, and the gunshots on the back roads of Mississippi.

It is cynical evidence of discrimination by the majority against the minority, and it is made even more invidious by being practiced openly, though officially condemned and outlawed.

In practical terms, it means older, more run-down, and more crowded school buildings, less experienced teachers, more tattered textbooks, and a diploma that is worth less than those handed out across town in the white school.

Although it is often called segregation, Northern style, de facto segregation of the schools—deeply rooted in other forms of segregation—is really a problem of urban areas whether they be in the North or the South. It exists, primarily, because of housing discrimination, and it contributes to further housing discrimination. Because the human products of segregated educational institutions are unequally prepared for the competition of modern life, de facto segregation contributes, too, to the Negro unemployment crisis.

Until recently de facto segregation was peculiar to the North, Midwest, and West, because de jure segregation (segregation practiced by law) was not allowed in those areas. But now it is beginning to spread to the urban South. In Atlanta, for example, de jure segregation was abolished several years ago. Now the increasing Negro population, coupled with the flight of the whites to the suburbs, is providing the city's school authorities with the same kinds of problems being experienced in New York, Chicago, and Los Angeles.

Back in 1954, when the Supreme Court handed down its decision in *Brown et al.* v. *Board of Education of Topeka et al.*, the big target was de jure segregation. Everyone's attention focused on segregation as it was practiced in the South. This was understandable. Segregation was worst in the American South, and the region was being required to meet Northern standards.

But the 1954 decision, and the Southern Negro movement it helped to create, led some Northern Negroes to question their own circumstances. One month after *Brown et al.*, Kenneth Clark, professor of psychology

Reprinted by permission of the author and the publisher from "Segregation, Northern Style," *American Education*, 3 (December, 1966-January, 1967), pp. 1-5.

at New York City College and one of those on whom the Supreme Court relied for expert information in writing the decision, charged the New York City school board with racial gerrymandering and with policies and practices resulting in inferior education for minority children.

New York City officials investigated the charges, and delivered a "Statement of Principle and Purpose," which said in part:

"We, therefore, interpret the May 17th decision of the U.S. Supreme Court as a legal and moral reaffirmation of our fundamental educational principles. We recognize it as a decision which applies not only to those cases in litigation, but also as a challenge to boards throughout the Nation to reexamine the racial composition of the schools within their respective systems in order to determine whether they conform to the standards stated clearly by the court."

In 1963, after nine years of sustained and well publicized reexamination, the Board reported that "New York City has exercised undisputed leadership in the field of school integration among all the cities of our country."

But now, a dozen years after *Brown*, the schools of New York City and dozens of other Northern, Midwestern, and Western cities remain segregated. It makes little difference to the minority groups that their segregation is termed de facto instead of de jure. Angry and alienated, they mount picket lines, hold school boycotts, and file court actions.

These years have been disappointing to those working to integrate schools outside the South. Said June Shagaloff, national director of education programs for the National Association for the Advancement of Colored People and perhaps the only civil rights organization official who works full time on de facto problems, "With one possible exception, I don't believe there's a single big-city school system in the country, or even a middle-sized school system, that is really dealing with this problem." *

Miss Shagaloff's emphasis was on the word "really"; certainly there are officials of big and middle-sized school systems who would disagree, but from her point of view there is only one city that is really doing something.

The one exception, she said, is New York City, where officials have agreed on their commitment to reorganize the school system to eliminate racial imbalance, but where they have been stymied by implementation difficulties. "Every place else," said Miss Shagaloff, "we're still fighting for a board policy to adopt a desegregation plan."

*Editors' Note: In 1968, Berkeley, California, became the first city in the United States with more than 100,000 citizens and a sizable Negro school-age population (41 per cent) to fully integrate every school and classroom.

Miss Shagaloff's objections are aimed primarily at the larger school systems; she has run into considerably less difficulty in smaller communities. "There are," she said, "between 35 and 45 suburban school systems that have adopted plans for total desegregation of their school system or have initiated very substantial desegregation plans."

Other researchers tend to agree with Miss Shagaloff's estimate of the gravity of the problem. Last spring, U.S. Commissioner of Education Harold Howe II told an audience that the sort of inequality produced by segregation Northern style can be "more complete and severe than that existing in many small Southern towns."

And the "Equality of Educational Opportunity" survey published this year by the Office of Education summarized its findings this way:

"In its desegregation decision of 1954, the Supreme Court held that separate schools for Negro and white children are inherently unequal. This survey finds that, when measured by that yardstick, American public education remains largely unequal in most regions of the country, including everywhere Negroes form a significant part of the population."

Evidence in the report points to the inescapable conclusion that segregation is practiced in the Northern, Midwestern, and Western schools, whether it is called "de facto segregation" or "racially unbalanced education," or "racial isolation." These terms are used by school and political authorities who feel that segregation is the understandable predicament of an urban area that has a high percentage of Negro youngsters, or that suffers from housing discrimination. In such communities, school integration—Negro and white children in the same classroom—is all but impossible.

Thus, de facto segregation may be termed a problem of the cities, and not exclusively a problem of the North. And it is almost certain to grow worse. When the 1960 Census was taken, 51 percent of all Negroes in the United States lived in what behavioral scientists call the "central cities." At the same time, 68 percent of the Nation's school-age Negro children lived in the central cities. (In the Nation's capital, 93 percent of the public school population is Negro.)

There is ample evidence that, in the urban ghettos, segregated education is inferior education, both in terms of the skills the student may be expected to learn and the self-esteem that is necessary if he is going to break out of his racial prison. With continued de facto segregation, the Nation can expect continued Negro unemployment and the troubles that are associated with it—bitterness, despair, and a tragic waste of the energies, intellectual abilities, and economic stimulation that could be provided by a healthy, vigorous minority.

Furthermore, the Nation can expect—if little or nothing is done—

increased alienation of the Negro minority toward everything that smacks of the white majority. Already some of the younger and more vocal Negro leaders are saying that whites aren't worth integrating with.

This fall [of 1966] a controversy arose over a modern, air-conditioned school which was to open in Harlem. Negro and Puerto Rican parents picketed and boycotted. They said they wanted integration, but there was some evidence that what they really wanted was a black voice in the operation of the school and the selection of personnel. Their statement said: "By demanding a decisive vote in the operation of 201, the community seeks to disarm a system that is systematically destroying the vast majority of Negro and Puerto Rican students."

Elsewhere, "black power" proponents are saying with increasing volume that Negro students should be taught in a black environment, one that makes them proud, rather than ashamed, of their color.

Such demands can't be dismissed as the exaggerations of leaders eager to accumulate power, or the rantings of modern-day Marcus Garveys seeking followers under the banner of black nationalism. Much of what they say is not exaggeration. The Northern as well as the Southern white community has been reluctant to offer more than token changes. And ghetto schools are inferior—inferior by any test.

The only way to diminish the influence of these leaders is by actually integrating the schools and other areas of American life.

This is a slow process. New York City may have called itself the undisputed leader in school integration in 1963, but a State education advisory committee reporting on the city's efforts in 1964, declared that "nothing undertaken by the New York City Board of Education since 1954, and nothing proposed since 1963, has contributed or will contribute in any meaningful degree to desegregating the public schools."

Two of New York's major obstacles have been housing discrimination and the white movement to the suburbs. In New York, as in most other large urban areas, a "neighborhood school" serves a community that is either all white, all black, or all Spanish-speaking. Thus, the number of predominantly white schools in New York has decreased while the number of predominantly Negro and Puerto Rican schools increased.

Frederick Williams, a 51-year-old native New Yorker and veteran of 28 years in the city's school system, is the assistant superintendent responsible for implementing integration.

"Undoubtedly the size and complexity of our system are major obstacles in achieving what we want to achieve," he said in a recent interview. "We're dealing with children for whom we have to personalize education. The larger the system, the more difficult this is to do. We can't really do this through a 'formula-type operation,' where we sit at headquarters and decide what is good, specifically, for every child in the city. All we can do is put out general guidelines, and then have school administrators translate them into meaningful educational practices."

New York City has tried a little bit of everything. It has offered Negro parents the opportunity to send their children to schools in white neighborhoods; it has "paired" schools in an adaptation of the Princeton Plan; it has rezoned schools; it has readjusted the feeder patterns from elementary into junior high schools; it has approved construction of two educational parks; and it has built new schools on boundaries between neighborhoods, rather than in the heart of all-white or all-Negro neighborhoods.

The results? Open enrollment was widely condemned and underutilized by Negroes, who felt the school board was placing the integration burden on them. School pairing led white parents to threaten to put their children in private schools. Little was accomplished by rezoning or the adjustment of feeder patterns. Educational parks are a long way off.

Efforts to build new schools on ghetto boundaries have been frustrated, too. Williams said that the school board often chooses school sites that border white and Negro neighborhoods, but by the time plans have been drawn, contracts have been let, and construction finally completed, the whites have moved out of "their" neighborhood, leaving the new school in an all-black area. In the relatively few integrated schools in New York City, ability grouping puts most white children in classes by themselves, and integration occurs only at lunch time.

So far, none of the attempts to order more heterogeneous classrooms has made more than a feeble dent in the segregated structure of New York City's schools. . . .

*   *   *   *

[It] is apparent to any New Yorker that it is taking the city an awfully long time to desegregate.

Similar delays occur in almost all major urban centers in the United States. For this reason, the U.S. Commission on Civil Rights was asked by President Johnson to study practices that contribute to racial isolation in 60 cities, North and South. "Such isolation," wrote President Johnson, "presents serious barriers to quality education."

*   *   *   *

There is evidence, however, that some smaller communities are doing better. "Where there have been changes," said June Shagaloff, "where school systems have desegregated, these have been suburban school systems."

Westbury, Long Island, for example, closed one Negro elementary school, reassigned its students and reopened the once segregated school as a kindergarten and preschool center. In Englewood, N.J., after the State education commissioner responded to NAACP complaints by ordering the local board to desegregate, school officials reassigned Negro students in grades one through five and used the empty "Negro" school as a central sixth grade.

Miss Shagaloff mentions East Orange, N.J., as a good example of what can be done by a "competent and courageous" superintendent of schools. The district abandoned its traditional building program and started construction of an educational park. In Darien, Conn., a virtually all-white, all-gentile community, the superintendent of schools started part-time pupil and teacher exchange programs with Negro schools in nearby Stamford and New York.

Mount Vernon, N.Y., plans a "children's academy," in which all students will spend two hours a day studying the arts, nature, and literature. The remainder of the school day will be spent in "neighborhood" schools, five of which are 75 percent Negro and six of which are 93 percent white.

The schools in Riverside, Calif., were partially integrated after one of three segregated schools was destroyed by fire but only after a petition urged the closing of all schools. Malverne, Long Island, claimed by integrationists to be one of the worst examples of educational bigotry in the Northeast, this fall agreed to comply with a three-year-old integration demand by James E. Allen, Jr., New York's State education commissioner. Allen has pressed school officials to do all they can to achieve integration and has urged Negroes to keep up their pressure.

"I think peaceful demonstrations by Negroes have done more than anything else to get us where we are," Allen said recently.

Other communities have been quietly working to desegregate. The absence of news stories about them is silent tribute to their success. Take, for example, Hartsdale, N.Y. Hartsdale is an unincorporated village about 25 miles north of New York City, in Westchester County. It is a commuter town with little industry. Its white residents are professional or semi-professional people working in New York City; most of the Negroes (about 35 percent of the population) work in construction, semiskilled, or menial jobs. In 1951, the school population was about half Negro, half white. There were two schools; one of them was 95 percent Negro and the other, 95 percent white. There was widespread housing discrimination. Aaron Lipton, principal of Hartsdale's Richard J. Bailey School, recently explained the change:

"One of our schools—back in 1951, this was—was an old, broken-down school, which was in the white neighborhood, and at that time it was very, very overcrowded. The Negro school, in the Negro neighborhood, was almost new, and was half full.

"Many people got together and decided that this was undemocratic. The problem was presented in terms of 'Why should our children go to this broken-down school when they have such a nice new school over there and it's not full?' And someone had the idea that perhaps, since the district was small enough, and we covered an area of perhaps five or six square miles, that maybe we ought to have all of the children of the district go to one school for kindergarten through third grade, another school for grades four through six, and another one for grades seven through nine. This would enable all the children to go to the same school. So in 1952, the schools were desegregated."

Soon after the desegregation of the schools, class "grouping" was started in Hartsdale. "What we mean by grouping," said Lipton, "is that every classroom has to have certain children in it. We feel that the most successful kind of grouping reflects the diversity of the community within each classroom." Thus, each of the classes "has intentionally the same number of boys and girls, the same number of Negro children and white children, the same number of children who are very successful, moderately successful, or unsuccessful" in school.

"We hire a superior staff, in my estimation," says Lipton, "a staff committed to education, not to the education of a small group of children . . . and we find that our bright and superior children are not being cheated by this experience. They're still hitting the top of the achievement tests." The Hartsdale administrators have found that the students who had placed in the highest quartile on achievement tests in 1959—who then had been rated at about one and one-half years above grade level— by 1963 had risen to more than two and one-half years above grade level. The students in the lowest quartile had risen from about two and one-half years below grade level to less than one year below the level.

Obviously, very few school systems can do precisely what Hartsdale has done. Physical or geographical factors make such a plan impractical or impossible for, say, Chicago or Grosse Pointe. But the situation in Hartsdale—and in a growing roster of communities: Roosevelt, Freeport, Buffalo, N.Y.; Detroit, Mich.; and Evanston, Ill., for example—does demonstrate that communities can so something if they decide to.

State policies have been adopted in New York, New Jersey, California, and Massachusetts. Illinois, Indiana, and California have taken legislative or administrative action. Robert L. Carter, the NAACP's legal counsel, believes that the Northern and Western courts are moving closer to a position that recognizes de facto segregation as a violation of the right to equal protection and recognizes that there are many ways to bring about desegregation.

June Shagaloff feels that the public school institution is "one of the most inflexible, rigid institutions in American life." She believes that change must be sought outside public schools and suggests that Negro parents become themselves a source of change. Four years ago, de facto school segregation was an issue in only six school systems in the Nation. Now it is a major item on the NAACP agenda in 140 systems in 22 states.

One of the more fortunate things that is happening in Hartsdale, Lipton feels, is that Negroes are coming into his office now and saying, "Why isn't such-and-such happening in this school?" Before, they might have thought that a trip to the principal's office was a waste of time.

Theron A. Johnson, who supervises the U.S. Office of Education's activities concerning de facto segregation, feels that "the most difficult part of desegregating the schools is the will and the desire and the intent to do it. Once you're past that one, you're all right," he says. "Once you've made the decision, then you can reorganize your grades, and you can place your buildings in certain strategic places, you can work arrangements with suburban areas and so on. The 'logistical setup' is not too difficult.

"Part of the problem in urban centers," says Johnson, "is the fact that education for all students has deteriorated. Urban education has to be better than what the surrounding areas offer.

"But the first job is the will to do something. And you know, in America, it's very interesting: once we make up our mind to do something, we do it."

JAMES S. COLEMAN

Toward Open Schools

Since the publication, in July, 1966, of the Office of Education's report to Congress and the President on "Equality of Educational Oppor-

Reprinted by permission of the author and the publisher from "Toward Open Schools," *The Public Interest* (Fall, 1967), pp. 20-27. © 1967 by National Affairs, Inc.

tunity," there has been much speculation and discussion concerning the policy implications of the report. The report itself, which focused principally on inequalities experienced by Negroes and other racial and ethnic minorities, contained only research results, not policy recommendations. Indeed, if recommendations had been requested, they could hardly have been given—for the facts themselves point to no obvious solution.

In some part, the difficulties and complexity of any solution derive from the premise that our society is committed to overcoming, not merely inequalities in the distribution of educational *resources* (classrooms, teachers, libraries, etc.), but inequalities in the opportunity for educational *achievement.* This is a task far more ambitious than has ever been attempted by any society:—not just to offer, in a passive way, equal access to educational resources, but to provide an educational environment that will free a child's potentialities for learning from the inequalities imposed upon him by the accident of birth into one or another home and social environment.

The difficulty that attends this task can be seen by confronting some of the results published in the report with one another. First, the inequality in results of elementary and secondary schooling for different ethnic groups, as measured by standardized tests, is very large for Negroes, Puerto Ricans, American Indians, and Mexican Americans. At the beginning of the twelfth grade, these groups were, on the average, three, four, or five grade levels behind whites in reading comprehension, and four, five, or six grade levels behind in mathematics achievement. Second, the evidence revealed that within broad geographic regions, and for each racial or ethnic group, the physical and economic resources going into a school had very little relation to the achievement coming out of it. This was perhaps the most surprising result to some persons: that variations in teacher salaries, library facilities, laboratories, school size, guidance facilities had little relation to student achievement—when the family backgrounds of the students were roughly equated. Such equating of background is necessary because, within each racial or ethnic group, the factor that showed the clearest relation to a child's achievement was his home background—the educational and economic resources provided within his home.

This pair of results taken together—the serious differences in educational output and their lack of relation to differences in the input of conventional educational facilities—create the complexity of the problem. For if it were otherwise, we could give simple prescriptions: increase teachers' salaries, lower classroom size, enlarge libraries, and so on. But the evidence does not allow such simple answers.

HETEROGENEITY AND ACHIEVEMENT

Another finding of the survey does give some indication of how different schools have different effects. The finding is that students do better when they are in schools where their fellow students come from backgrounds strong in educational motivation and resources. The results might be paraphrased by the statement that the educational resources provided by a child's fellow students are more important for his achievement than are the resources provided by the school board. This effect appears to be particularly great for students who themselves come from educationally-deprived backgrounds. For example, it is about twice as great for Negroes as for whites.

There are relatively small differences in the physical and economic resources of schools attended by Negro children and schools attended by white children (another surprising finding), but there are very large differences in the educational resources provided by their classmates. Classmates and schoolmates are usually rather homogeneous in economic and educational backgrounds, especially in large urban areas, and this homogeneity works to the disadvantage of those children whose family's educational resources are meagre. The disadvantage is particularly pronounced for Negroes, where historical patterns of school segregation and residential segregation, combined with the lower educational backgrounds of Negro families, place most Negro children in schools where the sum of educational resources brought to school by members of the student body is very small.

These results do offer a direct course of action in many communities where racial segregation of schools can be overcome by various means. For the results indicate that heterogeneity of race and heterogeneity of family educational background can increase the achievement of children from weak educational backgrounds with no adverse effect on children from strong educational backgrounds. Such integration cannot be expected to bring about full equality of opportunity for achievement; but the evidence does indicate effects that are far from negligible. In the large cities, however, where lower-class Negroes are both concentrated and numerous, this approach quickly exhausts its possibilities. There are simply not enough middle class children to go around.

Some observers have inferred from the Report that through racial integration of schools, and *only* through racial integration, will Negroes' educational achievement begin to match that of whites. The Civil Rights Commission has proposed that Congress pass a law requiring that all schools contain fewer than 50 per cent Negroes—a recommendation based partly on evidence in our report about Negro achievement in schools of differing racial and class composition. I believe such inferences are mistaken, and that the recommendations following from them are self-defeating. Racial integration of the schools is an important goal in its own right, affecting the very ability of our society to become truly multi-racial. It is important to know, as the Report shows, that this goal does not conflict with, and to some degree aids, the goal of increasing the educational achievement of lower-class children. But these two goals are not identical. The task of increasing achievement of lower-class children cannot be fully implemented by school integration, even if integration were wholly achieved—and the magnitude of racial and class concentrations in large cities indicates that it is not likely to be achieved soon.

RECONSTRUCTING THE ENVIRONMENT

I suggest that the matter may be better dealt with by inquiring more fully into the question of *how* a child's achievement is affected by the educational resources brought to school by other children. The evidence on this matter is not strong, but it is suggestive.

It is, for instance, a simple fact that the teacher cannot teach beyond the level of the most advanced students in the class, and cannot easily demand performance beyond that level. Thus, a comparison of Negro students (having similar family backgrounds) in lower class and largely segregated schools with those in middle class and often integrated schools shows that the former get higher grades than the latter, but their performance on standardized tests is lower. The student in a lower class school is being rewarded more highly for lower performance—not as much can be demanded of him.

It is also clear that going to school with other children whose vocabulary is larger than one's own demands and creates a larger vocabulary. Sitting next to a child who is performing at a high level provides a challenge to better performance. The psychological environment may be less comfortable for a lower class child (and there is some evidence that it is), but he learns more.

In short, there is some indication that these middle class schools have their effects through providing a social environment that is more demanding and more stimulating. And once we consider this, we realize that integration is not the only means, nor even necessarily the most efficient means, for increasing lower-class achievement. There may be other and better ways of creating such an environment.

For whatever the benefits of integration, it is also true that even in socially or racially integrated schools a child's family background shows a very high relation to his performance. The findings of the Report are quite unambiguous on this score. Even if the school is integrated, the heterogeneity of backgrounds with which children enter school is largely preserved in the heterogeneity of their performance when they finish. As the Report indicates, integration provides benefits to the underprivileged. But it takes only a small step toward equality of educational opportunity.

Thus a more intense reconstruction of the child's social environment than that provided by school integration is necessary to remove the handicap of a poor family background. It is such reconstruction that is important—whether it be provided through other children, through tutorial programs, through artificial environments created by computer consoles, or by some other means. The goal of increasing lower-class Negro achievement may be affected through a wide variety of means, which reconstruct a child's social and intellectual environment in any of several ways.

But if we recognize that racial and class integration does not in itself provide a full enough reconstruction of the environment, what happens then to the goal of racial integration in the schools? If more efficient methods for increasing achievement are found, as is likely to be the case, does this imply abandonment of attempts to overcome de facto segregation?

To answer this question requires a full recognition that there are two separable goals involved in current discussions for reorganizing schools. *The aim of racial integration of our schools should be recognized as distinct from the aim of providing equal opportunity for educational performance.* To confound these two aims impedes the achievement of either. It is important to know, as the Office of Education survey shows, that integration aids equality of educational opportunity; that white children perform no less well in a school with a large minority of Negroes than in an all-white middle class school; that Negro students perform somewhat better in such a school than in a predominantly Negro lower class school. Conversely, of course, greater equality of performance facilitates integration, making "grouping" or "tracking" within schools unnecessary. But integration is important to both white and Negro children principally for other reasons. We are committed to becoming a truly multiracial society. Yet most white children grow up having no conception of Negroes as individuals, and thus develop wholly unnatural and ambivalent reactions to Negroes as a group; most Negro children are in a similar circumstance. All educational policies must recognize the legitimacy and importance of the aim of racial integration. But we should not confound it with the aim of increasing equality of educational performance. Thus the proposals I shall make, though they stem from a single overall principle for reorganizing our schools, are directed to these two goals as *separable* goals.

FROM CLOSED TO OPEN SCHOOLS

The general principle underlying the proposals may be described as the transformation of schools from closed institutions to open ones—the creation of "open schools."

The general idea is to conceive of the school very differently from the way we have done in the past—not as a building into which a child vanishes in the morning and from which he emerges in the afternoon, but as a "home base" that carries out some teaching functions but which serves principally to coordinate his activities and to perform guidance and testing functions. The specific ways of "opening up" the schools are indicated below.

The essential aims of the elementary school, if the opportunity for further learning is not to be blocked, are the learning of only two things: reading and arithmetic. It is in teaching these basic skills that present schools most often fail for lower class children, and thus handicap them for further learning. Many new methods for teaching these subjects have been developed in recent years; and there is much interest of persons outside the schools in helping to solve the problem; yet the school is trapped by its own organizational weight—innovations cannot be lightly adopted by a massive educational system, and local arrangements that use community resources outside the school cannot easily be fitted into the school's organization.

In an open school, the teaching of elementary-level reading and arithmetic would be opened up to entrepreneurs outside the school, under contract with the school system to teach only reading or only arithmetic, and paid on the basis of increased performance by the child on standardized tests. The methods used by such contractors may only be surmised; the successful ones would presumably involve massive restructuring of the verbal or mathematical environment. The methods might range from new phonetic systems for teaching reading or new methods for teaching numerical problem-solving to locally sponsored tutorial programs or the use of new technological aids such as talking typewriters and computer consoles. The payment-by-results would quickly eliminate the unsuccessful contractors, and the contractors would provide testing grounds for innovations that could subsequently be used by the school.

One important element that this would introduce into schools is the possibility of parental choice. Each parent would have the choice of sending his child to any of the reading or arithmetic programs outside the school, on released time, or leaving him wholly within the school to learn his reading and arithmetic there. The school would find it necessary to compete with the system's external contractors to provide better education, and the parent could, for the first time in education, have the full privileges of consumer's choice.

One simple control would be necessary to insure that this did not lead to resegregation of the school along racial or class lines: no contractor could accept from any one school a higher proportion of whites than existed in that school, nor a higher proportion of students whose parents were above a certain educational level than existed in the school.

This means of opening up the school, through released time, private contractors, payment by results, and free choice for the consumer, could be easily extended to specific core subjects in high school. It should be a potentially profitable activity to the contractor, but with the profitability wholly contingent upon results, so that the incentives of these teachers and educational entrepreneurs are tied wholly to improving a child's achievement beyond the level that would otherwise be expected of him.

The use of released time and private contracts would be diversified in later years of school, so that a potential contractor could apply for a contract in any of a wide range of subjects, some taught within the school, but others not. The many post-high school business and technical schools that now exist would be potential contractors, but always with the public school establishing the criteria for achievement, and testing the results.

It would still remain the case that the child would stay within the school for much of his time; and in those schools that stood up well to the competition, most children would choose to take all their work in the school. At the same time, some schools might lose most of their teaching functions—if they did not deserve to keep them.

A second major means of opening up the school is directed wholly at the problem of racial and class integration, just as the first is directed wholly at the problem of achievement. The school would be opened up through intensifying the interactions between students who have different home-base schools. To create integrated schools in large urban centers becomes almost impossible; but to bring about social integration through schools is not. Again, the point is to discard the idea of the school as a closed institution, and think of it as a base of operations. Thus, rather than having classes scheduled in the school throughout the year, some classes would be scheduled with children from other schools, sometimes in their own school, sometimes in the other—but deliberately designed to establish continuing relationships between children across racial and social class lines. Certain extra-curricular activities can be organized on a cross-school basis, arranged to fit with the cross-school class schedules. Thus children from different home base schools would not be competing *against* each other, but would be members of the *same* team or club. An intensified program of interscholastic activities, including debates and academic compe-

titions as well as sports events, could achieve the aims of social integration
—possibly not as fully as in the best integrated schools, but also possibly
even more so—and certainly more so than in many integrated schools.

This second means of opening up the school could in part be accomplished through outside organizations acting as contractors, in somewhat
the same way as the reading and mathematics contractors described earlier.
Community organizations could design specific cultural enrichment programs or community action programs involving students from several
schools of different racial or class composition, with students engaging
in such programs by their own or parent's choice. Thus, resources that
exist outside the school could come to play an increasing part in education,
through contracts with the schools. Some such programs might be community improvement activities, in which white and Negro high school
students learn simultaneously to work together and to aid the community. But the essential element in such programs is that they should not be
carried out by the school, in which case they would quickly die after the
first enthusiasm had gone, but be undertaken by outside groups under
contract to the school, and with the free choice of parent or child.

A WIDENING OF HORIZONS

The idea of opening up the school, of conceiving of the home school as
a center of operations, while it can aid the two goals of performance and
integration described above, is much more than an ad hoc device for accomplishing these goals. It allows the parent what he has never had within the
public school system: a freedom of choice as a consumer, as well as the opportunity to help establish special purpose programs, clinics and centers
to beat the school at its own game. It allows educational innovations the
opportunity to prove themselves, insofar as they can attract and hold students. The contract centers provide the school with a source of innovation
as well as a source of competition to measure its own efforts, neither of
which it has had in the past. The interschool scheduling and interscholastic academic events widen horizons of both teachers and children, and provide a means of diffusing both the techniques and content of education, a
means which is not possible so long as a school is a closed institution.

A still further problem that has always confronted public education,
and has become intense in New York recently, is the issue of parental control versus control by the educational bureaucracy. This issue is ordinarily seen as one of legitimacy: how far is it legitimate for parents to exert
organized influence over school policies? But the issue need not be seen
this way. The public educational system is a monopoly, and such issues
of control always arise in monopolies, where consumers lack a free choice.
As consumers, they have a legitimate interest in what that monopoly of-

fers them, and can only exercise this interest through organized power. But such issues do not arise where the consumer can implement his interest through the exercise of free choice between competing offerings. Until now, this exercise of choice has only been available for those who could afford to buy education outside the public schools.

It is especially appropriate and necessary that such an opening up of schools occur in a period when the interest of all society has become focused on the schools. The time is past when society as a whole, parents as individuals, and interested groups outside the school were willing to leave the task of education wholly to the public education system, to watch children vanish into the school in the morning and emerge from it in the afternoon, without being able to affect what goes on behind the school doors.

GEORGE and EUNICE GRIER

The Costs of Discrimination in Housing

The United States today faces an all-out battle against one of its most protracted and fundamental domestic problems. The confrontation is long overdue, and the solution requires efforts that will have to be much more intense and far-reaching than most Americans probably now realize.

The problem is racial segregation and discrimination, and the task before the country is to undo the consequences of its prolonged and systematic repression of the rights of one-tenth of its population. In particular, it must deal decisively with the enforced segregation of these citizens into limited residential areas—geographic separation which carries with it profound social, economic, physical, and psychological effects. Recent large-scale population movements have complicated this task enormously, creating many new obstacles in the way of its solution. . . .

*   *   *   *

Reprinted by permission of the publisher from *Equality and Beyond* (Chicago: Quadrangle Books, 1966), pp. 3, 14-15, 32-36, 64, 84-89. Footnotes have been omitted. Editors' title.

THE HEART OF THE MATTER

At the root of most such dilemmas is residential segregation. If Negroes were more evenly dispersed throughout the metropolitan areas, not only would the concentration of urban problems be reduced but the resources available to deal with them would be immensely increased. And the tendency of those problems that center on race to extend themselves geographically and to perpetuate themselves in time would be sharply curtailed if not entirely eliminated.

For several years, legal prohibitions against racial discrimination in housing have received much publicity. These prohibitions, however, are neither exhaustive nor perfect. Enforcement procedures also have often been slow, cumbersome, and uneven. But even if the laws and their enforcement were complete and perfect in all aspects, they would not be sufficient to do the job that now exists.

*   *   *   *

As things now stand, the year 2000 will probably see Negro majorities in the core cities of most of the nation's major metropolitan areas, with a number of these cities being almost entirely Negro. The overriding fact is that most Negroes are simply too poor to afford private housing at the prices which now prevail in many of the newer suburbs. In 1959, the latest date for which complete statistics are available, approximately one-fourth of the Negro families in the North had incomes of $6,000 or more. Recently there has been a slow trickle of more affluent Negro families into predominantly white suburbs, and an increasing trickle of whites into more or less Negro neighborhoods—usually rehabilitated under private auspices—within the city. But neither movement touches the key problem: the low income of much of the Negro market.

The dilemmas posed to the United States by residential segregation are put in sharper focus by the current war against poverty. Can poverty among Negroes ever be eliminated in the face of their increasingly rigid segregation within the metropolitan centers? On the other hand, can metropolitan areas be desegregated as long as the majority of Negroes remain poor? As segregation continues to grow, and Negroes reach numerical predominance in more and more urban centers, will the central cities which house the bulk of the nation's industrial and commercial life find themselves less and less able to cope with their problems, despite massive federal aid? What then will be the answer for the metropolitan complexes where two-thirds of America's population currently reside, and where as much as 85 percent of the nation may live by the year 2000?

The task of overcoming and reversing the accumulated racial inequities of generations, and of eliminating the growing racial separation which accompanies and helps perpetuate them, is not yet hopeless. But each year in which effective action is delayed, the task becomes less and less manageable. To eliminate segregation now calls for national resolve and a sustained effort of many years. It will entail a varied yet coordinated set of basically national programs that must all be carried forward within the framework of the democratic ethos.

*   *   *   *

HOUSING AND NEIGHBORHOODS:
THE PHYSICAL AND ECONOMIC COSTS

During the postwar era the United States government has authorized almost five billion dollars of federal funds to renew and redevelop decaying neighborhoods. The bulk of these neighborhoods were occupied largely by Negroes, and segregation and the pressures it created were dominant factors in their decline. Local and state governments have contributed many hundreds of millions more to renewal and redevelopment programs. Further, while there is no estimating the monetary cost to both Negro and white families who have been victimized by speculators feeding upon racial panic, it may well be even greater than the total price taxpayers have paid for urban renewal. And this is to say nothing of the psychological and social costs.

Historically, the restriction and concentration of racial minorities into limited neighborhoods has been a prime cause of housing blight. Few things are more instrumental in the deterioration of a housing unit than too many people crammed into too little space. Because exploitation flourishes wherever people are denied free choice, segregated residential patterns also tend to contribute to the exacting of excessive prices for inferior housing, and to faltering maintenance as well. This has been especially true for rental units: landlords in Negro areas have long been notorious for practicing "slumlordism" in its most extreme forms.

Negro landlords are not much less likely to engage in such exploitative practices than whites. The general framework of market restrictions encourages exploitation. Any inherent sympathy toward individuals of similar skin color is usually overcome by the opportunity to profit from their disadvantage. The availability of a "captive market" seems to undo the humanitarian feelings of most people who deal with it. Or perhaps such a market simply attracts a disproportionate number of persons devoid of ordinary human scruples.

*   *   *   *

Though nonwhite homeowners in general fare considerably better than do nonwhite renters, they also fare considerably less well than white owners. Often the only housing they are allowed to buy is old and in poor condition. Many families undertake extensive repairs and renovations soon after assuming ownership, and the results can be observed in the improved maintenance of many neighborhoods that Negroes have entered in recent years. But some Negro families are forced to pay prices so exorbitant that they have little money left with which to keep up their properties. Moreover, monthly housing costs often are increased by extortionate financing arrangements—such as "lease-purchase" plans or high interest rate second and third mortgages—which Negroes must accept because "reputable" mortgage lending institutions either refuse their business outright or are unwilling to lend money on properties priced at the inflated levels many Negroes must pay. In all too many cases usurious costs are incurred because the properties available to Negroes are in the hands of speculators who insist on profiting outrageously not merely from the sale itself but from the financing as well.

Exploitation in such a "rigged" market largely accounts for the important finding, in several carefully conducted studies, that Negro entry into a neighborhood does not necessarily send its real estate prices plunging downward; indeed it often causes them to *rise* instead. The most thorough of these studies, *Property Values and Race*, conducted for the Commission on Race and Housing by the noted economist Luigi Laurenti, surveyed 10,000 transactions in all. The author found that prices rose in 44 percent of cases when Negroes entered, remained stable in another 41 percent, and declined in only 15 percent. These were *long-term* trends, and they were measured *relative to trends in carefully matched neighborhoods which remained all white.*

It does not follow from this that the relatively higher prices of homes in many racially changing neighborhoods benefit the white families who leave them. Rather, the money often goes into the pockets of the speculators who have helped panic the whites into selling for *less* than their homes would bring on a "free" or open market situation. The speculators then proceed to resell the homes to Negroes (often in a matter of days) for more than their normal market value.

The Laurenti study found chaotic price fluctuations in many of the neighborhoods it investigated—presumptive evidence both of racial panic and the success of sharp operators in exploiting it. Technically speaking, these block-busters represent an unscrupulous minority of the real estate industry—"outlaws" in a moral if not a legal sense. But their activities would not be profitable if the set of restrictions created by segregation were not accepted by the large majority of builders, brokers, and lenders —not to speak of large segments of the white public as a whole.

By adroitly holding back the Negro market, and permitting its housing needs to be satisfied only on a "waiting list" basis, reputable bankers and members of the building and real estate industries have contributed to the conditions under which their not-so-scrupulous colleagues can flourish. Working in tandem with the speculators, such individuals assiduously guard against the entry of Negroes into solidly white areas of the city. . . . Voluminous evidence from both social research surveys and testimony before legislative and executive bodies indicates that [this] is true of real estate boards in cities throughout the country.

*   *   *   *

HOUSING AND NEIGHBORHOODS: THE HUMAN COST

But the costs to white and Negro homeowners and to neighborhoods cannot be assessed in economic terms alone. At least as important are those costs which fall in the psychological realm—mental stress, misery, loneliness, the personal loss of being forced to leave a home and neighborhood one has grown to love. No dollar tag can be placed on such factors.

*   *   *   *

THE LIMITS OF LAW

The mere passage of a law, or the promulgation of an order or a judicial decision, is in itself no solution to a problem as complex and widespread as is the current pattern of racial segregation.

So far, for one thing, no state or local law against housing discrimination has been backed up with the enforcement machinery it requires to be fully effective. The same is true of the Presidential Order, which is being enforced chiefly by previously existing housing agencies, with their regular staffs and unchanged structures, aided by a small President's Committee on Equal Housing Opportunity. This committee, despite its national responsibilities, has less paid staff than is available to enforce the anti-discrimination housing laws of New York State alone.

But the most important limitations of law in this field do not lie in the area of enforcement. Far more serious is the fact that any present law must be superimposed upon a set of housing policies and programs which, at their root, actually sustain segregation. . . .

*   *   *   *

[Earlier] we discussed in detail both the forces which currently are extending the ghetto complexes and the obstacles which stand in the way of eliminating these forces. Let us briefly review the basic points in this discussion.

1. The growth of segregated living patterns has attained a momentum that now tends to be self-sustaining. Most of the young families

who will provide the future increase in the white population now reside outside the city. Virtually all of the young Negro families remain within it.

2. Unless this situation is promptly and decisively confronted, it may be irreversible. The baby boom of the postwar years is now reaching maturity. If the nation continues to meet the housing needs of new families as it has done in the past two decades, the next few years will see racial segregation grow to a scale dwarfing anything at present.

3. Anti-discrimination laws in regard to housing, no matter how comprehensive and how well enforced, cannot accomplish the task that needs to be done. Even if new housing were made available on an open-occupancy basis, economic barriers in conjunction with basic federal housing policies and practices would exclude most Negroes.

4. Segregation in housing makes desegregation in many other areas of society much more difficult to attain than it otherwise would be—in education (where it is almost impossible despite "busing" programs and similar arrangements); in many types of public facilities; and in employment. By impeding the efforts of Negroes to obtain equal preparation for work and life, and by hampering America's two chief racial groups from achieving a secure relationship based upon mutual understanding and respect, residential segregation thus perpetuates the social and psychological barriers that complete the vicious circle.

To attack these problems successfully will require total mobilization and a skillful reorientation of public and private resources: first, to assure that all new housing built in the future will incorporate a balanced racial composition; and second, to encourage the maximum redistribution of population in both central cities and suburbs, so that concentrations of one race or the other are eliminated as quickly as normal real estate turnover will permit.

This is not an argument in favor of forced redistribution of population, however. Such a "solution" would run so counter to the principles of American democracy that it would not be tolerated. But force is not needed; the normal mobility of the American people has recently been so great (about half of all households moved during the latter half of the 1950's) that redistribution can be achieved through the operation of free choice, if only sufficient resources are applied to make socially desirable patterns of residence as attractive to the public as socially undesirable ones have been made in the past.

Neither do we suggest that the goal should be a rigidly planned dispersal of Negro households, so many to each square mile. This also would be neither achievable nor desirable within the American democratic framework. The goal, rather, should be complete freedom of choice in place of residence without respect to racial barriers. Within such a framework of free choice, some substantial concentrations of Negro families would doubtless remain (just as Jews have tended to congregate in certain neighborhoods even after obstacles to reside wherever they choose have been largely eliminated), but the present monolithic character of the Negro ghettos, and the social evils which they encourage, would be broken.

*   *   *   *

We already possess the fundamental machinery with which to attack this problem. Impressive resources exist in both public and private sectors. The need is only to harness them to the task. The basic resources are these:

1. *The panoply of governmental programs that cover housing and the physical development of urban areas.* Prime examples are the programs of the federal housing agencies. As we have seen, these programs together did much in the immediate postwar years to expand and reinforce the country's patterns of segregation. They still do so to a certain extent today. Nonetheless, if they were redirected they would be equally effective in combating and helping to erase the very trends they in part created.

Important also are the federal and state highway programs, with their potential not merely for displacing large numbers of people but also for creating avenues between homes and jobs and for promoting the commercial and industrial development of the areas through which they pass. Potentially valuable also in combating segregation are the new federal programs that seek to improve public transit, to preserve open spaces around cities and develop recreational areas, and to supplement new housing with essential community facilities.

Important subsidiary resources are the burgeoning number of local planning and zoning agencies, some of them charged with developing comprehensive plans for the growth of whole metropolitan complexes.

All such programs must determine their immediate physical objectives in the light of fundamental social goals. Otherwise the programs are likely to frustrate the best interests of the whole society.

2. *Governmental resources in the economic area.* Chief among these in terms of immediate potential is the new anti-poverty program. But there are many other federal, state, and local resources which could help overcome the economic limitations that keep Negroes in the central city ghettos and prevent them from exercising their free choice in the selection of a home and a neighborhood. . . .

No single measure would do more to destroy the economic foundations of segregation than a total mobilization of both government and private industry to produce enough jobs, at decent rates of pay, for all who need them. Action that falls short of this cannot truthfully be considered a "war" against poverty.

*   *   *   *

The increased incomes that would result would provide the means for many Negroes to enter the private housing market outside the slums. Even a modest rise in incomes would help a startlingly large number of families. On a national scale, for example, if the incomes of urban Negro families were boosted overall by only $20 per family per week, it would mean an increase of over 40 percent in the number with incomes over $6,000 annually. Since a very high proportion of Negro families have more than one wage-earner, this rise could be accomplished through an *hourly* average increase of considerably less than the 50 cents which the $20-per-week statistic would suggest.

3. *Governmental resources in the social area.* Social and economic measures often are closely related—as in the anti-poverty program, for example. Other programs with mixed social and economic objectives are those in the field of public education; the many welfare programs that combine counseling and social services with monetary payments; public health programs; and an array of governmental services aimed at helping people overcome the personal problems which prevent them from achieving a fully productive role in the economy and from claiming all their rights as citizens.

*   *   *   *

4. *Private resources.* Although public power is absolutely necessary in dealing with a problem of the magnitude of racial segregation, a multitude of important resources in the private sector also can be brought to bear on it. Perhaps chief among them is the vast groundswell of civic and religious dismay concerning the denial of civil rights to Americans of color—a concern which so far has been focused in only a minor way on the problem of segregation in housing, and yet . . . has achieved startling results. The grass-roots fair-housing groups represent a source of vigorous and imaginative support for the highest aims of American democracy.

Another significant resource is the private housing industry, or at least the growing segment of it which now recognizes that segregation is detrimental to its own economic objectives as well as to the long-range welfare of the whole society. Among lenders, real estate brokers, and builders, there are now a good number who voluntarily conduct their businesses on a non-discriminatory basis, even in the absence of legal prohibitions. Furthermore, most of those who have been confronted by Ne-

gro applicants under anti-discrimination laws and ordinances, even if
they had opposed their enactment, have elected to comply with the law
rather than challenge it in the courts.

These, then, are the available resources. How can they best be used to
combat segregation? . . .

DONALD R. MATTHEWS and JAMES W. PROTHRO

The Limits of the Vote as a Political Resource

ESCALATING POLITICAL TENSION AND PEACEFUL COEXISTENCE

One characteristic of the new southern politics . . . will be a height-
ening of political conflict and tension. Despite some changes in white
attitudes in recent years, southern Negroes and whites remain deeply divided on the major issue of the region—racial segregation. This division
is not likely to disappear in the near future.

In the past the practical difficulties of running a democratic political
system under conditions of extreme conflict were "solved" by the simple
expedient of disfranchising the weaker of the two clashing groups—by
creating a mixed system of democracy for whites and autocracy for Negroes. The question now facing the South is whether its democratic procedures will continue to function—like its drinking fountains, busses, and
toilets—now that the "white only" signs have come down. Since political
systems are more complex than mechanical ones, the answer is not obvious.

As southern Negroes reenter the political system in massive numbers,
their racial attitudes and expectations suddenly become politically relevant . . . . Their political visibility can in turn trigger a white counter-
reaction, or "backlash," . . . . Negro demands and white reactions could
escalate to the point where democratic procedures would break down.

[We] isolated some mechanisms that tend to reduce this danger. Both
sides to the dispute tend to underestimate the seriousness of the cleavage, to

From *Negroes and the New Southern Politics* by Donald R. Matthews and James W.
Prothro, ©1966 by Harcourt, Brace & World, Inc., pp. 472-475, 477-481, and reprinted with their permission. Footnotes have been omitted. Editors' title.

believe that they have more supporters among the members of the other race than they actually have. These misperceptions—although scarcely comforting on other grounds—may tend, at least temporarily, to reduce the sense of conflict. The multiple values and multiple goals of southerners, Negro and white, result in a gap between what they prefer in race relations and what they will bear. Southern whites, for example, want better jobs, better schools, and many other things, not just segregation. They may have to sacrifice one objective for others. And, while southern Negroes want full racial equality, they are too realistic to start off by demanding the badges of social equality—such as intermarriage—about which whites are most sensitive. Negro political power, in the absence of massive federal activity to the contrary, will tend to grow more slowly in areas where white hostility is most intense. Finally, the leaders of both races in the region seem to have a more thoroughgoing commitment to democratic principles and procedures than the rank and file and a greater willingness to try to ameliorate racial strife.

Nonetheless, we must recognize the extreme difficulties of conducting biracial democratic politics in the South so long as most whites remain dedicated to racial segregation. Bargaining and compromises between leaders of the two races become extremely difficult when the rank and file hold diametrically opposite views.

Just how far the tensions between Negroes and whites will escalate toward chaos and massive violence is not now clear. This will depend ultimately on whether southerners find a rate of racial change that is fast enough to satisfy most Negroes but slow enough not to frighten most whites into panicky countermeasures. Pressures from the national government seem to be expanding the capacity of whites in most parts of the South to accept changes they would have found unthinkable a generation ago. By the time the Peripheral South becomes like the rest of the United States, the Deep South will probably be like the Peripheral South of old. Unlike the Republic of South Africa, the Deep South has no real choice.

SOUTHERN PARTY SYSTEMS IN FLUX

The most direct and immediate effect of growing Negro voting on southern party systems will be the addition of a large number of new Democrats to the region's electorate. No matter what measure of partisanship one examines—party voting, party registration, party identification, or party images—southern Negroes prove to be a far more Democratic group than their white neighbors. Indeed, they are probably the most overwhelmingly Democratic group in the nation.

But politics is a matter of balancing gains and losses. The net effects of increased Negro voting in the region are less certain and less favorable to the Democrats. The very actions that have given the Democrats such commanding support among Negroes have alienated many southern whites. Curiously, at least to those unfamiliar with the vagaries of the region's politics, the massive disenchantment of southern whites with the Democratic party has *not* yet led to corresponding, permanent gains for the Republicans. . . . [A] large majority of southern whites, including many who have not voted for a Democratic presidential candidate for years, still think of themselves as Democrats. And until these disaffected southern whites switch their party identification and party registration, the Republicans will be severely handicapped in their efforts to win state and local offices. Republican gains are being made at these lower levels, but they are far less spectacular than those scored by recent GOP presidential candidates.

One or two more presidential campaigns like that of 1964, in which the Republicans appealed explicitly to the racial prejudices of the white South, and an abrupt and thoroughgoing party realignment might well be brought about. But Senator Goldwater seems to have proved conclusively that his party cannot follow this strategy and win national elections, too.

The odds are, therefore, that southern white segregationists will be left without influential champions in *either* national party. The Republicans, to be sure, may try to appeal to southern segregationists by references to "states' rights," "decentralization," and "conservatism"—vague slogans that can be variously interpreted in New York and Mississippi. But the South's segregationists tend to be economic "liberals" for whom the Democrats have a powerful pocketbook appeal. The presidential Republicans may already have done about as much damage as they can to the anomalous Democratic coalition by appealing to the alleged "conservatism" of the white South—for the South is not an especially "conservative" region.

This means—especially when we remember that the Democrats will receive the support of almost all the new Negro voters—that two-partyism (or its approximation) will come to the South far more slowly than is generally expected. In the short run, southern politics will be characterized by vigorous party competition in presidential politics and Democratic dominance at other levels of the ballot.

This has to do only with the "normal" vote of southerners, however. In fact, both Negro and white southerners are unusually issue-oriented voters, and both are preoccupied by a single issue—race. The injection of racial controversies into particular campaigns can result in sharp but temporary divergences from the norm. This merely underscores the fact that the structure of party politics in the South is likely to remain unusually complex, confusing, and changeful in the years ahead. For while racial controversy can subvert old-style Democratic dominance, it also stands athwart all efforts to organize southern politics along seemingly more "rational" lines.

We are not at all sure, moreover, that a party system that aligned all Negroes, economic liberals, and integrationists against all white segregationists and economic conservatives would be particularly "rational." The costs of being on the losing side in such a system are dangerously high; such starkly polarized politics would heighten the political tensions in the South, which already are severe. The politics of race and the politics of class now divide the southern electorate in somewhat different ways; the noncongruence of these political cleavages tends to dampen and moderate the effects of both. The South desperately needs bridges between those who are dedicated to racial equality (mostly Negroes) and those who are fighting bitterly to preserve the racial *status quo* (mostly whites). The Democratic party is presently the most venerable and viable organization that contains large numbers of both. Common class interests tend to hold these people together despite their racial differences.

This, it seems to us, is the beginning of a "rational" and desirable party system for the South, one in which class-based issues are more important than racial ones. It is the upper-middle-class, economically conservative, racially moderate whites who need to be driven from the Democratic party into the Republican, not the region's segregationists. Then, and only then, will a politics of class prevail over a politics of race in the South as in the rest of the nation. This kind of party realignment will not be built in a day.

* * * *

TRANSLATING VOTES INTO PUBLIC POLICY

Political pundits have assumed that the vote will automatically give southern Negroes influence over public policy commensurate with their numbers. Once Negroes are voting in substantial numbers, the argument goes, southern state and local officials will either respond to Negro demands or suffer at the polls. Negroes will then be able to use their political leverage to force governments to eliminate segregation in other realms of life. Hence the special significance of the vote to southern Negroes.

Attractive as this argument is, it is much too simple. The linkages between mass attitudes, as expressed in elections, and public policy are exceedingly complex and little understood. The best research we have suggests that the translation of votes into power, and power into policy, is by no means automatic, and that public officials and political leaders have far more freedom of maneuver in dealing with their constituents than had been initially realized. The governmental response to Negro votes, then, may not be at all automatic in the South or anywhere else. The experience of northern Negroes—who have been voting in large numbers for many decades and yet are still distinctly "second-class citizens" —is not very comforting to those who would place primary reliance on the vote as the "solution" to the Negro problem in the South.

The Vote as a Political Resource

A number of resources can be translated into political power—votes, money, prestige, information, skill, organization, and so on. Individuals and groups possess varying amounts of these resources. The amount of *potential* political power they have is *not* directly determined by the amount of *any one resource* they have. Rather, it depends on how much of *all* these resources they control. (In the typical case there is likely to be a good deal of dispersion, with those having a great deal of one resource not having much of the others.) People's actual power depends, further, not just on the level of their total resources but also on whether they choose to expend these resources to further their political goals. The local millionaire, for example, may have a tremendous power *potential* because he is wealthy, but little actual power because he is more interested in chasing nubile blondes and buying yachts than in seeking political influence. It is therefore possible for individuals and groups with limited political resources who invest them heavily in politics to be more influential than those with vast power potential but no inclination to use their resources for political purposes. In the usual case, the proportion of all political resources actually used for political purposes tends to be small. The result is a great deal of "slack" (or unexpended resources) in the political system.

Southern Negroes have but one political resource in abundance—votes. Southern whites, most of whom still oppose the Negro's political objectives, tend to have the lion's share of *all* political resources, including votes. The competition between the two groups for control over public policy will tend to be very uneven unless southern whites fail to use their overwhelmingly superior resources for political ends. No doubt there has been a great deal of "slack" in the utilization of political resources by southern whites in the past. But the more threatened they feel by evidence of rising Negro political power in the future, the more their disproportionate resources will be invested in politics and the less "slack" there will be. Racial inequalities in political resources other than the vote, then, probably will result in southern Negroes' receiving less influence over policy than their proportionate share of the electorate would seem to dictate.

Even the vote itself has limitations as a political resource for southern Negroes. They are in a minority almost everywhere in the South. (In the relatively few communities where Negroes are potentially a clear majority of the electorate, white resistance to Negro voting tends to be most vehement, and the barriers to the effective use of the ballot, once achieved, are likely to be greatest.) In order to win, southern Negroes generally have to enter into coalitions with at least some white politicians and voters. In situations characterized by an overwhelming white consensus in favor of segregation, biracial coalition-building is almost impossible. A good many Negroes in the South may finally win the right to vote only to find themselves in a more or less permanent political minority.

Where a significant minority of moderate and integrationist whites is in being—as in Peripheral South cities . . . —Negro-white political coalitions are easier to arrange. But opponents of biracial coalitions need merely take steps to increase the salience of the racial issue to the electorate at large, and the Negro-white coalition usually dissolves. In view of the corrosive effects of the racial issue and the lack of other stable political structures in one-party systems, Negroes in the South may have to rely primarily on joining *ad hoc* coalitions on an issue-by-issue basis. On many state, local, and "style" issues, for example, the Negroes' most likely allies are the economically conservative but racially moderate middle classes; in presidential politics and on class issues, however, they may receive greater benefits from highly volatile, "populistic" coalitions with heavily segregationist white workers.

Such a complex and fluid political situation, characterized by high tension levels and limited "slack," places heavy demands on political leaders. For one thing, bargaining and negotiations between white and Negro leaders must be almost continuous and call for highly developed political skills. In the second place, followers may become confused by rapidly shifting strategies and alliances. They must be given clear cues and constant guidance lest they inadvertently throw their votes away. All these things southern Negro leaders must be able to do, and do well, before the Negro vote can have a major impact on public policy, *even in areas where biracial coalitions are formed.* The desperate shortage of capable Negro leaders . . . and the possibility that this shortage will become even more severe in the future . . . not only affect how often Negroes go to the polls, but how effectively they use their votes once they get there.

Types of Negro Goals

Southern Negroes seem to have a better chance of achieving some types of racial objectives than others by way of the ballot box. Other modes of attack—litigation, demonstrations, and federal intervention—are likely to be more fruitful than the vote in grappling with many kinds of civil rights problems.

First, Negro votes are an effective resource in altering segregationist practices when *the costs of abandoning segregation are relatively low for the white community.* For example, police brutality tends to decline and, to a lesser extent, the entire administration of justice tends to improve after southern Negroes become active members of the electorate. The psychic and monetary costs of such reforms for whites are modest. Where, on the other hand, the white community perceives the costs of abandoning segregation as high—such as in the areas of housing or school desegregation —the Negro vote seems to have little impact. The coefficient of correlation between the proportion of the Negro adult population registered to vote and the existence of desegregated schools, by county, in 1958 was +.03! Change in this area tends to be brought about through litigation and federal action. Negro political muscle demonstrated at the local polls seems entirely irrelevant.

A second factor that affects the ability of the Negro vote to bring about desegregation is the *visibility of the issue to the white community.* If the benefits of the reform are confined to the Negro ghetto, and if the change can be brought about without a great deal of publicity, then the Negro vote seems to carry more punch. Negro policemen, for example, have been hired in many southern communities and assigned to responsibilities in Negro residential areas with scarcely any publicity or controversy. Hiring Negro firemen, however, tends to be much more difficult. Either Negro and white firemen must share the same living quarters or else the community must build a new firehouse. And a new firehouse takes money, often a bond issue. So hiring Negro firemen is both more costly and more visible, and hence harder to achieve.

Third, the power of the Negro vote increases to *the extent that whites perceive the issue as involving matters of fairness and impartiality.* One of the greatest resources of Negroes in their struggle for equality is the obvious congruence of many of their demands with the "democratic" and "good government" ethos. Reforms that can be justified by simple and clear appeals to the whites' sense of fair play and impartiality have a relatively good chance of being adopted. Thus nondiscrimination in public hiring practices is far easier to achieve than a policy of compensatory opportunities that seems, on its face, to discriminate in favor of Negroes. Police brutality and discrimination in electoral administration are obviously unfair, and very few white southerners are prepared to defend either practice as inherently desirable.

Finally, the vote can help southern Negroes to achieve racial equality only in the *public sector of community life.* Even a responsive government is of little help in altering injustice in areas where the government has no legal authority or informal influence. As the more blatant, legal, "southern" forms of segregation are replaced by more subtle, *de facto,* "northern" forms, the vote as a weapon in the civil rights struggle will become less and less potent.

The Value of the Vote

This is not to argue that the vote is of little or no value to southern Negroes. It is to argue, however, that the concrete benefits to be derived from the franchise—under the conditions that prevail in the South— have often been exaggerated.

To be sure, much of the extravagant talk about the vote being *the* key that will unlock the door to racial equality for southern Negroes should be discounted as political hyperbole. It is dangerous talk nonetheless. Statements to this effect by responsible public officials, from the President of the United States on down, and by scores of prominent Negro leaders, just might be taken at face value. The result might be to lull nonsoutherners into thinking that the southern Negroes' struggle for equality has been won when the tide of battle has merely begun to shift, to lead southern Negroes to expect miracles from the vote and to become deeply embittered when the miracles fail to materialize, and to lead southern whites to panic at the prospect of a "black domination" of the region that will never come. The vote for southern Negroes is a necessary but not a sufficient condition for racial progress in the South. So are continued pressures from the non-South and realism and understanding from Negro and white southerners.

The concrete, measurable payoffs from Negro voting in the South will *not* be revolutionary. But these are not the only reasons for valuing the franchise. The effects of taking part in the process of self-government *on the participant*—on his self-esteem and his sense of civic responsibility— must not be ignored. One middle-aged Negro interviewed in the course of this study was asked why he so deeply wanted to vote. He replied simply: "To be a man." This is reason enough to justify all the efforts and sacrifices that have been made to reenfranchise the Negroes of the South. Race will remain a serious problem in the South until southerners—Negro as well as white—accept the moral worth of Negroes as a matter of course. The vote and its exercise by southern Negroes will help both groups move toward this new day.

V.

Due Process of Law

The struggle for democracy, put briefly, has been to make the use of power responsible and thereby enlarge men's area of freedom. One phase of that restraint on the use of governmental power has been the evolution of the concept of due process of law, to insure that the great power of the state will not be used arbitrarily against its citizens. The concept of due process of law in Anglo-Saxon history can be found as early as the Magna Charta's insistence that

. . . no free man shall be taken or imprisoned or disseised or outlawed or exiled or in any way destroyed, nor will we go upon him, nor will we send upon him except by the lawful judgement of his peers or by the law of the land.

These words ring well to Western ears even today, but in the three-quarters of a millenium since those words were reluctantly agreed to by King John their fulfillment has been uneven and faltering, though persistent. The holds of the cockleshell ships bringing the English to these shores carried tomes of English law, and during 150 years of colonization the protection of these laws was transplanted here. Indeed, the most serious complaint of colonials against the King in the events preceding Lexington, and the one which found much sympathy in England, issued from that base of law. It was that Parliament was acting against "the law of the land" by abridging the protections of free Englishmen held for so long in history that "the memory of man runneth not to the contrary."

Much of the indignation of the colonists can be read in the Declaration of Independence in the charges detailing the King's abuses—abuses against which later Constitution writers were to insist on safeguards. Some of these were thought so serious as to be inserted in the original Constitution (for example, the ban on *ex post facto* laws, Art. I, Sec. 9-10), while more numerous limitations on federal power appear in the Bill of Rights and on state power in the amendments following the Civil War. Congressional actions to implement these safeguards, plus innumerable Supreme Court decisions, have since given specific meaning to the broad Constitutional phrasing.

But authoritative statements in impressive documents are not self-executing, for not everyone jumps to obey the Constitution's requirements. Several reasons account for such slack between command and behavior. For one thing, except for the Thirteenth Amendment, the Constitution restrains only governments and their agents, not private persons. Then, too, many don't even *know* what the current legislation is in such matters, and even fewer know what the Court has prescribed on any subject. Further, community definitions of any safeguard may differ from the authoritative definition. In this case, even though knowing what is required, the community may not care to comply, and its officials will be hard put to impose national standards on local ones.[1]

There is much evidence in our past of this national-local conflict over protection of the weak, the outsider, the dissenter. It is hard to be humane when one is human: one's sense of fair play struggles with outraged injury; compassion is undermined by fear. The winner in this human struggle does not always write the kind of sanguine history recognized by the Daughters of the American Revolution, for, as we have indicated, there has been much violence against the minority in our history. But when the state of due process of law today is compared with what it was when we enshrined that value in the Fifth or Fourteenth Amendment of the Constitution—or even what it was thirty years ago—it is clear that we have come far in reducing the unequal and arbitrary administration of justice. Some of the reasons why this is so were explained by John Roche in the first chapter of this book.

At the national level, where the Bill of Rights provides somewhat detailed protection of due-process rights against encroachments by the federal government, the Supreme Court has been relatively inactive. However, in the past thirty years, the Court has been increasingly militant in utilizing the Fourteenth Amendment to protect individuals against the often excessive zeal of the police and the courts in state and local government. In this it has, in effect, gradually incorporated some of the specific requirements of the Bill of Rights into the Fourteenth Amendment and has made more specific and comprehensive the meanings of due process.

A brief listing of even some of these Court requirements imposed fairly recently indicates the scope of its effort:

—Those arrested must be notified what conduct is criminal.
—The accused must be notified of the charges against him.
—Search or seizure without a valid warrant is not allowed.
—Evidence obtained illegally is not admitted as evidence in court.
—Severe limitations have been placed on wiretapping.
—Confessions obtained by coercion or deception are not allowed.

[1] An empirical study of this problem is Jack W. Peltason's *Fifty-eight Lonely Men* (New York: Harcourt, 1961).

—A person has the right to counsel after arrest, at trial, and upon appeal.

—Many due-process rights have been extended to juveniles.

—Juries may not be selected in a discriminatory fashion.

—Arresting officers must warn an accused of his right to remain silent and his right to counsel.

These new dimensions of freedom have not always been popular, nor always successfully implemented. The Court's decisions, where they run afoul of local police practices, can often be evaded by pleas that they were not considered relevant; if someone thinks otherwise, he is "free" to undertake the long and expensive litigation to prove it. Of late, opposition to new Court requirements of due process has escalated beyond law-enforcement officials to the general public. Beneath the swirl of contending claims and charges lies a set of opposing values which law professor Herbert L. Packer explores in the opening article in this chapter. He notes that there are two "models" of the purpose of the criminal process: one emphasizes efficiency of operation in order better to control crime; the other stresses the need to maintain the dignity and rights of the individual. Packer's comments on the origins of this recent clash and his suggestions to the police are calm counsel in this often stormy area. In an article not provided here, law dean Edward L. Barrett, Jr., has emphasized how the entire criminal-justice process is affected by the overwhelming volume of crimes, arrests, and prosecutions; if even 5 per cent more defendents insisted on a full trial, the whole system of the administration of justice would be overwhelmed. Barrett's close study of California, one of the most efficient and enlightened state court systems in the country, suggests strongly that Packer's model of efficiency for the sake of crime control may be the prevailing model, particularly for the poor.[2]

The notion that one should be humane to the weak is thought to be part of the heritage of Western civilization. Christians see it as a reflection of Christ's caution that "as you did it to one of the least of these my brethren, you did it to me." But humanity for the lowly appears in many non-Christian cultures—the admonitions of the Torah of Judaism, the criminal-justice system of some of the Chinese dynasties, the welcome to strangers by the desert Bedouin and the Alaskan Esquimaux, the gentle advice of the Indian Emperor Ashoka well before Christ, and so on. Thus, as a counterpoint to that savagery which makes men oppress and slay, there runs the impulse—often sputtering and uncertain—to protect those most vulnerable to naked power.

One emerging consideration in the administration of justice, related to the foregoing, is how the poor fare in our system of justice.

[2]Edward L. Barrett, Jr., "Criminal Justice: The Problem of Mass Production," in Harry W. Jones, ed., The Courts, the Public, and the Law Explosion (Englewood Cliffs, N.J.: Prentice-Hall, 1965), pp. 85-123.

In a series of recent studies of this subject,[3] it has been made graphically clear that among the many things needed by the economically disadvantaged is legal protection in both criminal and civil matters. The dimensions of this social injustice in the administration of criminal law are seen in the article by political scientist Stuart Nagel. His findings are based on a 1962 study of 194 counties in all fifty states with a total of 11,258 criminal cases in state law and 36,265 criminal cases in the federal courts. He focused on the most frequently reported crimes —larceny and assault (846 assault and 1,103 grand-larceny cases in the states, and 196 assault and 785 interstate larceny cases at the federal level). He asks, "Who gets what kind of criminal justice?" The answer will shake anyone whose notions of justice are based on clichés.

As to civil law, the poor have special needs which recent programs, administered under the Office for Economic Opportunity, are seeking to fill. Possibly heart and will are not enough in such programs, for the best of efforts can have unintended side effects. We have just begun to experiment on developing the concept of the "rights" of the poor, and some believe that the efforts to assure these rights may cause more problems than they solve.[4]

The most publicized recent criticisms of the Supreme Court have been directed at its efforts to ensure that an arrested person is clearly and quickly acquainted with his rights. Part of this criticism asserts that the Court is loosing on society a horde of criminals who escape conviction through court-provided loopholes. However, the facts are quite different. In almost all instances where Court decisions overturn convictions, proceedings are begun again, and in the overwhelming number of cases the defendant is again convicted, in a manner untainted by violation of rights to due process.[5]

One of the basic rights about which there has been an outcry is the right to counsel. The Court included this as a basic right of due process in a case brought as the result of a handwritten brief by a pauper in a Florida jail.[6] One important study which examined various kinds of counsel provided for the poor and the resulting difference this

---

[3] Jacobus tenBroek, *The Law of the Poor* (San Francisco: Chandler Publishing Company, 1966). Jerome E. Carlin, Jan Howard, and Sheldon L. Messinger, "Civil Justice and the Poor," *Law and Society Review* (November, 1966), pp. 9-89; Carlin and Howard, "Legal Representation and Class Justice," *UCLA Law Review* (January, 1965), pp. 381-437; Note "Neighborhood Law Offices: The New Wave in Legal Services for the Poor," *Harvard Law Review* (February, 1967), pp. 605-650.

[4] For an introduction to criticisms along these lines, see Martin Mayer, *The Lawyers* (New York: Harper, 1966, 1967), Chap. 8.

[5] For a detailed analysis of the effects of states adopting Court requirements, see Stuart S. Nagel, "Testing the Effects of Excluding Illegally Seized Evidence," *Wisconsin Law Review* (Spring, 1965), pp. 283-310.

[6] For a fascinating account of these events, see Anthony Lewis, *Gideon's Trumpet* (New York: Random House, 1964).

makes in the disposition of a case, found that the provision of counsel
(whether private counsel or public defender) doesn't prevent the overwhelming number of accused from pleading guilty—not because of
"police brutality," but because of the advice of their own counsel.
Indeed, law professor Abraham S. Blumberg, in another study, suggested that a lawyer may be less important in many cases than is
generally imagined. He found that often the lawyer's prime function
was to negotiate permission for his client to plead to a lesser offense
in return for a plea of guilty (thereby averting a trial); this process is
commonly known as "copping a plea." The symbiotic relationship
among judge, prosecutor, and defense attorney is a realistic way of
viewing the role of counsel, for Blumberg argues that each of these
parties has some reason for wanting a guilty outcome without going
to trial.[7]

What difference does it make that the Court has required warnings
of silence and legal aid of police before interrogation—seemingly a
great leap forward in protecting the accused? All the empirical
studies so far in print agree that while the process of criminal prosecution and investigation has changed somewhat, there has been little
if any decrease in the number of confessions or increase in the work
of lawyers. James Ridella, whose research is included in this chapter, found this to be true in a survey of 26 major cities. Law professor
Michael Wald and his colleagues found this to be true in a carefully
controlled study of New Haven, Connecticut. As they report, "Not
much has changed after *Miranda*."[8] Indeed, such findings suggest
that the Miranda decision may have exaggerated the fears of its opponents and the hopes of its supporters. Some analysts see numerous
ways that law-enforcement officers can evade the requirements, and
have offered alternatives which would truly protect the defendant—
and would truly give police supporters something to bemoan.[9]

Thus the movement to define safeguards more broadly may not
have changed the administration of justice very much. Most of those
arrested are convicted, usually without trial and often by the
"copping-a-plea" process encouraged by the defendant's counsel. Confession rates seem to be unaffected; in fact, Wald and his associates
reported a strange tendency for confessions to increase with increased

---

[7]Dallin H. Oaks and Warren Lehman, "Lawyers for the Poor," *Trans-action*
(July-August, 1967), pp. 25-29; and Abraham S. Blumberg, "Lawyers with Convictions," *Ibid.*, pp. 22-24.

[8]Michael Wald *et al.*, "Interrogations in New Haven: The Impact of Miranda,"
Yale Law Journal (July, 1967), pp. 1519-1648, at p. 1613.

[9]Sheldon H. Elson and Arthur Rossett, "Protection for the Suspect under Miranda
v. Arizona," *Columbia Law Review* (April, 1967), pp. 645-670. For support and criticism of the Court over these recent decisions, see the entire issue of *The Journal of Criminal Law, Criminology and Police Science* (September and December, 1966).

warnings. Added to this are the findings that (1) only about 15 per cent of all cases go to trial, and only 60 per cent of this small number involve a jury;[10] and (2) judges believe there is little difference between the quality of the defense and that of the prosecution.[11] Thus it appears that we have a vastly different notion of the criminal process from that fostered by the Perry Mason view of the legal process held by much of the general public.

Still other needs and demands are continually being thrust on due process to expand its meaning. We have chosen three such developments to illustrate this evolutionary aspect. From Alan Westin's comprehensive study of the consequences for privacy of new developments in technological surveillance (for example, "bugging," psychological tests, and computerized data collection), we have selected excerpts of the last chapter, which presents his factual conclusions. His thoughtful recommendations for needed protections are omitted from our selection, but should be read by those concerned with this problem. The head-on encounter between freedom of the press and the right to a fair trial has brought on a confrontation between newspaper publishers and the American Bar Association. Central to this controversy is the alleged effect of publicity on the jury's deliberations. For a decade now, there has been extensive research into many aspects of jury behavior, including this claim of the effect of publicity. Journalism professor Donald M. Gillmor reviews this research in our next selection; his footnotes, which are not included here, provide a good bibliography to this research.

Then, as a final item in this chapter, we present Judge Robert Gardner's evaluations of a problem which is just beginning to receive attention: the lack of due process in our treatment of juveniles. Juveniles constitute half or more of all arrests, but until the 1967 opinion of *In re Gault* the Supreme Court had not begun to apply to juveniles the protections assured to adults. Now the traditional social-welfare approach to juvenile crime and the due-process ideals are placed in jarring opposition.

This clash is a good point for closing, as it illustrates the kind of conflict between basic values which underlies all civil-rights disputes. In this area of due process, as Packer indicates in our opening selection, efficiency and order face individual rights. On the one hand there is a concern for protecting the security of the community (by means of efficient crime control) which the community demands of its law-enforcement officials. On the other hand there is also a concern by many jurists and civil-libertarians that the individual's claim to secu-

---

[10] Harry Kalven, Jr., and Hans Zeisel, *The American Jury* (Boston: Little, Brown, 1966), Chap. 2.

[11] *Ibid.*, Chap. 28.

rity should also be recognized. [12] Clearly, the Supreme Court has moved to the individual's side in recent years, although accompanied by protest from many alarmed community elements. The outcome of this conflict is not yet clear, but it seems a fair judgment from available evidence that the results of the Court's efforts are not always quite as profound as is feared or hoped.

---

[12] For a study of how the police in one large city are caught between these competing concerns, see Jerome Skolnick, *Justice Without Trial* (New York: Wiley, 1966).

HERBERT L. PACKER

Individual Rights or Public Order: Two Models of Justice

We stand today at a moment of comparative pause and quiet in the kinetic and turbulent development of the relation between the courts and the police in this country. . . .

. . . [In] this rare moment of repose, fleeting as it is, there is an opportunity to reflect on where we are and to consider some of the long-run implications of the situation in which the agencies of the criminal process today find themselves. . . .

*   *   *   *

. . . Five years ago all the talk . . . was about the effect of *Mapp* v. *Ohio* [1961] on police search and arrest practices. Five years before that, it was the *Mallory* [1957] rule. Since *Mapp* we have had in rapid succession a series of decisions—*Gideon* [1963], *Douglas* [1963], *Malloy* [1964], *Griffin* [1965], to mention only a few—that promise profoundly to influence law enforcement practices at the police and prosecutorial level. It is a mistake to look at each of these in isolation and to argue about them as if they were separate and discrete phenomena. They are not. They represent a trend which needs to be identified and analyzed as such. Let us consider what this trend is, what forces have shaped it, what it portends for the

From "The Courts, the Police, and the Rest of Us," *The Journal of Criminal Law, Criminology and Police Science* (September, 1966), pp. 238-243. Reprinted by special permission from the *Journal of Criminal Law, Criminology and Police Science*, Copyright © 1966 by the Northwestern University School of Law, Volume 57, Number 3. All but two footnotes have been omitted.

future, and what kind of response to it should be forthcoming from the agencies of law enforcement.

As I have elaborated elsewhere, the kind of criminal process that we have is profoundly affected by a series of competing value choices which, consciously or unconsciously, serve to resolve tensions that arise in the system. These values represent polar extremes which, in real life, are subject to almost infinite modulation and compromise. But the extremes can be identified. The choice, basically, is between what I have termed the Crime Control and the Due Process models. The Crime Control model sees the efficient, expeditious and reliable screening and disposition of persons suspected of crime as the central value to be served by the criminal process. The Due Process model sees that function as limited by and subordinate to the maintenance of the dignity and autonomy of the individual. The Crime Control model is administrative and managerial; the Due Process model is adversary and judicial. The Crime Control model may be analogized to an assembly line, the Due Process model to an obstacle course.

What we have at work today is a situation in which the criminal process as it actually operates in the large majority of cases probably approximates fairly closely the dictates of the Crime Control model. The real-world criminal process tends to be far more administrative and managerial than it does adversary and judicial. Yet, the officially prescribed norms for the criminal process, as laid down primarily by the Supreme Court, are rapidly providing a view that looks more and more like the Due Process model. This development . . . has been in the direction of "judicializing" each stage of the criminal process, of enhancing the capacity of the accused to challenge the operation of the process, and of equalizing the capacity of all persons to avail themselves the opportunity for challenge so created.

The nature of the trend is obvious enough. What has brought it about and how durable is it? A definitive answer to this question would comprehend a large slice of the history of our times, but I should like to venture a few tentative and speculative observations on the point. Let us start with the Supreme Court itself. To some extent, the Court's decisions are not simply evidence of the trend but are in themselves a contributor to it. Typically, the Court's intervention in any given phase of the criminal process has started with a highly particularistic decision dealing on a narrow basis with the facts of a particularly flagrant or shocking case brought before it. That was true of the first right to counsel case, *Powell* v. *Alabama* [1932], and it was true also of the first confession case, *Brown* v. *Mississippi* [1936]. The confession cases are particularly instructive on this issue. For approximately twenty years following *Brown* v. *Mississippi*, a number of confession cases came before the court. As the standards it sought to lay down emerged, they placed great emphasis on the "special circumstances" of the cases. A given confession was deemed involuntary because of the defendant's personal characteristics—illiterate, of low intelligence, immature, a member of a disadvantaged minority group—or because of coercive forces at work in the interrogation process, or because of some combination of these factors. In those decisions, the Court tried, among other things, to influence police behavior by dealing, in its traditional way, with the facts of the specific case before it. But the gap between aspiration and reality proved too great to bridge in the Court's traditional way. And so, the movement has been to ever increase-ing generality of statement: from *this* confession was coerced for the fol-lowing particularistic reasons unique to this case, to *all* confessions are bad when they are obtained from an arrestee who has not been promptly brought before a magistrate, as in the famous *Mallory* rule announced for the federal criminal courts in 1957. *Escobedo* may perhaps turn out to mark the beginning of a similar line of generalized development for the state courts.

The great criminal procedure decisions of the last few years can all be regarded as exemplifying this movement toward increasingly generalized statement, sparked by the court's despair over the prospect of significantly affecting police practices through its more traditional activity. The court has sensed a law-making vacuum into which, rightly or wrongly, it has seen itself as having to rush. *Mapp* v. *Ohio*, in extending the exclusion-ary rule on unreasonable searches and seizures to the state courts, was explicitly based on the proposition that no other presently available means of control held out any hope for deterring police disregard for the dictates of the Fourth Amendment (which had been held applicable to the states in *Wolf* v. *Colorado*, in 1949). *Gideon* v. *Wainwright* substi-tuted a blanket rule on right to counsel explicitly because the earlier case-by-case approach of *Betts* v. *Brady* [1942] had failed to bring about universal compliance with what the court perceived as needed reform in the provision of counsel to indigent defendants.

Moves of this sort by the Supreme Court are, in my view, moves of desperation. Nobody else is exerting control over the law enforcement proc-ess, so the justices think that they must. But they can do so, in state cases at any rate, only in the discharge of their duty to construe the Constitu-tion in cases that come before them. And so, the rules of the criminal process, which ought to be the subject of flexible inquiry and adjustment by law-making bodies having the institutional capacity to deal with them, are evolved through a process that its warmest defenders recognize as to some extent awkward and inept: the rules become "constitutionalized." The Bill of Rights becomes, as Judge Henry Friendly's gibe has it, a code of criminal procedure.

It is easy enough to poke holes in, not to say fun at, this development. But what it represents is an increased consciousness that our criminal process in its everyday functioning does not live up to minimum standards of fairness or, for that matter, of efficiency. That increased consciousness comes from a number of sources, of which I shall mention only two.

Perhaps the most powerful propellant of the trend toward the Due Process Model has been provided by the Negro's struggle for his civil rights and the response to that struggle by law enforcement in the Southern states—as well, it needs to be said, by law enforcement in some Northern cities. What we have seen in the South is the perversion of the criminal process into an instrument of official oppression. The discretion which, we are reminded so often, is essential to the healthy operation of law enforcement agencies has been repeatedly abused in the South: by police, by prosecutors, by judges and juries. Police brutality, dragnet arrests, discriminatory official conduct may be debatable issues in the cities of the North; but they have been demonstrated beyond doubt in the streets of Selma and Bogalusa and a dozen other Southern communities. Powers of arrest and prosecution have been repeatedly and flagrantly abused in the interest of maintaining an illegal, not to say unconstitutional, social system. We have had many reminders from abroad that law enforcement may be used for evil as well as for beneficent purposes; but the experience in the South during the last decade has driven home the lesson that law enforcement unchecked by law is tyrannous.

I do not wish to be understood as suggesting that the imputation of the abuses that I have mentioned to law enforcement generally is rational or fair. I simply suggest that it has taken place. As Walter Arm, former Deputy Police Commissioner of New York in charge of community relations, recently observed: "Never before have public expressions of confidence in police been so meager." He added that the status of New York's police has suffered because "the New York patrolman was automatically equated with the 'red-necked sheriff'; and the New York department was criticized for the use of police dogs and fire-hoses in the South, although no such measures were ever employed—or thought of—in our city."

As we all know, the Negro's plight is also, and at least as importantly, a problem of urban poverty in the large cities of the North and West. Our heightened national consciousness about the problems of urban poverty likewise contributes to and sustains the trend in the direction of the Due Process Model. The urban Negro's plight is joined to that of the Puerto Rican, the Mexican-American, and other submerged groups. Law enforcement may not be a cause of social injustice, but it must reckon with the consequences of social injustice. It is broadly recognized that the urban poor, and particularly those who belong to minority groups, provide most of the raw material for the criminal process. As the idea develops and is promoted by governmental programs that the legal rights of the poor require special attention, politically and economically muscular pressure for reforms in the criminal process continues to make itself felt.

It is far from clear that this powerful trend is going to continue at anything like the velocity that it has exhibited in the past few years. I suspect that any sharp accentuation of the Viet Nam war, to mention only the most obvious factor, will tend to slow down the rate of change in the criminal process. However, the trend may well be in its broad outlines irreversible, if for no other reason than that once the problems have become visible, it is unlikely that the national sense of injustice (to borrow Edmond Cahn's phrase), whether manifested by the Supreme Court or by other agencies of government, will be easily turned off. Making whatever allowances one ought to make for consolidation or swings of the pendulum, it would still represent the worst kind of wishful thinking for law enforcement people to believe that they can persuade those who need to be persuaded that all is for the best in this best of possible worlds.

If I am right about the nature of the present trend (of which there seems little doubt) and about its durability (about which there may be more), the question arises: how should law enforcement officials adapt themselves to the drastically changed legal environment in which they must henceforth operate? . . .

The police are a sorely-tried group—there is none more so in our society —and I do not propose that their burdens should be increased. Indeed, I would venture to assert that if the mood I am about to suggest were to become prevalent, the burdens devolving upon the police might both appear and be lighter than in the past. My first bit of advice is simply this: calm down. Repeated experience with the procedural innovations thrust upon the criminal process by the Supreme Court has demonstrated, if it has demonstrated anything, that the dire predictions of imminent doom that seem automatically to follow each new departure are, to put it mildly, overstated. Whether they are genuine or simply tactical, these outbursts of emotion do nothing except possibly convince many who are basically sympathetic with the demands of law enforcement that where there's smoke there's fire.

I do not by any means suggest that the police should roll over and play dead. Constructive participation in the current dialogue between the courts and law enforcement is, to paraphrase Holmes, not a duty but only a necessity. "Constructive participation" does not include, in my view, the kind of name-calling to which some law enforcement people seem habitually to resort when things are not going quite as they would like them to.

It is widely recognized that community relations is a major problem facing the police today. But it is often overlooked that the community in question is wider than simply those parts of the population with whom the police come most often in contact. It includes opinion leaders of all sorts, including the country's intellectuals and—a point which seems to me too often ignored—it includes the Supreme Court itself. To anywhere from five to nine members of the Court, depending on how hair-raising the facts of the particular case appear to be, the police are suspect. I do not think that the discretion which all or almost all disinterested observers agree the police must have in close cases will be ungrudgingly afforded so long as the courts—and this is by no means limited to the Supreme Court—remain unconvinced that the police regard the rights of the accused as anything but a nuisance and an impediment.

This attitude toward the police will not be changed by words. It will take deeds. As an instance of what I am talking about, let me refer to the current controversy over civilian participation in the police disciplinary process. In selecting this instance to discuss, I do not mean to suggest that I regard "the" civilian review board as a panacea or as the incarnation of the good, the true and the beautiful. Indeed, the entire controversy has become unreasonably polarized because of the unsubstantiated extremes to which both proponents and opponents have gone. More subtly, a good deal of the problem inheres in the reification of the civilian review board, in the notion that there is a "thing" called a "civilian review board" which must be either embraced or rejected in its entirety. Nothing could be further from the truth, and I am surprised that the astute men who direct our police departments have seemingly failed to realize it.

The reason that the civilian review board issue has become such a hot one is precisely because it exposes the nub of the controversy over police practices. As I have suggested elsewhere, the question of just what the rules are by which the police should be made to govern themselves in their phase of the criminal process may be less important than the question of how those rules, whatever they are, are to be enforced. If I may take the liberty of quoting myself:[1]

"In today's crisis of confidence, the question of sanctions is *the* central question. The main source of hostility to the police among minority groups is the helpless frustration engendered by the certain knowledge that, whatever the police do, there is no way in which they can be called to account for it. . . . No code of police practices that does not provide effective sanctions for police lawlessness can so much as begin the long repair job that will be required to win minority group acceptance of even the most necessary police functions."

---

[1]Packer, *Policing the Police: Nine Men Are Not Enough*, New Republic, Sept. 4, 1965, p. [21].

I do not think that the police can any longer have it both ways. They cannot enjoy the discretion which it is argued they need and at the same time insulate themselves from effective outside scrutiny of how they exercise that discretion. As long as the criminal process in the courts has to serve as the only effective vehicle for the correction of abuses, through the reversal of convictions, the courts will go on policing the police. It is in the long-run interest of law enforcement to develop viable alternatives.

There can hardly be any disagreement with the following proposition: "A review board procedure serves two basic functions: maintaining discipline within the Department and satisfying citizen complainants. A procedure that satisfactorily performs one function does not necessarily discharge the other."[2] That statement, with which, as I say, it seems difficult to disagree, is the predicate for the recommendation, now historically controversial, by Mayor Lindsay's law enforcement task force that a seven-man review board, consisting of four civilians and three police officers, be set up to supplant the existing three-man police board.

*   *   *   *

What I . . . wish to say is simply this: that a police response in totally negative terms to proposals of this kind seems to me both wrong in principle and strategically foolish. First, for the principle. I do not understand it to be argued that *any* civilian (which means to say, nonpolice) role in the police disciplinary process is inappropriate. The argument is over the appropriate structure and timing of civilian intervention. Must it inhere purely in the political check that is always available or is there room at the adjudicative level for a civilian voice to be heard? To reject categorically and in advance the idea of *any* civilian participation seems to me to deny that the police are a part of society. Be that as it may, nothing could be more injurious to the notion that the police are responsive to community relations, than the indignant, not to say hysterical root and branch opposition to any and all such proposals.

The sensible strategy for the police, it seems to me, is not to reject the idea of a civilian review board but rather, to accept it, to domesticate it, to make it their own. There are a number of ways to do this. First, let us consider the question of board composition. There is no *a priori* reason why the administration and disposition of complaints against the police should have to be in the hands exclusively of police or exclusively of outsiders. There is every reason why both should be present. . . .

Second, it makes a great deal of difference whether the board has independent disciplinary powers or simply has a recommending function.

---

[2] Report to Mayor-Elect John V. Lindsay by the Law Enforcement Task Force Appointed for the Period of Governmental Transition, p. 15, Dec. 31, 1965.

Much of the expressed opposition to such boards appears to rest on the view that it is anomalous for outsiders to mete out discipline to the police. Neither the Rochester nor the Philadelphia review structure in fact confers the actual power to impose sanctions on the civilian board. The power is purely a recommending one. And it is worth noting that the Philadelphia board, which is the only one that has had a sustained experience, has clearly not produced results loaded against the police. For example in 1961-62, 108 cases were closed, 96 were settled to the satisfaction of the complainant without hearing or the complaint was withdrawn after investigation. In the 12 cases in which a hearing was held, there was a decision adverse to the policeman in only 6.

Third, there is a variety of devices available to ensure that the all-important investigative function—ascertaining the facts underlying a complaint against the police—does not fall into unfriendly hands. Indeed, the Philadelphia board relied exclusively on the police department for doing its investigative work.

* * * *

. . . Civilian participation in the disciplinary process is only one, and perhaps a minor, aspect of the evolution of such devices [for controlling the exercise of police discretion]. I have dwelt on it because it is the one currently most pressed, and therefore the one that provides a testing case for the hypothesis that what the police really want is to be free of all external control. Unless the responsible leaders in police administration concern themselves actively with disproving that hypothesis, the courts will continue to see themselves as the only mediators between the police and the rest of us, with results that will continue to be pleasing to no one, least of all to the police.

STUART S. NAGEL

The Tipped Scales of American Justice

The Fourteenth Amendment to the Constitution of the United States asserts that no state or local government shall "deny any person within

Reprinted by permission of the author and the publisher from "The Tipped Scales of American Justice," TRANS-ACTION Magazine (May-June, 1966), pp. 3-9. Copyright © 1966 by Washington University, St. Louis, Mo. A chart has been omitted.

its jurisdiction the equal protection of the laws." The due process clause of the Fifth Amendment by judicial interpretation provides a similar restraint on the federal government. Other clauses in the Bill of Rights guarantee the right to a lawyer, a grand jury indictment, a speedy trial, and a trial by jury. Do all defendants in American courts get the full benefit of these guarantees?

Many criminologists, lawyers, and other observers say that they do not. The equality before the law guaranteed by the Fourteenth Amendment often turns out in practice to be much like the equality proclaimed on George Orwell's *Animal Farm*—all men are equal, but some groups are more equal than others. Justice, some observers say, may have a blindfold, but it may also have a price, a complexion, a location, and even age and sex; and those with enough money, the right complexion, in the right court, and even sometimes of the right age and the right sex, can often get better treatment. The "least equal" in America are generally those the Fourteenth Amendment was apparently designed specifically to protect—the Negro, the poor, and the ignorant.

The Supreme Court, in an opinion in 1956, stated that "there can be no equal justice where the kind of trial a man gets depends on the amount of money he has." The Attorney General's Committee on Poverty and the Administration of Federal Criminal Justice, headed by Professor Francis A. Allen, then of the University of Michigan Law School, in its 1963 report documented the charge that the poor suffer in the courts because of their poverty. The committee recommended reforms in the bail system, in legal representation, in appeals, and at other steps in the long ladder from arrest to release or conviction.

These propositions would seem to be further supported by common sense. Bail, lawyers, appeals, parole, frequently require money and professional help which are in short supply among the poor. Policemen, prosecutors, judges, and jailors are all human products of our times and nation and, therefore, like the rest of us, are capable of error, prejudice, and "taking the easy way." Our trials are based on the adversary system, in which two more or less evenly matched sides are supposed to meet in the cockpit of a courtroom, under rules designed to insure fair play, and contend until the side with the stronger case wins. How can the indigent, the ignorant, and the victims of discrimination hope to be strong adversaries?

In answer to this question, many prosecutors, law enforcement officers, and editorial writers contend that discrimination in the administration of justice is minor and relatively unimportant. What they believe is much more important—and more damaging—is that safeguards for defendants

have already thrown the scales of justice out of balance, and more safeguards could make it almost impossible to get convictions.

Perhaps the picture is muddied partly because not enough broad reliable research has been done on the American system of justice, based on
a large, nationwide sample. What has been needed was an analysis of a
lot of data taken at all stages of criminal procedure, from all over the
country, and including both federal and state cases. This article is based
on such an analysis with a concentration on grand larceny and felonious
assault cases.

HOW SAFE ARE SAFEGUARDS?

Disparities in justice may appear at any stage of the criminal process
—and most groups suffer both apparent advantages and disadvantages
from them. For instance, in larceny cases non-indigent defendants are
more apt to get probation or suspended sentences than indigent ones, but
are also more apt to draw longer sentences if they don't get probation,
possibly because of the larger amounts of money which they steal. Also,
one defendant's handicap may be another's special privilege. An adult
male who does not get a grand jury hearing is possibly being denied a
fundamental right; a woman or juvenile who doesn't get one is possibly
being given special, informal treatment.

Let us examine these stages briefly, and see what safeguards at each
level can mean to an accused.

Preliminary Hearing

The preliminary hearing is the first stage on which data are available.
The main purpose of a preliminary hearing is to allow the presiding
official (police magistrate, justice of the peace, or judge) to decide whether
there is enough evidence against the accused to justify further action. If he
decides there is not, then an innocent person may be spared considerable
humiliation, expense, delay, and inconvenience. The hearing is preliminary to the prosecutor's formal accusation or to a grand jury indictment,
which it can prevent. The preliminary hearing also has other advantages
for an accused: (1) it deters the use of the third-degree; (2) it allows counsel
to appear and plead for the accused, particularly with regard to bail;
(3) and it reveals the fact that the accused has been arrested and detained,
so that *habeas corpus* (which can bring about immediate release), right to
a copy of the complaint, and other guarantees can be secured. In short,
the preliminary hearing is a safeguard for the rights of the accused; and
its denial is a limitation to those rights.

Of the 1,168 state cases coming from counties that have provisions for
preliminary hearings and on which information was available, the ac-

cused received no preliminary hearing in 434. In 357 of these he waived his right to a preliminary hearing—possibly without realizing its importance; the rest were recorded as "no preliminary hearing, reason unknown." Information as to the preliminary hearing was not available in the federal data.

Bail

The next important protection for a defendant is the right, or the ability, to be released on bail. Bail reduces his hardship, especially if he is innocent, and gives him a better chance to investigate and prepare his case. Of the 1,552 state cases on which information is available, 44 percent (689) were not released on bail. Of these, 562 were eventually found guilty, 71 found not guilty, and information was not available for 56. Of the 71 not convicted, 20 had stayed in jail for two months or less, 13 for over three months, and we have no information for 38. Five of those not convicted, nor released on bail, in effect served jail terms of six months or more although found guilty of nothing.

Defense Counsel

Lawyers generally concede that few persons (including lawyers) are capable of properly preparing and arguing their own cases—especially when confined. Having a lawyer, preferably of your own choice, is therefore a fundamental right.

All the state cases were felonies, punishable by more than a year in prison. Yet 183 of the 1,561 cases had no lawyer at all, and only 13 of these were recorded as having waived counsel. (Under the Supreme Court ruling in the famous case of *Gideon versus Wainwright*, decided in 1963, all indigent state defendants must hereafter be assigned counsel for any felony. The 1962 data for this study, however, precede Gideon.) In federal court, all defendants must have counsel of some kind, and the cases were divided according to whether the lawyer was the defendant's own. At least 390 of the 1,151 federal defendants did not have a lawyer of their own choosing.

A lawyer is considered essential for investigation, negotiation with the prosecutor, examination of witnesses, and the presentation of legal and factual arguments to judge and jury. A court-appointed lawyer is better than none, and often better than some, but he can easily suffer from lack of experience, sympathy, enthusiasm, and especially finances and time, since he will probably be appointed late, and may have to take much expense money out of his own pocket.

Grand Jury

What percentage of cases went before a grand jury? Like the preliminary hearing (and the trial) the grand jury process is designed mainly to protect and to minimize the harm done to the innocent. The alternative is to let the prosecutor alone judge whether the accused should be held for trial. The state data did not separate those indicted by a grand jury from those who were not. Of the 915 federal cases involving either grand jury or the prosecutor alone, 344 involved only the prosecutor—although of these only half the defendants formally waived the right to a grand jury hearing.

Delay

The American Law Institute Code of Criminal Procedure provides that if a defendant is held for more than three months without trial due to no fault of his own, then he must be set free without danger of rearrest for the same crime, except for extremely extenuating circumstances. A long delay before trial, especially in jail, can penalize the innocent or over-punish the guilty, as well as make witnesses less available and reliable.

The federal data unfortunately do not distinguish between those who await trial in jail and those who can afford to wait at home. Nevertheless it does reveal that, inside or out, there was, for almost half the cases, more than two months delay from arrest until release or trial (whichever came first). In the state cases, of the 405 *not* released on bail, 162 were kept in jail more than two months. (Two months was chosen as the watershed for all cases, half being delayed less, and half more.)

Trial by Jury

Generally, there is less chance that twelve jurors will agree unanimously on conviction than one judge (especially a so-called "hanging judge"). Therefore a defendant usually has a greater chance of acquittal before a jury. In addition, if he is a member of a disadvantaged group (uneducated, working-class, or Negro) he stands a much better chance of encountering somebody like himself on a jury than on the bench.

On the other hand, our data show that seeking a jury trial may mean greater delay. It may also mean that if the defendant is found guilty, he is less likely to get probation than if he only had a bench trial. (The stiffer penalties for those convicted by juries may reflect the possibility that the more severe cases come before juries.) But on balance, the chance at a trial by "a jury of his peers" is a strong safeguard of the rights of a defendant.

Nevertheless, in the state data, 63 percent of those cases going to trial did so without a jury; 48 percent of federal trials were held without juries.

Conviction and Sentencing

About four of every five tried defendants, state and local, are found, or plead, guilty. The approximately 20 percent found not guilty, of course, had been put to the expense and anxiety of criminal proceedings. Of those considered guilty, 83 percent pleaded guilty—25 percent to lesser offenses than the original charge, possibly after negotiating with the prosecutor. Almost half the defendants found guilty were given suspended sentences of probation. Slightly more than half of those convicted and sentenced received sentences of more than one year.

THE UNEQUAL DEFENDANTS

These are the major stages in standard criminal procedure. And it is within this framework that disparities because of poverty, race, sex, age, and residence must be understood. The question is not whether the "average" accused person gets complete justice but whether some people and some groups suffer (or benefit) more or less than others—and if so, how and why.

Let us examine some of these disparities.

Economic Class

In the state data, "indigent" is defined, generally, to mean not able to afford one's own lawyer—a legalistic rather than a sociological definition. The poor, then, must usually have court-appointed lawyers, or none. In the federal cases, where indigency is not specified, the poor may be defined as those with assigned counsel.

In the pre-sentencing stages, 34 percent of indigents up for felonious assault in state courts did not get preliminary hearings—compared to 21 percent of non-indigents. This was also true, if not as markedly, in state grand larceny cases. Bail, since it requires the ability to raise money, shows the greatest disparity between those who have money and those who do not. About three-quarters of all indigent state cases did not raise bail and stayed locked up, with all this means in unearned punishment and inability to prepare for trial, while 79 percent of non-indigent assault cases, and 69 percent of larceny, did raise bail and got out.

In *having a lawyer*, an interesting reversal occurs: In most states one must be poor to have assigned lawyers, the rich hire their own, and it is the middle group that may be the most apt to be undefended. (Since the *Gideon* decision, as noted, merely having a lawyer is perhaps no longer a major disparity; what *kind* of a lawyer, of course, is something else.)

In the state cases, the indigent were delayed in jail awaiting trial more than the non-indigent. This, obviously, is related to their relative inability to raise bail. In the federal figures delay is measured irrespective of whether or not the defendant is in jail—and here the indigent have *shorter* waits. A court-appointed lawyer would be inclined, apparently, to put in less time and trouble on his case than a private lawyer, and not be as apt to ask for delays; he might also want to get his bail-less client out of jail as soon as possible, and so be less likely to delay the trial.

The federal data show that the indigent are much less likely to have a grand jury indictment than the non-indigent. Perhaps they lack knowledge and are more easily persuaded to waive this right. Perhaps also this ignorance, coupled with appointed attorneys' desires to be rid of their cases, accounts for their relatively high frequency of bench, rather than jury, trials. The state indigents also have proportionately fewer jury trials—but here the difference between them and the non-indigent is much less, perhaps because state juries are usually presumed to be of a lower class than federal juries, and middle-class defendants may show less preference for them.

About 90 percent of all indigents studied were found guilty. Though the percentage of non-indigents found guilty was also high, it was consistently lower (averaging about 80 percent). The greatest disparity was in the federal cases, where all indigents had court-appointed lawyers, and this may indicate that poorer representation had something to do with the higher rate of conviction. The poor also tend to feel more helpless, and may be more easily persuaded to plead guilty.

Not only are the indigent found guilty more often, but they are much less likely to be recommended for probation by the probation officer, or be granted probation or suspended sentences by the judge. Of the defendants on whom we had data in this study, a sizeable majority of indigents stayed in jail both before and after trial, unlike non-indigents.

The federal data show that this is true also of those with *no* prior record: 27 percent of the indigent with no prior record were *not* recommended for probation against 16 percent of the non-indigent; 23 percent indigent did *not* receive suspended sentences or probation against 15 percent non-indigent. Among those of both groups with "some" prior record the spread is even greater.

Why these class disparities? They reflect, at least partly, inferior legal help. But even when the lawyer works hard and well, the indigent faces the handicap that he is, and looks, lower class, while those who determine his destiny—probation officer and judge—are middle-class. Therefore, apart from the other disabilities of the poor, class bias among judicial personnel may work against them.

Sex

Are women discriminated against in criminal proceedings as in other walks of life? The findings are much less definite for sex than for poverty, partly because the sample was too small. (Women simply do not commit as many larcenies—and especially assaults—as men.) What differences do emerge seem to be in favor of women, especially in sentencing. It is apparently assumed that women cannot—or, chivalrously, should not—endure as much as men. On the other hand, it is possible that women can be persuaded to give up their rights more easily, and that procedures with them tend to be less formal.

Men are much less likely to be released on bail they can afford than women. In trial, women are more likely to be found innocent, and if guilty more likely to be put on probation or given suspended sentences. Studies in women's prisons have shown that women develop fewer defenses against the pains of incarceration than men and perhaps suffer more, and it is possible that judges and juries know or sense this. Or perhaps they simply find the idea of women in prison, away from their families, offensive.

Race

Most Negroes are poor. A great many poor people are Negroes. So the figures about indigency and race must overlap. But they are not identical, and the differences are important. Generally, the poor suffer even more discrimination than Negroes in criminal justice; and Negroes may suffer more from lack of money than from race.

For instance, a Negro is more likely to get a preliminary hearing than a poor man. He is not as likely as the white defendant to be released on bail, but much more likely to be released than the indigent defendant. Since many Negro defendants are also indigent, the Negro is slightly more likely to have a lawyer than a white defendant, given the indigency prerequisite for receiving a court-appointed lawyer. When the Negro has a lawyer, his lawyer is much more likely to be court-appointed than the lawyers of white defendants. In the federal larceny cases, 52 percent of the Negroes did not have their own lawyers as contrasted to 25 percent of the whites.

Like the indigent, the Negro awaiting trial with his court-appointed lawyer tends to have *less* delay than the white defendant. In fact, being subjected to delay seems to be a sign of high status rather than discrimination. Delay while released on bail may be desired by the defendant because it can benefit the guilty defendant by prolonging his freedom and weakening the memories of witnesses.

The Negro is much less likely than the white to have a grand jury indictment in either federal assault or larceny cases. If he goes to trial he is even more unlikely to have a jury trial. Indeed, 86 percent of the Negroes in federal assault cases failed to receive a jury trial, contrasted to a 26 percent figure for white defendants. It appears that the constitutional rights of a grand jury indictment and of trial by jury are mainly for white men. Perhaps Negroes believe white juries to be more discriminatory than white judges. But it is also possible that Negroes commit the less severe larcenies and assaults, and so do not as often require grand or petit juries.

Negroes, compared to whites, are particularly discriminated against when it comes to probation or suspended sentences. This is evident in the assault convictions, but is more dramatic for larceny; 74 percent of guilty Negroes were imprisoned in state larceny cases, against only 49 percent of guilty whites; in federal larceny cases the score is 54 percent to 40 percent. With prior record held constant, the disparity still holds up.

Why the difference in treatment between Negro assault and Negro larceny? Are not crimes against the person usually considered more reprehensible than those against property? The answer possibly is that larcenies by Negros are more often (than assaults) committed against white men, who are more likely to be worth robbing; but assaults occur most frequently within one's community, in this case against other Negroes. Disparities in sentencing may therefore be double, determined not only by the color of the skin of the criminal, but of his victim too.

It is interesting to note that there is a greater race disparity in federal probation *recommendations* than in probations *granted*. This may be because probation officers deal more subjectively with people, while judges (who are also better educated) tend to put more emphasis on objective factors, like the nature of the crime and the law.

On the other hand, of those actually imprisoned, the Negro defendants (particularly in larceny cases) tended to receive lighter sentences. This may be because, like the indigent defendants, they tend to steal smaller amounts; but it is probably also because the mild white offender is more likely to escape imprisonment altogether.

Generally, and surprisingly, discrimination against the Negro in criminal proceedings was only slightly greater in the South than in the North. It was, however, consistently greater in the South at all stages, pre-trial, trial, and sentencing. Discrimination in the South, predictably, was also greater at the state level than the federal level, possibly because federal judges are more independent of local pressures than state judges.

Age

Younger defendants (below 21 in the state data, 22 in federal) generally are less likely to receive the safeguards the older defendants do, but are more likely to get lighter sentences.

Thus 66 percent of the young did not have their own lawyers in federal assault cases compared to 36 percent of the older defendants. They are less likely to face either grand or trial juries. There is, however, no substantial difference in preliminary hearing or bail. Much of the lack of formal procedure may actually be an advantage, reflecting a protective attitude by the courts toward the young (as toward women), and the belief that informality of procedure diminishes the "criminal" stigma, and leads more easily into rehabilitation. This is, of course, the rationale behind separate juvenile courts. The lack of a personal lawyer probably also reflects some poverty —people 21 and under seldom have much money of their own.

Young defendants are more likely to be recommended for probation, more likely to get it (or suspended sentences), and those few who do go to prison generally receive shorter sentences. (The one exception—longer sentences for youthful federal larcenists who are imprisoned—is probably unrepresentative because of the small sample, or perhaps because only the most hardened cases actually go to federal prison.) Younger people, of course, usually have shorter prior records, and this could count for some of the disparity; but the main reason is probably the belief that the young (again like women) are not as responsible, are more easily rehabilitated, and suffer more hardship in prison.

Urban vs. Rural, South vs. North

The sample does not distinguish between *defendants* from the North or the South, the city or the farm—but it does distinguish between *courts* in different locales. Which were the fairest? The answer might sometimes surprise those who automatically accept the stereotype of Northern-urban civil-libertarianism, as opposed to Southern-rural anti-civil-libertarianism.

In the state data, an urban county was defined as one with more than 100,000 population; the federal data used a similar but more sophisticated definition. For both, "South" meant the original eleven states of the Confederacy. The six border states were considered neutral, and the "North" encompassed all the rest. As it developed, most cases (especially the larcenies) were tried in urban courts. Generally, North-South differences in treatment were greater than urban-rural differences.

In preliminary hearing and bail, urban-rural differences were small and inconclusive, but North-South differences were large and consistent—and not to the credit of the North. Thus 38 percent of Northern assaults had no preliminary hearing in spite of laws providing for them, compared to only 10 percent in the South. The South is more traditional toward law and custom, perhaps. The bail difference may also be due to the fact that more Northern defendants were classified as indigents.

Not having any lawyer at all was disproportionately rural and Southern; of the eleven Southern states, eight did not have laws providing for compensated counsel. (*Gideon vs. Wainwright* originated in a Southern state, Florida, and the South will now have to change its ways.) But in the federal cases, where assigned counsel was available, the rural and Southern defendants were *more* apt to have their own hired lawyers than in the cities and the North. That more defendants were labeled indigent in the North, and lawyers cost more there, may be an explanation.

The urban and Northern courts are more congested; defendants wait longer for trial. In the state assault cases, 56 percent of urban defendants sat in jail for more than two months, contrasted to 31 percent of rural defendants, and there is a similar 25 percent spread for federal larceny cases. Much has been written about congestion and delay in urban civil cases, but delay in criminal cases also needs attention, especially in the Northern cities.

In assault cases, jury trials and grand jury indictments are more common in the South than in the North; in larceny cases, however, it is the other way around. (The findings are similar in rural and urban courts, although not as consistent.) Urban and Northern courts are more likely to *imprison* for *assault*; the rural and Southern, for *larceny*. Perhaps these disparities reflect the "frontier" morality still lingering in the open country and the South, in which a man is expected to be prepared to personally defend his honor (and therefore assault is not so terrible) but a crime against property is something else again.

In the congested cities and the North, perhaps, crimes against the person seem more terrible, whereas property tends to be considered corporate and impersonal. Moreover, people in settled areas are more conditioned to rely on professional police, not personal defense and retribution. No great differences exist North and South, urban and rural, in percentages of convictions. But there is a good deal of difference in length of sentences. Rural and Southern courts are harsher, at least at the state level—66 percent of Southern state larceny sentences were for more than a year, contrasted to 35 percent in the North. Assault shows about the same spread. Rural-urban differences are parallel, if less marked. Southern states make the greatest use of capital punishment.

Federal versus State

Because of different constitutions and judicial interpretations, federal defendants have greater access to the grand jury and to counsel (when the data were collected) than state defendants. Delays are much shorter at the federal level. Shorter delays mean less need for bail, and the grand jury hearing diminishes the importance of the preliminary hearing. A slightly higher percent of federal trials are tried before juries.

Both federal and state trials end in guilty findings (or pleas) about 80 percent of the time; both find assault defendants guilty less often than larceny defendants. Probation and suspended sentences are more common in federal court—but, perhaps because the milder cases are already winnowed out, federal assault sentences are longer.

As detailed earlier, disparities unfavorable to Negroes are slightly greater in the states. Juveniles are more likely to be deprived of safeguards at the federal than the state level—but also given lighter sentences. In the broad outline, however, the same disparity patterns show up in both.

*   *   *   *

Significant disparities in the administration of justice do exist. Some groups are more likely than others to receive preliminary hearings, release on bail, better lawyers, grand jury proceedings, jury trials, acquittals, shorter sentences.

Some of these differences are justifiable. The severity of the crime and the prior record, should affect the sentence (though not due process). Women and juveniles should perhaps be given more consideration. Some crimes may have greater importance in one place than another, and minor adjustments made accordingly. Nevertheless, the majority of disparities discussed in this article are probably not socially justifiable and run contrary to our democratic philosophy and to those laws which are supposed to guarantee due process and equal treatment.

CORRECTING THE BALANCE

What can be done about it? Remedies vary with the specific disorder. But these discriminations in the courts partly reflect the same discriminations in our society. The indigent would not get different treatment if there were no indigent; Negroes would not be discriminated against as Negroes if there were no race prejudice. If general American performance matched American oratory and promise, equality in the courts would come quickly enough. Thus the problem of criminal procedure disparities is inherently tied to attempts to remove distinctions that are considered undesirable between the city and the country and the North and the South, and to attempts to further emancipate women, as well as to decrease the numbers of the indigent and the uneducated, and to eliminate general racial discrimination.

Meanwhile, what is being done with regard to a more piecemeal attack on specific disparities?

Partly as the result of the recommendations of such groups as the Attorney General's Committee on Poverty and the Administration of Federal Criminal Justice, the Vera Foundation in New York City, and the National Bail Conference, the federal courts have been releasing many more people considered trustworthy *without bail*, pending trial. There is some evidence that state courts are starting to follow suit. Illinois now has a law requiring that most defendants waiting trial be released if they can afford a 10 per-cent down payment on the bail bond—the interest usually charged by com-mercial bondsmen. Philadelphia, New York, and St. Louis have followed the Vera recommendation to set up bodies that investigate defendants and advise judges whether they are good risks for release without bail. The fact is that judges have almost always had the authority to forego bail for trustworthy defendants—but few have been willing to use it with what little information they could pick up from the bench. In these cities at least they are using it now, and with increasing frequency.

Since *Gideon versus Wainwright*, all felony defendants can probably be assured of *some* kind of representation. In addition, a large scale campaign to provide *competent* counsel has been started by the National Legal Aid and Defender Association, and the American Bar Association. The Admin-istrative Office of the U.S. Courts is currently conducting an educational program to encourage more rational sentencing practices and a statistical program to show more clearly just what those practices are. Though the evidence is very spotty, there does seem to be a general trend, especially in the large cities, toward better trained and better educated policemen, probation officers, and court officials. The civil rights movement, by focus-ing publicity on disparities, is also bringing change.

Bringing the facts to light can expedite needed change. The disparities exist partly because the facts have been denied, ignored, disbelieved, or simply unknown to a large public. The facts are available, and they keep accumulating. We may reasonably hope that when a similar study is done five or ten years from now it will show less disparity in the administration of criminal justice.

A more detailed analysis of the data presented in this article may be found in Stuart S. Nagel, "Disparities in Criminal Procedure," 14 *U.C.L.A. Law Review* (1967), 1272-1305.

JAMES RIDELLA

The Effects of Miranda: Does Protecting the Accused Endanger Society?

*   *   *   *

The *Miranda* case was one in a series of cases concerned with the rights of the criminally accused. *Miranda*, however, was both an extension of preceding cases and an attempt to clarify the constitutional safeguards which had been enunciated in such preceding cases as *Gideon* v. *Wainwright*, *Massiah* v. *United States*, and *Escobedo* v. *Illinois*. The *Miranda* decision was less a result of any ambiguity in these cases than a response to the frustration, indecisiveness, and confusion displayed by law enforcement officials over the earlier cases. *Miranda* clearly and directly admonished police officers to adhere to the following procedures:

Prior to any questioning, the person must be warned that he has a right to remain silent, that any statement he does make may be used as evidence against him, and that he has a right to the presence of an attorney, either retained or appointed. The defendant may waive effectuation of these rights, provided the waiver is made voluntarily, knowingly and intelligently. If, however, he indicates in any manner and at any stage of the process that he wishes to consult with an attorney before speaking there can be no questioning. Likewise, if the individual is alone and indicates in any manner that he does not wish to be interrogated, the police may not question him. The mere fact that he may have answered some questions or volunteered some statements on his own does not deprive him of the right to refrain from answering any further inquiries until he has consulted with an attorney and thereafter consents to be questioned.

WHY THE CONTROVERSY?

The *Miranda* controversy surrounds two competing viewpoints: those who argue that the rights of persons accused of crimes are an essential component of the concept of individual rights and those who consider cases like *Miranda* an encroachment upon effective law enforcement, a placing of handcuffs on the accuser rather than the accused, with the ultimate result being a breakdown of law and order.

*   *   *   *

Reprinted by permission of the International City Managers' Association from "Miranda: One Year Later—The Effects," *Public Management* (July, 1967), pp. 183-190. A table and a photocopy of a police form have been omitted.

BEHIND THE CONTROVERSY

To find out if the controversy had much factual basis, the International City Managers' Association contacted police departments in U.S. cities over 250,000 population to ascertain whether data had been collected from which the effects of *Miranda* could be evaluated. (Data that did not support the critics' viewpoints would, obviously, render their arguments meaningless, while data supporting their arguments could mean that a basic change was required in our law enforcement system, rather than that the Supreme Court had acted without wisdom.)

Although many of the 26 police officials who answered the survey voiced strong opinions against *Miranda*, they lacked an accumulation of data on the pre-*Miranda* period to compare and objectively evaluate events after *Miranda*. Eight officials opposed *Miranda* without any data to support their opinions.

However, in those departments that did conduct studies (Detroit, Los Angeles, New Orleans, and St. Louis), two major results emanated from the *Miranda* decision:

—The effectiveness of law enforcement has not been hampered as a result of *Miranda*, however,

—The law enforcement process itself has been changed.

Other police departments (Boston, Chicago, New York, and Philadelphia) are now researching the effects of the decision.

One study conducted by Evelle J. Younger, district attorney of Los Angeles County, to assess the effects of *Miranda* reached the following conclusions:

—Confessions are essential to a successful prosecution in only a small percentage of criminal cases.

—The percentage of cases in which confessions or admissions were made has not decreased, as might have been anticipated, because of the increased scope of the admonitions required by *Miranda*.

EFFECT OF CONFESSIONS

An analysis of events in Los Angeles County is especially significant since it has the nation's largest caseload. Of the 828 defendants against whom felony complaints were issued (during the three-week study period), 471, or 57 per cent, made confessions, admissions, or other statements. In the 11 instances in which confessions were ruled inadmissible because of a failure to comply with *Miranda*, complaints were still issued since there appeared to be enough evidence without such statements. In only 1 per cent of the cases (three) in which statements had been made was the request for a complaint rejected, because *Miranda* made the statements inadmissible.

The Los Angeles County study also indicated that there was no decrease in the ratio of complaints issued to complaints rejected, no decrease in the percentage of admissible extrajudicial statements obtained in comparison to an earlier study period, and that the *Miranda* ruling did not appear to be affecting the success of prosecution at the preliminary or trial stage.

The Los Angeles County study is significant because it indicates that confessions are not as much a necessity for successful prosecutions as many of the Supreme Court's critics contend and that the *Miranda* decision does not result in mute defendants or suspects.

A comprehensive survey was conducted by the Detroit police department in an effort to determine the effects of the *Escobedo-Miranda* decisions. Cases for the year 1965 (after *Escobedo* but prior to *Miranda*) were compared to the year 1961 (before *Escobedo*). Although this survey occurred before the *Miranda* decision, it is useful in assessing the implications of *Miranda*.

*   *   *   *

The Detroit statistics indicate that in such crimes against the person as homicide and forcible rape confessions were higher in the post-*Escobedo* period. While confessions were not essential in any of the forcible rape cases and in only 11.7 per cent of the homicide cases, the rate of confessions for homicide cases was 54.5 per cent.

The areas in which a reduction in the number of confessions occurred are robbery and burglary. Even for these crimes the confession rate was about 50 per cent while the number of cases for which confessions were essential was less than 25 per cent. For robbery, the more dangerous of the two to the person, confessions were essential in 19 per cent of the cases while the confession rate was 45 per cent.

Thus it cannot be said, as the Supreme Court's critics have done, that the Supreme Court opinions make our streets more dangerous and provide a haven for criminals. Since *Miranda* made the earlier constitutional directives much clearer, there is every reason to anticipate—as the Los Angeles and Detroit experiences seem to indicate—the continuance or development of favorable trends insofar as Supreme Court decisions can produce any changes in the area of criminal law. This is further supported by an analysis of criminal cases in St. Louis.

FURTHER STUDIES

The St. Louis police department—recently commended by the President's Commission on Law Enforcement and the Administration of Justice for its success in holding down the city's crime rate—reported the following information for the period June 13, 1966 to March 7, 1967:

1. Total index offenses   19,480
2. Total arrests for index crimes   6,246
3. Warrants refused because of failure in warnings procedure   7
4. Total request for counsel by indigents   15

Only one-tenth of 1 per cent of those arrested were released as a direct result of the *Miranda* decision. All of these releases occurred before August 26, 1967, and none have occurred for this reason since then. Curtis Brostron, Chief of Police, stated that the over-all effect of *Miranda* has been negligible in St. Louis. He gave the following reasons:

—Proper instruction and familiarization of the police.

—Most cases that are proceeded with are built on independent evidence and do not require the suspect's statement.

—The proof that the warnings have been given and a waiver granted by the defendant prior to taking his statement have not been restrictive.

—There has been a low demand for counsel by indigent suspects.

Events in St. Louis seem to demonstrate that two aspects of the Supreme Court's decisions involving the rights of the criminally accused—cited by its critics as inevitably destined to produce an emasculation of the law enforcement process—are not likely to have this effect.

Requests for counsel by the indigent have been minimal and have not stopped or even unduly hindered the legal-judicial system. Even if the demand by the indigent for counsel should increase, it can be currently anticipated and planned for. In addition, although police have the burden of proof to demonstrate that an accused has waived his constitutional rights "voluntarily, knowingly, and intelligently," the St. Louis police do not feel hampered by this stipulation.

The matter of an accused waiving his constitutional rights was studied for a four-month period in New Orleans, Louisiana. The New Orleans police department reported that 36 per cent of the 1,214 persons arrested during that period waived their rights. Thus, *Miranda* and similar decisions affect interrogation in 64 per cent of these cases. However, this does not necessarily mean that these suspects could not be questioned.

THE RESULTS

It seems apparent from these studies that the changes in law enforcement anticipated with fear by many have not materialized: suspects have not suddenly stood mute, confessions have not disappeared, and demands for counsel have not been overwhelming. Provision of counsel itself does not seem to present a problem of excessive demand but rather one of establishing a system for making counsel available to those who require it.

This is not to say that no changes have resulted from *Miranda's* explanation and clarification of an accused person's constitutional rights. However, the most fundamental change is not related to the incidence of crime but to the nature of the law enforcement process itself. St. Louis Police Chief Brostron described it this way:

. . . the over-all effect of *Miranda* is not appreciably raising the crime rate but increasing the workload of the police officer. The *Miranda* decision requires greater effort in building a case on independent evidence rather than confessions and it has, if anything, caused us to re-evaluate our procedures in light of the new requirements.

Thus, the Supreme Court's image of the ideal accusatory system is becoming a reality. As the Court stated:

. . . our accusatory system of criminal justice demands that the government seeking to punish an individual produce the evidence against him by its own independent labors, rather than by the cruel, simple expedient of compelling it from his own mouth.

Although attitudinal transitions have occurred in relation to the merit of the Supreme Court's disposal of cases involving the criminally accused, [a] polarity . . . still prevails amongst law enforcement officials and the controversy persists. For example, San Diego Police Chief W. S. Sharp commented:

The *Miranda* and other decisions have obviously caused officers of this department to alter their interrogation and investigative techniques. It is true we have lost a certain number of confessions but in reviewing the entire picture our efforts have not seriously been impaired.

. . . we are not currently experiencing any problems. It has not been necessary for us to increase our personnel because of the decisions.

In contrast, L. H. Caylor, Chief of Police in Dayton, Ohio, said, ". . . the day of the suspect admitting his criminal action is almost gone." Houston Police Chief H. B. Short, said the decision ". . . has definitely handicapped this department and the law abiding citizens we serve." E. M. Pond, Chief of Police in Wichita, Kansas, added, "We would [desire] that all courts could base judicial proceedings on truth and fact of guilt or innocence rather than imaginary violations of criminal rights."

The Supreme Court, by giving explicit recognition to the inherent compulsion of police interrogation in the *Miranda* decision, has done at least two things:

—It has provided a guarantee of the individual's constitutional rights when accused of a crime that is more viable than merely relying upon the individual's ability to appeal under the due process clause of the Fifteenth Amendment—i.e., the individual's rights have been spelled out and conformity is required by the police. In the absence of police adherence to the express stipulations of *Miranda* a violation of the individual's rights will automatically be said to exist.

The police have thus received a positive mandate to protect the rights of an accused and have been told how to do this. Furthermore, police must explain any failure to do so. Consequently the individual no longer has the burden of actively seeking those rights which were his to begin with.

—It has emphasized the true nature of police work in a society which utilizes an accusatory rather than an inquisitorial system. Police have become more intent upon securing external evidence of a person's guilt rather than placing excessive reliance upon his own confession.

THE PROBLEMS

*   *   *   *

The most immediate problem faced by police departments after *Miranda* has been the establishment of a method by which an accused could be informed of his constitutional rights. Most officers have been provided with a card or form containing a simple statement of this information. Police officers read aloud from the form and then allow the person being arrested to read it. The form used by the New Orleans police department also serves as a waiver if signed by the suspect. Whenever a suspect is uncertain about waiving his rights he is advised not to do so.

Because the *Miranda* decision emphasizes the desirability of obtaining independent evidence of a suspect's guilt rather than placing excessive reliance on obtaining a confession, many police departments have increased or are trying to increase department manpower in anticipation of heavier workloads. However, this does not appear necessary because the rate of confessions has not declined sharply since *Miranda*. If manpower increases result they must be attributed to a general concern for the democratic, constitutional underpinnings of criminal law rather than to one Supreme Court decision. In its last term, the Supreme Court split almost evenly between favoring the state (the police) and favoring criminal defendants.

LEGAL ADVICE

Although police are now equipped to quickly and efficiently give the statement of constitutional rights required by *Miranda* they still encounter many problems which require immediate action within the bounds of legal procedures. Failure to act could mean the escape of a criminal, yet illegal action would ultimately have the same effect. In the past police have not had ready access to legal advice (with New York City's Police Legal Bureau a notable exception) since municipal legal departments—already heavily burdened—could not take on the additional function of advising police about their daily on-the-spot activities.

To attack this problem Northwestern University, with the support of a five-year grant from the Ford Foundation, has established a police legal-advisor training program. The program spans two years and is open to law school graduates. In the first year participants divide their time between the classroom and the police department of Chicago, or one of its suburbs. During their second year they serve on a metropolitan police force with their salary paid by the Ford Foundation. They also work on a thesis so that they may receive an LL.M. degree. After the second year they may be placed on the city's payroll if the city wants to hire them.

Wayland Pilcher, working in Corpus Christi, Texas, is typical of the participants in the police legal-advisor program. For four hours in the afternoon Pilcher may lecture police rookies, discuss warrants with detectives, or look up answers to officers' questions at the city's law library. From 8:00 P.M. to 1:00 A.M. he cruises in a radio car—volumes of the 1966 Revised Texas Code of Criminal Procedure and the annotated state statutes in his trunk—ready to render an immediate opinion when requested by an officer.

At least 19 cities have indicated an interest in trying advisors who can both give on-the-spot advice and also serve as a valuable training aid in police training programs which usually devote little time to criminal law procedures. In Chicago, Charles Rogers, a Northwestern trained advisor, is now aide and legal coordinator on Police Chief Orlando W. Wilson's staff. Rogers produces a monthly law training bulletin for the department. [1]

Another significant problem for police departments stems from the Supreme Court's stipulation that any waiver of an accused's rights must be "voluntarily, knowingly, and intelligently" obtained. The burden of proof rests with the police to demonstrate that these qualifications exist.

New York City has been experimenting with a complete monitoring of interrogations to determine the effects of *Miranda* on this aspect of police work and to provide an independent record of interrogations. Under the first phase of this project the city continuously monitors the interrogation room at one of the precinct station houses. A sound recorder is in operation 24 hours a day, whether or not the room is in use. The objective of the experiment—in addition to providing a record of whether a person waived his rights—is to determine the most effective method of monitoring within reasonable cost limits. All felonies and some misdemeanors are monitored and all suspects are given a written notice that the monitoring is taking place. The *Miranda* warning is given. If given earlier, a statement to that effect is made with the suspect asked to repeat any statements he made at an earlier time.

THE TOTAL EFFECT

The total effect of the Supreme Court ruling in *Miranda* and other cases does not hinder police activities. Rather the innovations made following *Miranda* should enable police to function within Supreme Court guidelines and perform their work more effectively.

As more emphasis is placed on the acquisition of independent evidence the police will become more involved with the causes of crime. They can then work not only to apprehend criminal suspects but to reduce the incidence of crime by directing their efforts toward its causes, as suggested by the President's Commission on Law Enforcement and Administration of Justice.

If police departments follow this course of action—not adhering to policies which psychologically demean the individual—police-community relations should improve. Fair treatment of suspects by police and access to legal counsel by those who require it should have this same effect of diminishing resentment directed toward the police.

Police departments have been given a firm basis for changing their practices in a way which can be conducive to individual well-being and community harmony. Even those who are reluctant to initiate changes that would upset settled patterns of behavior and cause criticism to be heaped upon them can say they have no choice but to comply with the Supreme Court's decisions. Compliance, however, is a positive concept and those who do not recognize the role of a *police* system in a *democratic* society simply issue an invitation for greater external direction for that which could be remedied internally.

Science, Privacy, and Freedom

A RESTATEMENT OF THEMES

To begin, let me restate the main conclusions that have been presented, since it is on these foundations that I shall rest my analysis of the "forces" and "choices" that confront us.

1. A technological breakthrough in techniques of physical surveillance now makes it possible for government agents and private persons to penetrate the privacy of homes, offices, and vehicles; to survey individuals moving about in public places; and to monitor the basic channels of communication by telephone, telegraph, radio, television, and data line. Most of the "hardware" for this physical surveillance is cheap, readily available to the general public, relatively easy to install, and not presently illegal to own. As of the 1960's, the new surveillance technology is being used widely by government agencies of all types and at every level of government, as well as by private agents for a rapidly growing number of businesses, unions, private organizations, and individuals in every section of the United States. Increasingly, permanent surveillance devices have been installed in facilities used by employees or the public. While there are defenses against "outside" surveillance, these are so costly and complex and demand such constant vigilance that their use is feasible only where official or private matters of the highest security are to be protected. Finally, the scientific prospects for the next decade indicate a continuing increase in the range and versatility of the listening and watching devices, as well as the possibility of computer processing of recordings to identify automatically the speakers or topics under surveillance. These advances will come just at the time when personal contacts, business affairs, and government operations are being channeled more and more into electronic systems such as data-phone lines and computer communications.

2. In the field of psychological surveillance, techniques such as polygraphing and personality testing that probe the intimate thought processes of their subjects have swept into widespread use since World War II. Because they are supposed to offer "scientific" examination of individuals,

From Alan Westin, *Privacy and Freedom* (New York: Atheneum, 1967), pp. 365-369. Originally published as "Science, Privacy, and Freedom: Issues and Proposals for the 1970's," in *Columbia Law Review*, Vol. 66. Reprinted by permission of the author and the *Columbia Law Review*.

these techniques have become commonplace in the personnel-selection systems of many corporations, private organizations, and government agencies, and are used for a variety of other purposes as well. At the same time, advances in drug research indicate that we may be approaching the point at which the administration of a drug (with or without the subject's knowledge) may render him a truthful person under questioning; already, arguments in favor of such narco-analysis under new drugs have appeared in police and legal journals. Finally, research in brain-wave analysis establishes that "reading" certain signals of the brain is now possible; if in the coming decades this progresses to the ability to distinguish the more complex messages involved in thoughts and emotions, direct interrogation of the mind may become the "ultimate weapon" in penetration of privacy.

3. In the area I have called data surveillance, the rapid pace of computer development and usage throughout American society means that vast amounts of information about individuals and private groups in the nation are being placed in computer-usable form. More and more information is being gathered and used by corporations, associations, universities, public schools, and governmental agencies. And as "life-long dossiers" and interchange of information grow steadily, the possibilities increase that agencies employing computers can accomplish heretofore impossible surveillance of individuals, businesses, and groups by putting together all the now-scattered pieces of data. This danger is augmented by current proposals from some private and government spokesmen who advocate the adoption of a fully-computerized and automatic credit system to replace cash transactions, a single-identifying-number system for every person in his dealings with public authorities, and similar "total" computer systems.

4. In each of these areas of surveillance, most of the scientific advances did not arise through efforts to develop instruments for invading the privacy of the citizenry. Rather, they grew out of research to solve broad problems of American society—space travel and communication, medical research, diagnosis and treatment of mental illness, mobile television broadcasts, rapid analysis and use of general data, and a host of similar purposes. Once the scientific advances were made, however, often at levels of cost that only government could supply in the stages of basic research and prototype development, many of the techniques were then adopted swiftly by both government agencies and private interests for purposes of physical, psychological, or data surveillance. The technology we have been discussing has thus been "socially useful" in origin, and potentially "neutral" in relation to privacy. Yet the ease with which the new techniques have been used for penetration of privacy, their relatively low cost in relation to the resources of those wishing to employ these tech-

niques for surveillance, and the ready accessibility of the "parts" or "processes" indicate that existing legal and social rules for policing the borderline between "proper" and "improper" use have proved inadequate. Furthermore, the test psychologists and computer scientists involved in applying the new surveillance techniques have often been so sure of their own purposes and ethics that they have been insufficiently sensitive to the issues of privacy created by the uses of these processes. This preoccupation with scientific solutions to social problems has sometimes tended to place the professionals in various fields in opposition to what they regard as "unscientific" and "emotional" positions asserting "new" claims of privacy.

5. The response of American society to these technological and scientific developments since 1945 has been uneven and often without the consistency that comes with self-consciousness. But the studies of civic reactions to five key problems—subliminal suggestion, electronic eavesdropping, polygraphs, personality testing, and the computer—show steadily growing sensitivity to privacy claims in the press and among national civic groups. Group positions vary, depending on who is doing the surveillance, who is being surveyed, and the purpose for intruding. But so many areas have been affected by the new techniques and so many group interests have been directly threatened that statements deploring the erosion of privacy and the tactics of "Big Brother" have been issuing steadily from every position along the ideological spectrum, from extreme right to radical left. While some might read the record differently, I conclude from the five depth-studies that a "minimum position" in support of privacy is emerging. This unites both liberal and conservative camps, and awaits only a clear enunciation of basic standards and the development of a creative evaluative process before it becomes a national consensus which can be drawn upon by legislators, judges, and private authorities to deal with the specific problems of privacy under technological pressure.

6. In probing the functions which privacy serves in democratic systems— its psychological, sociological, and political utility—we found that privacy is an irreducibly critical element in the operations of individuals, groups, and government in a democratic system with a liberal culture. For the individual, there is a need to keep some facts about himself wholly private, and to feel free to decide for himself who shall know other facts, at what time, and under what conditions. At the same time, there is an equally powerful need in each person to disclose "personal" or "private" matters to others, as well as a strong impulse to penetrate the privacy of others, not only in terms of his peers and local gossip but also by "eavesdropping" on the activities of leading elites of the society through exposés by the

press, government investigations, court trials, etc. While some aspects of this urge for penetration of another's privacy can be considered "voyeuristic" in the personal sense and "populistic" in their political aspect, this is so clearly a fact of behavior, and serves such a key role in a mass society, that its presence must be noted by anyone seriously concerned with privacy norms in our society. There is also a close correlation between the availability of privacy from hostile surveillance and the achievement of creativity, mental health, and ethical self-development, though there is always a shifting standard of balance in these matters and a heavy layer of cultural relativism.

Privacy as a need in organizational life was amply demonstrated in considering the internal affairs of businesses, civic groups, and ideological protest movements. Without time for preparation and internal rationalization of views and differences, private groups cannot fulfill the independent role envisaged for them by the values of a pluralistic, democratic society. Whether to allow such nutritive privacy for a particular group, and how much, are always policy questions for law and government. Thus a scale of privacy depending on the social prestige and assumed social contributions of groups has been a standard feature of our society, with the major religious organizations placed at one end of the scale and "subversive" groups at the other. In addition to the need of individual groups for privacy, there is also a need for privacy in negotiations *between* private groups, such as labor-management bargaining sessions, intercorporate negotiations, and a variety of similar relations in the civic and political sphere.

A core area of privacy is also essential to the successful conduct of democratic government, whether the setting is the private conference of the Supreme Court, meetings of the White House staff with the President, executive sessions of legislative committees, the conference-committee stage of legislation in Congress, exploratory negotiations with foreign governments, or "frank" sessions behind the scenes at international conferences or at the UN. In situations of all types, privacy is a critical ingredient for the process of accommodation and resolution upon which peaceful settlement of conflicting interests rests. In most instances, the privacy required is a temporary one, and the interests of a democratic society in knowing what its elected and appointed officials are doing can be properly served by pulling back the curtain of privacy after the bargains have been struck and implemented. At that stage, democratic statesmen are held responsible for their acts. Just when the time for disclosure has been reached, and whether privacy is proper at all for a particular process of government, are issues that will receive different answers according to the type of problem, the degree of agreement in the nation on the policies being pursued, the presence of built-in conflicts over privacy created by our separation-of-powers system, and many other factors already discussed. But the need for privacy in democratic government, and the dangers of mislabeling this need by calling it "secrecy," have been the burden of the discussion in this chapter.

7. Finally, in the chapter on privacy and the law, it was seen that concern for protecting privacy has been part of American constitutional law, common law, federal and state legislation, and administrative rules from the very beginning of our national history. A deliberate concept of balancing competing interests was at the heart of American privacy law, as in the "reasonable man" standard for common-law privacy rules and in the federal and state constitutions' ban against "unreasonable" searches. This chapter (and the case studies on civic reactions) showed that the current legal framework is now inadequate to defend the American equilibrium on privacy from new surveillance techniques. However, there has been a strong ferment in American law in the past decade, a beginning of the process necessary to develop in law and social norms what was once assured by physical and technological realities in the older republican society. Despite this recognition that American law is in the process of change, two deep concerns remain: first, that the new legal doctrines should reflect sensitively the needs for both privacy and disclosure; and, second, that major attention should be paid to the role of voluntary, privacy-supporting actions by private authorities and organizations, especially in areas where legal intervention is unlikely or would probably be ineffective.

DONALD M. GILLMOR

External Influences on Juries

Because of its dramatic role and its central importance in the trial process, the American jury has been the focal point of a number of pioneering social-scientific investigations. By far the most significant of these was the University of Chicago Law School Jury Project . . . directed by Harry Kalven, Jr., Hans Zeisel and Fred Strodtbeck, and sponsored by the Ford Foundation.

Reprinted by permission of the author and the publisher from *Free Press and Free Trial* (Washington, D.C.: Public Affairs Press, 1966), pp. 201-210, 220. Footnotes have been omitted. Editors' title.

Jury Project collected basic data on jury behavior through statistical analysis and refinement of existing court records, post-deliberation interviews, simulated cases before experimental juries, and the recording of a limited number of actual jury deliberations. Public opinion surveys were used to determine population attitudes toward the jury system. Other phases of the study sought to analyze the methods and results of jury selection. Trained observers were assigned to a series of jury trials to witness the trial, interview the judge and counsel, and interview the jury panel at the end of the trial. With the approval of the court and counsel for both sides, six actual jury deliberations were tape recorded, primarily to validate the other investigative methods.

Among the over-all purposes of the study were: (a) to determine if the jury perceives its function the same way the law conceives it; (b) to determine if the jury understands the judge's instructions; (c) to see if the jury's criteria for a verdict are consistent with those laid down by the law; (d) to see if the jury comprehends the evidence; and (e) to determine if the jury is moved by "rational" or by emotional factors.

As part of the study, 1,500 jurors who had served in 213 different criminal cases were subjected to intensive interviewing. Among the findings: juries were unanimous on the first ballot in 30 per cent of the cases; in the remaining 70 per cent there was a lack of unanimity on the first ballot. But in 90 per cent of these cases the majority on the first ballot ultimately won its point. The broad conclusion is that most criminal cases are decided during the trial, not during jury deliberations.

Similar conclusions were reached in a study by Weld and Danzig at Cornell University. A simulated trial designed to create the real atmosphere of a court room was divided into stages, with jury members at each stage indicating their belief in guilt or innocence—and recording their opinions before all of the evidence was heard. Judgments fluctuated considerably during the proceedings as individuals reacted differently to the same testimony. Judgment was often affected by admiration for or antagonism toward the counselors. Even these jurors, above average in intelligence and education, did not seem to reach decisions through a logical analysis of the case, and apparently no juror attempted to maintain an attitude of doubt until he had heard all of the evidence.

Early in the trial at least 25 per cent of the jurors reached a fairly definite decision, but later testimony seemed to change this certainty. In this regard, the opening and closing statements of the attorneys were important.

In another segment of Jury Project, 500 trial judges filled out questionnaires—one for each jury trial over which they had presided. Fifteen hundred criminal-case questionnaires were returned. In 83 per cent of these cases the judges and jury had agreed on the verdict and in 17 per cent there was disagreement. Judges appeared more prone to convict than did jurors. If all defendants in the 1,500 cases had been tried by a judge the number of acquittals would have been cut in half.

In a detailed study of the decision differences of juries and judges in personal-injury suits, it was found that the percentage of agreement between judge and jury remained almost constant whether or not the judge summarized the evidence, whether or not written instructions were given the jury, and whether or not the judge commented on the weight of the evidence. There is a strong suggestion here that at least in personal-injury suits these procedural controls make the jury neither more nor less like the judge.

Edwin Schur observes that theoretically the selection of jurors is geared to finding value-free persons, and any opinion on the case or type of problem involved may serve to disqualify the prospective juror. But he adds: "Actually, of course, we know that the selection proceeds on radically different grounds, each attorney scrupulously dedicated to the selection of those jurors whose value systems will most favor his client's cause." Jury Project noted that 60 per cent of the lawyers' *voir dire* time was spent in indoctrinating jurors and only 40 per cent in asking questions designed to separate favorable from unfavorable jurors.

Strodtbeck sought to evaluate the importance of . . . variables in jury deliberations: differentiation between the roles of men and women [and] social status . . . . Analysis indicated that men dominate jury deliberations —they initiate long bursts of talking directed at the achievement of a verdict. Women were found to be more likely to react emotionally to the contributions of others.

*   *   *   *

[In the social status study, the] findings indicated that men and high-status persons had higher participation, influence, satisfaction and perceived competence for the jury task than did women and persons of lower status. Jurors with high participation rates in deliberations were perceived to be more competent—respondents, should they be on trial, would choose such persons as jurors.

*   *   *   *

A group of Georgia investigators attempted to determine the effect of the jury foreman's prestige and method of leadership on the behavior of the jury. . . .

. . . Although characteristics of the jurors had been matched to insure equivalent groups, the mode of leadership had no consistent effect on jury behavior. The study also showed that although the foremen were generally able to change the opinions of individual jurors regarding what constitutes equitable damages, the juries reached their decisions on damages through a deliberate, arithmetic averaging of individual opinions. Members of the jury, realizing that a consensus had to be attained, in some cases voted against their personal convictions.

* * * *

James found that participation during deliberations varied directly with the amount of the individual's education. The more highly educated jurors gave more emphasis to procedural matters and instructions from the judge, while the less well educated tended to pay more attention to trial testimony, personal experience and opinion. Education, however, did not influence persuasiveness or persuasibility. James also found that 50 per cent of the deliberation time was spent exchanging personal experiences, 25 per cent was spent on procedural matters, 15 per cent on reviewing facts and 8 per cent on discussing the instructions.

Another type of jury study is that concerned with the *a priori* bias injected into juries by the manner in which jurors are chosen. Robinson found a great discrepancy in the occupational makeup of grand jury venires compared with what would be expected from a probability sample of the community as a whole. In a 13-year period he found 894 professionals, semiprofessionals, proprietors, managers and officials when, judging by their numbers in the community, there should have been only 299—an overrepresentation of 595. In the same period only 26 craftsmen, foremen and kindred workers were selected (instead of 167) and only two unskilled workers (instead of 200). "In view of the well-known correlations between socio-economic status and political and economic attitudes," Robinson concludes, "there is a strong presumption that the occupational bias will result in political and economic bias as well."

* * * *

Jury Project did not deal with the impact of newspaper publicity on the jury. In a letter to Judge Herbert F. Goodrich, director of the American Law Institute, Jury Project coordinator Kalven assessed that problem:

"Our materials as to the impact of newspaper publicity on the jury are even less satisfactory. *As a matter of prudence we decided not to interview in major criminal cases where there was trial by newspaper. And we have been unable to think of a way of importing the stimulus of the news to our experimental jury routine.* As a result the vast majority of the cases we have studied simply do not present the problem of the newspaper. We do, however, have evidence that the jurors take with surprising seriousness the admonition not to read the paper or to discuss the case with other people. . . . Our over-all impression . . . is that the jury is a pretty stubborn, healthy institution not likely to be overwhelmed either by a remark of counsel or a remark in the press. The chief reason for this is that in most cases the jurors are initially in some disagreement and there are champions for both sides of the case in the jury room. Thus a prejudicial remark which is likely to please one side is equally likely to irritate the other and would be offset by counter-argument. But this is unfortunately only a general impression. . . ." (Emphasis added.)

Since this letter was written, at least one attempt has been made to assess the possible impact of pre-trial publicity. Kline and Jess used eight 6-man juries in mock trial situations at the University of Minnesota. Control and experimental juries were assigned to each of four trials. Prior to the trial, the jurors were exposed to two kinds of material. The experimental groups received information designed to be prejudicial about the case they were deliberating. The control group received an "unbiased" version of the story. The information was "planted" in a newspaper and radio news tapes purported to have been recorded off the air. Each jury was told by the judge to disregard any evidence obtained outside the courtroom or that was not admitted into evidence.

*   *   *   *

In each of the four trials at least one member in each of the experimental juries made reference to the information contained in the news stories. In the control juries no such references were made. This could be explained by the fact that in the experimental juries "new" information was provided by the news accounts, whereas in the control-jury situation the material in the news stories was similar to that offered as evidence.

In three of the four cases the experimental juries decided not to use the extraneous "prejudicial" evidence due to internal group pressures. In these three cases both the control and experimental juries found for the defendant —despite the outward appearance of it being a plaintiff's case. In the fourth case, both experimental and control juries found for the plaintiff. It was in this case that the experimental jury based a portion of its rationale for decision on the "prejudicial" material presented in the news stories.

The finding that all four experimental juries made reference to the "prejudicial" evidence in their deliberations points up the possibility of the prejudicial impact of publicity and the need for further research in this sensitive area.

*   *   *   *

In general, the Kline and Jess study supported the findings of Weld and Danzig and the Jury Project to the effect that jurors decide how they will vote prior to deliberations. Of the 42 jurors who returned questionnaires, 35 indicated that they had made up their minds prior to deliberations. In this experiment, contrary to what was found in Jury Project, the judge's instructions apparently had the desired effect on three of the four experimental juries, but it's at least possible that students would be more responsive than nonstudents to such a legal admonition.

In another recent study of the effect of newspaper publicity on prospective jurors, Simon suggests that jurors take seriously the judge's instructions that they lay aside opinion formed prior to the presentation of evidence. Using an experimental design similar to Kline and Jess, but with tape-recorded trials, she found that prior to the presentation of evidence the effect of "prejudicial" publicity caused the jurors to think the defendant more guilty. This difference dissipated upon hearing the evidence in the case. She concludes that these results suggest that the dangers to fair trial by pre-trial publicity are yet to be proven.

A few tangential field studies have been made in recent years. A report on a public opinion survey . . . was attached to the Alger Hiss motion for a change of venue on the grounds of newspaper-fostered prejudice in New York City. Of the New Yorkers questioned, 45.1 per cent said they had formed opinions on the guilt or innocence of Hiss, compared to only 33.8 per cent of those questioned in Rutland, Vermont, to which city Hiss sought to have his second trial removed. But there were unexpected results. In New York, 21.8 per cent of the interview sample believed Hiss to be guilty and 12.1 per cent thought him innocent. In Rutland, 23.1 per cent thought him guilty and only 5.9 per cent thought him innocent. The fact that less coverage of the case and more anti-Hiss sentiment occurred in Rutland did not support the asserted conclusion that trial there would be fairer. The effect of inflammatory reporting in large, metropolitan communities, where it is most likely to occur, is especially open to question. Some judges in these communities believe that the continuous succession of sensational reporting tends to produce no impression.

In 1953, Elmo Roper applied scientific principles to a legal issue. He was engaged by the NAACP to determine by public opinion poll whether prejudice against a Negro, accused of the rape of a white woman, was higher in the Florida county in which the trial was scheduled than it was in three surrounding counties. Roper concluded that the atmosphere would be more temperate in the other counties and his findings were submitted with an application for a change of venue. But the court refused to consider this "newfangled" approach to legal questions, characterizing the results of the survey as "hearsay."

*   *   *   *

[A] recent study of pre-trial coverage by North Carolina newspapers showed that of 568 crime stories in 330 issues of the papers examined, 60 included confessions and admissions of guilt and 45 carried references to prior criminal records. Sixty-three per cent of the stories contained no such details at all; in the 37 per cent that did, lawyers were the source in less than two per cent of the cases while slightly more than 18 per cent of such references were attributed to police, sheriffs or other investigators. Another 15 per cent were attributed to "others," usually witnesses. The investigators, John B. Adams and John Jennrich, felt that the statements credited to police officers were probably quoted from privileged documents such as warrants for arrest. But these sources were not cited specifically in news stories. A noteworthy finding was that lawyers were not the primary source of prejudicial pre-trial statements they are presumed to be. Adams and Jennrich conclude that newspapers should be more specific in their use of attributions.

* * * *

Until more reliable evidence concerning the influence of inflammatory press publicity upon judges and jurors has been gathered and incorporated into legal thinking, the press has an obligation to evaluate concomitant private and public rights in deciding what to print; and, in this regard, two assumptions will have to be considered: (1) the public interest sometimes demands that information violative of private rights be published; and (2) on occasion the mass media are capable of impairing the rights of an accused without any overriding social interest being served. It follows that the American editor, being relatively exempt from judicial or other governmental restraints, has a moral question to face in deciding whether or not to publish facts in his file. He has no moral right and therefore should have no legal right to be deliberately in error. Considerations of a professional or commercial nature are secondary to questions having to do with the life or reputation of a defendant. Although rights are interdependent and none is purely private or wholly public, social rights are ultimately the sum total of individual rights. We therefore deliberately destroy an individual right at our peril. But in those instances when public and private rights appear to be irreconcilable, a choice may have to be made. A civilized society respects human life, liberty and happiness: it also recognizes that freedom of speech and press is close to the central core of all freedoms. Neither can be held lightly. Where a choice must be made, it must be made in the clear conscience that, in the particular circumstances, either the individual or social right is overriding.

Any attempt to assess the influence of publicity in creating "a community pattern of deep and bitter prejudice" . . . would necessarily take into account the level of public interest in the case, the initial attitudes of the community, the question of pendency, whether or not the speech at issue legitimately strengthens the spirit of inquiry, the probable effect of the publication on witnesses, whether the case is civil or criminal, and the nature of the crime itself. . . .

ROBERT GARDNER

Juvenile Justice: The Worst of Both Worlds

There is evidence in fact that there may be ground for concern that the child receives the worst of both worlds: that he gets neither the protection accorded to adults, nor the solicitous care and regenerative treatment postulated for children.
Justice Abe Fortas of U.S. Supreme Court

The words of Justice Fortas in the Kent case last year [1966] express eloquently the concern felt by many observers concerning the treatment of young people in our juvenile courts. They formalize the charge often heard that children in those courts are treated as second-class citizens. True or false?

On May 15 of this year [1967], the U.S. Supreme Court announced its decision in a case entitled, "Application of Gault." Here, the Justices took a hard look at the juvenile court. It obviously did not like what it saw. In tracing the history, the Supreme Court said:

"The highest motives and most enlightened impulses led to a peculiar system for juveniles, unknown to our law in a comparable context. The constitutional and theoretical basis for this peculiar system is—to say the least—debatable. And in practice . . . the results have not been entirely satisfactory.

"Juvenile court history has again demonstrated that unbridled discretion, however benevolently motivated, is frequently a poor substitute for principle and procedure . . . Under our constitution, the condition of being a boy does not justify a Kangaroo Court."

Last February, after 18 months of intensive study, the President's Commission on Law Enforcement and the Administration of Justice, filed its report, "The Challenge of Crime in a Free Society." The report was shocking. For 340 fact-filled pages, it painted a depressing picture of a sick

Reprinted by permission of the author and the publisher from "Juveniles Face the Worst of Both Worlds in Court," *Los Angeles Times* (November 19, 1967).

society—destroying forever the comfortable concept that crime is the vice
of a handful of people.

But the most disquieting portions of the report were those relating to
young people, according to the commission's study, the most lawless group
in the country. And it was for the agency charged with responsibility for
that group, the juvenile court, that the commission issued one of its most
scathing indictments.

"Studies conducted by the commission, legislative inquiries in various
states, and reports by informed observers, compel a conclusion that the
great hopes originally held for the juvenile court have not been fulfilled.
It has not succeeded significantly in rehabilitating delinquent youth nor reducing, nor even stemming, the tide of delinquency or in bringing justice or
compassion to the child offender."

[Is there] an underlying weakness in the administration of justice
for young people in our juvenile courts?

To answer [this question] we must go back to the turn of the century
—to the origin of the juvenile court movement.

The year was 1899.

The place, Chicago.

A group of concerned citizens, properly horrified at the sight of impres-
sionable youngsters being handled in the same court with hardened adult
criminals, created the first juvenile court. The idea met with instant success
and soon each state had its own juvenile court. No less an authority than
Dean Roscoe Pound of the Harvard law school, hailed the creation of the
juvenile court as "the greatest advancement in the administration of justice
since the Magna Carta."

(In 1937, Dean Pound wrote, "The powers of the Star Chamber were a
trifle in comparison with those of our juvenile courts." It would appear that
Dean Pound's initial enthusiasm for the court dimmed with the years.)

The architects of this new law were basically behavioral scientists—sociologists, psychologists, psychiatrists, reformers. Thus, they created a new
court which Justice Fortas describes as "rooted in social welfare philosophy"—not in traditional legal principles. Unhappily, they forgot one of
the lessons of history—that in its relations with the individual, the state
needs to be controlled; that, to again quote Justice Fortas, "Unbridled
discretion, however benevolently motivated, is frequently a poor substitute
for principle and procedure."

These "principles and procedures" were handed down to us after a long
and sometimes bloody history, as the basic protections which the individual
must have when confronted with the power of the state. These protections

which take the form of "rights" act as a buffer or a bulwark between the state and the individual.

NECESSITY OF BASIC RIGHTS

Granted that in its refinement of certain of these rights the U.S. Supreme Court has recently rendered some controversial decisions which are the subject of spirited debate, nevertheless, no thinking person argues with the desirability and necessity of these basic rights which represent the culmination of centuries of experience in history's effort to balance the rights of the individual and the rights of the state in a free society.

Among these commonly accepted rights are: when a person is charged with an offense in which his liberty is at stake he is presumed to be innocent until the contrary is proven; that the proof of his guilt must be beyond a reasonable doubt; that he has the right to be released on bail pending the determination of his guilt or innocence; that he has a right to a speedy trial, to a public trial, to a trial by a jury; that he has the right to be confronted by the witness against him; that he has a privilege against self-incrimination, and that he has a right to be represented by an attorney at all stages of the proceedings.

But what about the juvenile court?

In their effort to establish a court based on social welfare principles, the architects of the juvenile court created a new and different court based on a philosophy of protection of the child. In this court the State would act through the juvenile court judge and in the proper case take jurisdiction of the juvenile for his welfare, protection and guidance.

In so doing, the court completely abandoned the existing philosophy of the criminal court, that an individual is responsible for his own actions and punished when he commits an antisocial act—a crime. Thus, a court based on a fiction was created, a fiction that a juvenile cannot commit a crime. Instead he commits an act which would be a crime if he were an adult. But, since he is a juvenile, it (the crime) is merely an indication of an underlying social problem which, in turn, indicates that he needs the protection of the juvenile court. This fiction, said Justice Thomas A. White of the California Supreme Court . . . "presents a challenge to credulity and does violence to reason." Nevertheless, the fiction exists.

Based on this fiction, the juvenile court is a civil court, not a criminal court, and since it is not a criminal court and the juvenile is not charged with a crime, he is not entitled to the basic rights of an adult charged with a crime. Thus, the juvenile courts, according to the President's commission, acted as though they were "hospital clinics whose only object was to discover the child's malady and to cure him"—all with a complete lack of the safeguards fundamental for the protection of the individual.

CALIFORNIA COURT IN 1903

*   *   *   *

This, then, is the broad picture of the history and the philosophy of the juvenile court movement. What is the situation in California today?

California came into the juvenile court picture in 1903 and since that time its history has been one of strife—strife between the conflicting points of view of two groups. At the risk of oversimplification, they might be called the Purists and the Constitutionalists.

The Purists are those who believe thoroughly in the social welfare, protective philosophy of the juvenile court with its loss of constitutional rights. The Constitutionalists are those who believe that regardless of age, the young person before any court should be afforded the same basic constitutional rights of an adult.

Prior to 1961 the Purists were clearly in control. Under the California Juvenile Court Law and decisions interpreting that law, it was held that a minor was *not* entitled to be released on bail pending the disposition of his case; to be advised of his right to an attorney; to be confronted by witnesses against him; to subpoena witnesses on his behalf at public expense; to a jury trial; to court-appointed counsel; to demand that the proof of his alleged wrongdoing be beyond a reasonable doubt, or to timely notice of the proceedings.

Thus, under the very informal practices of the juvenile courts, whether or not the minor was afforded a fair hearing depended entirely on the discretion of the judge trying the case.

CHECKERBOARD OF INCONSISTENCIES

By the late 1950s, the juvenile court had become a checkerboard of inconsistent practices and procedures. In 1957, Gov. Goodwin Knight appointed a citizens' committee to study and evaluate the administration of juvenile justice in this state. In November, 1960, the commission, under Justice Robert Kingsley, then dean of the University of Southern California law school, reported its recommendations to Gov. Edmund G. Brown and these recommendations were adopted almost in their entirety by the Legislature in the Juvenile Court Law of 1961, widely hailed by its architects as "The Bill of Rights for Young People."

The Juvenile Court Law of 1961 was a gallant, and in many ways, a successful effort to bridge the gap between the social welfare concepts of the Purists and the legalistic complaints of the Constitutionalists. Nevertheless, there were serious questions concerning certain aspects of that law which became a matter of interest to several divergent groups.

Among these was the Juvenile Courts Committee of the Conference of California Judges which followed the 1961 law and presented to the Legislature each year, somewhat unsuccessfully, programs to increase the rights of young people appearing before the juvenile court.

At the same time the California State Bar became more interested in the problems of the juvenile court as attorneys began to appear in that court and the State Bar began to include in its legislative program each year suggested improvements in the juvenile court law in the field of constitutional rights for young people.

Under the impetus of the Gault case and its criticism of the juvenile court's lack of respect for constitutional rights of young persons, and as a result of the forces already at work in this field, certain amendments concerning the rights of juveniles were approved by Gov. Reagan.

Without trying to indicate which laws were passed in 1961 and which in 1967, it may now be reported that the Juvenile Court Law of the State of California provides, insofar as the rights of the minor are concerned:

—That he and his family and his attorney are entitled to adequate notice of the proceedings and of the nature of the charge placed against him.

—That he is to be advised of his constitutional rights by the police officer when first apprehended, and by the probation officer on his first contact with that agency.

—That he is to be advised of his right to an attorney and an attorney must be appointed for him if he or his family are unable to afford counsel.

—That he is entitled to the right of confrontation by and cross-examination of witnesses, and the privilege against self-incrimination.

—That he is entitled to subpoena witnesses at government expense.

—That he is entitled to a full record of the proceedings and the right to appeal, with a free copy of the transcript of the proceedings as in the adult court

Still missing are certain rights which an adult has in the criminal court. These are: (1) the right to be released on bail pending the disposition of his case, (2) the right to a jury trial, and (3) the right to demand that the proof of his alleged wrongdoing be beyond a reasonable doubt.

CONCEPT IS SOUND

The court is still a civil court; the fiction persists; the child still does not have the full rights of an adult charged with the same offense.

The juvenile court concept is sound—that there be a separate court for the handling of young people in which the primary accent is on rehabilitation. Whether sufficient procedural safeguards have now been established to strike the delicate balance between the rights of the child and the rights of the State, remains a subject of debate. Rather obviously, the battle between the Purists and Constitutionalists will continue. In the meantime, the child will continue to get some of the best and some of the worst of both worlds.

However, it would appear fundamental that when a person's good name, his character, his reputation, and his liberty are at stake, it does not matter whether he is 16 or 60—his basic constitutional rights should be identical.

VI.

Prospects for the Future

No single volume can encompass all of current research and thinking on the status of civil liberty in our time. Writing on developments in criminal justice[1] and equality[2] alone pours from the publishers, and the Supreme Court continues to redefine and broaden the limits on the freedom of the individual. These times mark a high point in our history for considering the meaning and implications of the brief clauses in our Constitution which deal with the individual's freedom. One is impressed by the degree to which contemporary legal scholars, social scientists, and philosophers are exploring systematically the practice (or nonpractice) of liberty. Thus this volume can only sample such research and commentary. Yet we hope that the perspectives of liberty discussed here may move the student to explore other writings of this kind or even to explore the implications of these writings in his own community.

While much still remains unknown about the ways in which Americans enjoy, or are denied, their constitutional guarantees, there are, nevertheless, pervasive themes. One theme is the fashion in which any American's effort to "secure the blessings of liberty"—in whatever era or form—is an effort to live his life as he sees fit. Not all such efforts can be realized (ability may be lacking) or can be permitted (the cost to the community is too great to permit the pyromaniac—we use the term both literally and figuratively—to roam free). But through time one senses the manifold efforts of multifaceted publics to search out those areas of freedom in which they can develop their potentials and pursue their dreams. Whatever the dream our people seek to realize is not yet clear, and the search is far from being over.

---

[1] For example, see Rita James Simon, ed., *The Sociology of Law* (San Francisco: Chandler Publishing Company, 1968).

[2] For example, see Arnold and Caroline Rose, *Minority Problems: A Textbook of Readings in Intergroup Relations* (New York: Harper, 1967); Lee Rainwater and William L. Yancey, *The Moynihan Report and the Politics of Controversy* (Cambridge, Mass.: The MIT Press, 1967); and Louis A. Ferman *et al.*, eds., *Negroes and Jobs* (Ann Arbor: University of Michigan Press, 1967).

Another pervasive theme in this time of new departures is the effort to find the means or strategies which optimize liberty. In our nation's beginnings, the great fear was the tyranny of a national government; so the great means of defense were a federal government of limited powers and strong local government. But in our time, some groups have reversed this outlook, seeing in the national government a powerful defense against tyranny and injustice at the local level. Too, the rise of the great, impersonal institutions within which we live today has occasioned fears that these combinations make our life "cabinned and confined"—particularly if private concentrations of power become linked to big government.[3] However, some have argued that the growth of bureaucracy creates more, not fewer, areas of freedom for men: it eliminates arbitrariness and extends opportunity and resources to men without them.[4]

Thus new dimensions to civil rights are now emerging, while old problems still remain around which these dimensions revolve. In this last chapter, we will look at some ways that new meaning can be given to the concept of liberty. We see new dimensions of freedom emerging as the result of two forces: new laws and new ideas.

The force of law in enlarging the scope of freedom has been seen throughout this book. Yet it is part of the American folk wisdom that "you can't legislate morality"; that is, laws cannot make people think or act against their deep-felt wishes. Therefore, it is thought, laws extending freedom to minorities, for example, in the matter of racial segregation, cannot work in the face of a majority with a strong contrary view. Look, we are told, at the failure of Prohibition! And yet it cannot all be that simple. After all, few support slavery today while many did a century ago, and certainly a law (the Thirteenth Amendment) played a large role in transforming those attitudes. Political scientist William K. Muir, Jr., in a summation of a specialized study on this subject, answers the query, "Can law change deep-rooted attitudes?"

Of course it can. It has done so—in reshaping in less than a generation this nation's views about racism; in altering in even a shorter time police attitudes toward criminal behavior; in ennobling the city dweller as the backbone of American democracy; in imparting an understanding of poverty; in recasting our ideas about leisure; in maintaining certain attitudes of good sportsmanship apparently essential to a competitive market economy; in stemming religious prejudice; in establishing heightened standards of honesty in public service. . . .

---

[3] See C. Wright Mills, *The Power Elite* (New York: Oxford University Press, 1956); and William Whyte, *The Organization Man* (New York: Simon and Schuster, 1956), for examples of this view.

[4] Anthony Downs, *Inside Bureaucracy* (Boston: Little, Brown, 1967), Chap. 21.

Judiciously used, law can and does manipulate our deep-rooted attitudes, our personality.[5]

Muir's general assertion about the effectiveness of law in changing attitudes requires fuller explanation. While his point is generally accepted among social scientists aware of the law's strengths—as well as limits—in this respect, the idea is still new to many Americans. For clarification of the processes involved, our first selection in this chapter presents psychologist Gordon Allport's analysis of the manipulative and educational roles of law.

Law, however, is a final product of social action behind which must be the interplay of social groups seeking enhancement of their goals and values—material values as well as symbolic ones. Undoubtedly the most visible group action on the American scene now is that surrounding the efforts of the American Negro to achieve the reality of a dream offered him a century ago. For more than a decade, the nation has watched this action move from litigation in calm court chambers to civil disobedience in hot Southern towns to bloody riots in equally hot Northern cities.

Minority groups have long been aware, from painful experience, that the view many of us have had of broad consensus on the principles of, and commitment to, individual freedom was a caricature, if not a charade. This recognition had led various groups in American history to view the preservation of freedom as dependent on effective group action. It is difficult to know the relationship between a minority group's political and economic power and its share of freedom. Certainly the ability of various groups to dramatize the extent of their deprivation has had observable impact on the enactment of legal safeguards; perhaps the most dramatic of these instances has been the Civil Rights Acts of 1964, 1965, and 1968.

The extent to which group action is effective in preserving liberty depends on the specific goals sought, on the way those goals are pursued, and on the group's resources. Negro frustration at the unwillingness of society to assure greater opportunity for self-respect and the good life had led some Negro groups to embrace the notion of "Black Power." The debate over this term's meaning and utility is complex and not always clear.[6]

One form of group action is violence, no matter how ugly some may view it; our history is not lacking in such action. That it may have some utility for Negroes in obtaining long-overdue action by government is a real possibility. The reader will recall that the six-city study from the Lemberg Center for the Study of Violence in Chapter IV

---

[5] *Prayer in the Public Schools* (Chicago: University of Chicago Press, 1967), p. 138.

[6] A clear exposition and rebuttal are David Danzig's "In Defense of 'Black Power,' " *Commentary* (September, 1966), pp. 41-46; and Bayard Rustin's " 'Black Power' and Coalition Politics," *ibid.*, pp. 35-40.

showed that Negroes believe riots are an effective means of group protest—*as do whites*, to a surprising degree.[7] But it would be a mistake to believe that most, or even a large minority, of Negro Americans endorse violence. Sociologist Gary T. Marx has found in a national study that commitment to militancy by Negroes is highly associated with support also of many of the procedural elements of democratic ideology.[8]

Just as law may be conceived of as the final product of group action, so in turn groups act in response to the motivating force of ideas and ideals. In concluding this chapter, and this book, we present two writers who examine old concepts in new ways and offer suggestions about future dimensions in the growth of liberty. William Eaton, an attorney and a political scientist, presents a heretofore unpublished view of the Ninth Amendment as a potential source for future constitutional redefinitions of civil rights.

As noted earlier, the President's Commission on Civil Disorders laid the cause for much of the inequality of condition among the races at the door of white racism. The Report, early in its remarks, says bluntly:

What white Americans have never fully understood—but what the Negro can never forget—is that white society is deeply implicated in the ghetto. White institutions created it, white institutions maintain it, and white society condones it.

Most whites have found it difficult to accept this accusation, but the charge should at least cause us to rethink some of what equality really means. It may be that prevailing concepts of equality, such as "equality before the law" or "equality of opportunity," are shields behind which we may hide our lack of commitment to greater equality of condition for minorities. Political philosopher John Schaar argues in the final article of this book that our present thinking about equality may actually lead to increased inequality. He suggests how we might reformulate the notion of equality in order to mitigate some of the more onerous disparities among men.

Reinterpretations of basic concepts such as those offered by William Eaton and John Schaar are the wellspring of ideas which in the past have energized men to act to extend civil rights and liberties. While one may disagree with some of their views, it is certain that these writers are confronting the central problem in trying to expand freedom: How do we create an intellectual and moral climate in America which discourages intolerance, anxiety, and injustice in the face of ideas or characteristics different from our own?

This is not some academic matter unrelated to reality. As a nation we are in the midst of a soul-searching inquiry into this question,

[7] An earlier national survey of biracial attitudes is William Brink and Louis Harris, *Black and White* (New York: Simon and Schuster, 1966).
[8] *Protest and Prejudice* (New York: Harper, 1967).

especially as it applies to our treatment of the ethnic minorities. If civilizations are to be judged by the quality of the main questions they pursue, then surely this one, central to the democratic culture, is an ennobling one.

GORDON W. ALLPORT

You Can *Legislate Morality*

DOES LEGISLATION AFFECT PREJUDICE?

[The] Supreme Court toward the end of the last century justified its conservative decisions on the grounds that the law was powerless to counter "racial instincts." This laissez faire attitude marked much of the social thinking of that period. A leading sociologist of the day, William Graham Sumner, asserted "stateways cannot change folkways." Even today the same view is often heard: "you cannot legislate against prejudice."

The point sounds plausible, but actually it is weak in two respects. First, we can be entirely sure that discriminative laws *increase* prejudice—why, then, should not legislation of the reverse order *diminish* prejudice?

Secondly, legislation is not in fact aimed at prejudice at all, at least not directly. Its intent is to equalize advantages and lessen discrimination. Only as a by-product of the improved conditions do people gain the benefits that come, as we have seen, from equal status contact and from normal acquaintance . . . . Increasing the skills of minority groups, raising their standard of living, improving their health and education, have similar indirect effects. Further, the establishment of a legal norm creates a public conscience and a standard for expected behavior that check *overt* signs of prejudice. Legislation aims not at controlling prejudice, but only its open expression. But when expression changes, thoughts too, in the long run, are likely to fall into line.

* * * *

. . . While it is true that unless a fairly large percentage of the people are in favor of a law it will not work, yet it is false to say that folkways must always take precedence over stateways. It was the Jim Crow laws in the south that in large part *created* folkways. Similarly, we have seen that FEPC

Reprinted by permission of the publisher from Gordon W. Allport, *The Nature of Prejudice*, 1954, pp. 469-473. Addison-Wesley, Reading, Mass. Editors' title.

legislation quickly creates new folkways in a factory or department store. Within a very few weeks, Negroes, Mexicans, or Jews are accepted as a matter of course in occupations where for decades they had been excluded.

It is often said that the way must be paved for remedial legislation through education. Up to a point this statement is undoubtedly true. Debate, hearings, and an aroused electorate are all essential. But when the initial work has been done, then the legislation in turn becomes educative. The masses of people do not become converts in advance; rather they are converted by the *fait accompli.* It is a well known psychological fact that most people accept the results of an election or legislation gladly enough after the furore has subsided. Even those who strenuously favored a Democratic candidate for office accept without resentment the Republican who is elected. And those who fought against FEPC or civil rights legislation ordinarily abide by the majority decision if these laws are passed. They allow themselves to be re-educated by the new norm that prevails.

What we are here speaking of is the basic habit of democratic society. After free, and often fierce, debate, citizens bow to the majority will. *They do so with a special kind of willingness if the legislation is in line with their own private consciences.* On this point civil rights legislation has a marked advantage. . . . [Most] Americans have a deep inner conviction that discrimination is wrong and unpatriotic. While their own prejudices may make them squirm and protest in opposition to proposed laws, they may also sigh with relief if the law, in accord with their "better natures," is passed—and enforced. People need and want their consciences bolstered by law, and this is nowhere more true than in the area of group relations.

Actually, in the United States, stateways—at least as expressed in the Constitution—are in advance of folkways. The Constitution is clear in its intentions that total democracy shall prevail. Thus the "official" morality of this country is high, although private morality is in many respects low. The contrast with certain other lands, for example Germany under Hitler, is striking. There the official morality (discrimination, persecution, expropriation of minority groups) was low, and the morality of many private citizens immeasurably higher. But in the United States official morality sets a high ideal. Furthermore, it is expected that the laws of the land shall lead and guide the folkways. Even the violators may approve them in principle. Traffic laws, we know, are often broken, but no one wants to live without them.

While laws do not prevent violations altogether, they certainly act as a restraint. They will deter whoever is deterable. They will not deter the compulsive bigot or demagogue. But neither do laws against arson deter the pyromaniac. Laws, we may say, restrain the middle range of mortals who need them as a mentor in molding their habits.

A final argument in favor of remedial legislation is its ability to break into vicious circles. When group relations are bad, they tend to worsen. Thus, the Negro who is deprived of opportunities for equal employment, equal educational opportunities, equal facilities for health and growth, sinks into an inferior position. He is then regarded as a lower species of mankind and treated with contempt. His opportunities continue, therefore, to deteriorate, and his situation becomes worse. Neither private efforts nor education can break into this aggravated tangle. Only strong, publicly supported legislation can do so. Police powers may be needed to start the spiral of improvement in housing, health, education, and employment.

When discrimination is eliminated, prejudice . . . tends to lessen. The vicious circle begins to reverse itself. The termination of discrimination in employment, housing, and in the armed forces has had the result . . . of creating more friendly ethnic attitudes . . . . And experience proves that the difficulties of integrating hitherto segregated groups is ordinarily less than anticipated. But it often takes a law, or a strong executive order, to start the process moving. The "principle of cumulation," as Myrdal calls it, holds that raising the Negro plane of living will lower prejudice on the part of the white, which in turn will again raise the Negro plane of living. Benign circles of this order can be established under the initial prompting of law.

. . . It is not entirely true that legislation must wait on education—at least not on complete and perfect education, for legislation itself is part of the education process.

We are not saying that any and every law designed to improve group relations is wise. There are plenty of poorly designed laws. Some of them may be so vague and unworkable that even their educative and conscience-guiding effect is nil. Laws of censorship and suppression are in the long run self-defeating. And while certain laws should perhaps carry stern penalties, it is a generally sound principle that minority group legislation should rely as far as possible on investigation, publicity, persuasion, and conciliation.

There is a special reason why this is true. A prejudiced person is extremely touchy on the subject. A man may accuse himself of prevarication or theft, but seldom of prejudice. We have time and again noted . . . the unconscious forces at work in the prejudiced mind, and the ready defenses and justifications that protect one from insight into his hostilities. It is, therefore, wise to assume that the violator of an antidiscrimination law is unwilling or unable to feel guilt, that he must be allowed to save face, and that a conciliatory approach will gain the desired end better than will punishment.

We have said that laws will, by and large, be obeyed if they are in line with one's conscience, and if they are tactfully administered. We should add an additional condition: they should not be felt to be imposed by an alien will. The South has a legendary resistance to "Yankee interference." Even a law otherwise acceptable may be resisted if it is felt to be a personal (or regional) affront. We are not saying that laws will fail to operate successfully unless they are initiated by one's own legislative representatives, but that the flavor of "alien domination" will probably lessen their effectiveness. Prejudices are not likely to be reduced by laws which, in the manner of their passing, arouse other prejudices.

*   *   *   *

WILLIAM EATON

New Dimensions of Freedom in the Ninth Amendment

The enumeration in the Constitution, of certain rights, shall not be construed to deny or disparage others retained by the people.

Ninth Amendment

The unspecified rights of the Ninth Amendment concern the values by which a free society lives. Though it was ratified in 1791, along with the rest of the Bill of Rights, it was not until June 7, 1965, that the United States Supreme Court used the Ninth Amendment to support any of its decisions. In *Griswold v. Connecticut* the Court held that a Connecticut law prohibiting the use of contraceptive devices was an unconstitutional invasion of the right of marital privacy. No single constitutional provision was the basis for the holding. Rather, the Court's conclusion was derived from the concept that "specific guarantees in the Bill of Rights have penumbras, formed by emanations from those guarantees that help give them life and substance." The right of privacy was founded on guarantees contained in the First, Third, Fourth, Fifth, and Ninth Amendments. A concurring opinion of three Justices, written by Justice Goldberg, went beyond the Court's holding to urge the Ninth Amendment as the chief ground for decision, and presented the first detailed discussion of that Amendment to issue from the Supreme Court. Four Justices rejected the Ninth Amendment as a basis

Printed and edited by permission of the author from *The Other Rights of the Ninth Amendment*, a previously unpublished paper. Footnotes have been omitted. Editors' title.

for deciding the case. The Amendment has thus been introduced, if tenuously, into the body of constitutional law after lying nearly dormant for 175 years.

The Constitution makes several provisions guaranteeing unspecified rights, similar to the provisions of the Ninth Amendment. The problems which arise in interpreting such provisions can be illustrated by referring to a few examples from the Fourteenth Amendment. The due process clause of the Fourteenth Amendment provides that, "No State shall . . . deprive any person of life, liberty, or property, without due process of law." The Court has had frequently to consider what "liberties" might be comprehended by this clause. The Court has suggested that the due process clause "denotes not merely freedom from bodily restraint but also the right of the individual to contract, to engage in any of the common occupations of life, to acquire useful knowledge, to marry, establish a home and bring up children, to worship God according to the dictates of his own conscience, and generally to enjoy those privileges long recognized at common law as essential to the orderly pursuit of happiness by free men." Further, the "liberty of parents and guardians to direct the upbringing and education of children under their control" has been upheld against a state law requiring compulsory public education for all children. Nor may a state exclude a person from the pursuit of an occupation in a manner which contravenes the due process clause.

The same due process clause occurs in the Fifth Amendment, applicable against the federal government rather than against the states. A recent case presents an arresting example of the potential scope of "liberty" under its provisions. The Supreme Court had ruled that racial segregation in public schools is in violation of the equal protection clause of the Fourteenth Amendment when practiced by states or their subdivisions. A companion case banned racial segregation in the District of Columbia, under federal jurisdiction. Yet no constitutional provision prohibits the federal government from denying equal protection of the laws as the Fourteenth Amendment prohibits the states. What the Court did, therefore, was virtually to derive a federal equal protection clause from the due process clause of the Fifth Amendment. As we shall see presently, this development is highly suggestive of one use to which the Ninth Amendment might be put.

The principles by which the Court has sought to identify such unspecified liberties as those of the Fourteenth Amendment's due process clause are of even greater interest than the specific rights announced. The Justices have stated that they must look to the "traditions and conscience of our people" to determine whether a principle is so rooted there "as to be ranked as fundamental." Or they have sought those "fundamental principles of liberty and justice which lie at the base of all our civil and political institutions." Similarly, the Court has disallowed state action which "shocks the conscience," or which violates the "decencies of civilized conduct." The "canons of decency and fairness which express the notions of justice of English-speaking peoples" have been invoked. Appeal has been made to procedures which assure the "protection of ultimate decency in civilized society," and which do not violate "immutable principles of justice." Governmental action has been found constitutionally invalid which does "more than offend some fastidious squeamishness or private sentimentalism," and which "offends even hardened sensibilities." The list of phrases could be expanded, but the difficulty is apparent enough: such phrases as these do not indicate with any precision or predictability what the Court will find to be a "fundamental personal liberty" within the meaning of the Constitution.

The Court knows that in seeking to identify unspecified rights in the Constitution it has a very broad territory in which to search. The Justices have sought, by use of the phrases quoted, to discover "immutable principles of justice" by which to guide and limit their deliberations. The implication is that such principles exist "out there" somewhere, and that the Court can find them and apply them to its work. But no matter how long we pour over the formulas which the Court has offered, we cannot discover what the limits of the Court's interpretations will be or what limits there should be. Not only are the results unpredictable, but the procedures of the Court in arriving at them are obscure. The same problem would arise in a further elaboration of the Ninth Amendment's unspecified rights. We must look further to understand the difficulties in this matter.

THE AMERICAN ENLIGHTENMENT

It can be said of the Ninth Amendment that there are "emanations" from the body of the Constitution, from the other original Amendments, and from the age in which the Constitution and the Bill of Rights were written, which make of it almost a summary of its time. The Constitution and its original Amendments are saturated with the idea that there exist for all citizens, or persons, rights beyond those which have been explicitly guaranteed.

The early case of *Calder v. Bull* expresses this philosophy. Justice Chase stated that there are "certain vital principles in our free Republican governments," founded in "the general principles of law and reason," which limit legislative power and prevent its abuse. Likewise, Justice Miller, speaking for the Court in a later case, held that, "There are limitations on . . . power which grow out of the essential nature of all free governments. Implied reservations of individual rights, without which the social compact could not exist, and which are respected by all governments entitled to the name."

The statements of these cases flow directly from the philosophical position expressed in the Declaration of Independence, and subscribed to generally by the men of the American Enlightenment. "These truths are self-evident," and when they came before the courts, the "self-evident" truths were incorporated into the law as judicial principles. The foundation for "self-evident" truths was in an idea of permanence which infused the thinking of the time. These truths were thought to be part of a universal system, existing apart from man's own thoughts, which was immutable and enduring. Ideas as to how this order was constituted were based on a particular understanding of science and nature. This science rested largely on the mechanics of Sir Isaac Newton, which posited the universe as a regularized, limited, describable, friendly place, in which man could perfect himself through knowledge and reason, according to the universal pattern laid down for him. It was a world virtually without evil, a kind of gigantic clockwork, wound by some mysterious force, ticking away inexorably, predictably, and regularly.

The Ninth Amendment is one of the chief efforts of the Constitution to preserve the "unalienable rights" which were thought to inhere in such a world. But the Constitution and its first ten Amendments were adopted nearly two centuries ago. The way the men of the American Enlightenment saw themselves and their world differs as much from the modern perception man has of his condition as musket balls differ from ballistic missiles. The serene countryside of Monticello, and the towns of Williamsburg or Philadelphia, represented life much as it had always been. The twentieth century has produced a kind of life never known before. What changes in our ideas of fundamental rights might be indicated in the wrenching of the old foundations accomplished by science, urbanization, the hydrogen bomb, the probing of the subconscious, the industrial revolution—already being compounded by the automation revolution—and all that these things imply for the way man views himself in his world?

THE SHOCK OF CHANGE

As permanence was the mainspring of Enlightenment thought, so change is the energizing concept of modern thought. The engine of change is modern science, and ideas of permanency as old as Genesis have been blown down by the force of its applications.

Basic science now makes radically different assumptions about the composition of the universe from those of Newtonian science. The physics of the Enlightenment included the "law" of the conservation of matter and energy: Whatever else happened, the quantities of both would remain the same. Einstein's formula, $E = mc^2$, is a conversion table for changing energy into matter, or matter into energy. Its utility is demonstrated in every atomic explosion. A principal supposition of bedrock stability was thus shattered. A most graphic example of the destruction of permanency as a model of thought is in one of the discoveries of quantum mechanics. It had always been supposed that some essential stuff, whether it be called a molecule, an atom, or something more sophisticated, existed out of which all else was made. This "building block" theory was carried from Newtonian science into the early assumptions of quantum physics. Success in probing subatomic particles destroyed the theory. The tiniest of all "things," those particles which might have been expected to be "essential" and "permanent," turn out to have hardly any existence at all. The "W" particle, for example, only one of a host of similar particles, has a life span of 100 millionth of a billionth of a second. It is as though the "elements" which we seek, when we think we have found them, turn into a puff of wind and vanish before our eyes.

These and other discoveries of science have shattered almost every principle of permanence believed in in the eighteenth century. This has led at last to a strange realization about all "permanent" principles. Man invented these principles himself—every last one of them. They are all the product of his brain, and their continued vitality depends upon how the brain accepts, rejects, or rearranges them. All of the systems of science or law which have been recorded from the past illustrate man's efforts to construct principles by which to live.

Nothing "exists" to the mind initially but a mad jumble of impressions. The mind must shape these impressions into systems of thought by which to understand and control its own experience. Perhaps the best summary of this realization was that of the Nobel physicist, P. W. Bridgman, when he concluded simply that "we never get away from ourselves." And these selves of ours, through changing thought patterns in our minds, seem to insist on constantly altering the world in which we live. So it is with the rights which are referred to in the Constitution and its Amendments.

The "unalienable" rights of which the Founders spoke are not part of some pre-existing "immutable" system at all. Better than that. They are the ingenious inventions of some men to keep other men, called dictators, legislators, philosopher kings, and the like, from killing them, torturing them, throwing them into prison, or robbing them of their property. The power of such invented rights rises not from any mysterious "inalienability," but from the perception that they furnish principles by which to accomplish desired ends. The idea of individual rights has been created as a weapon against irrational and uncontrolled use of power. For it is obvious, looking at history, that fair and just treatment of all men has been a most uncommon and alienable form of political action. Tyranny is far more "self-evident" in human experience than are individual rights. But when man invented the *idea* that he has a right to be treated better, he fashioned a weapon by which to destroy tyranny and pave the way for tolerance and moderation.

Changing concepts of science, and the new technology which follows these changes, require alterations in the statement and application of basic rights. The right of privacy, carried to a new state of development in the *Griswold* case, can be interpreted in such terms. Justice Brandeis was the first to give judicial expression to this right. He did so in his famous dissent in *Olmstead v. United States*, where he opposed the use of wiretapping—a new technical possibility for the invasion of privacy—to secure evidence for criminal convictions. Brandeis argued that the Constitution protects Americans "in their beliefs, their thoughts, their emotions and their sensations." He contended that it confers, as against government, "the right to be let alone—the most comprehensive of rights and the right most valued by civilized men." He saw every "unjustifiable intrusion" by the government upon this right, "by whatever means employed," as a violation of the search and seizure provisions of the Fourth Amendment, and the use in criminal proceedings of evidence so obtained as a violation of the self-incrimination provisions of the Fifth Amendment. It was by this fusion of the provisions of these two Amendments that Brandeis fashioned the new right of privacy. It was an early example of the use of "emanations" from the specific rights guaranteed by the Constitution to create new rights called forth by new circumstances.

In the modern condition where change is the foundation of society, the idea of fundamental rights, not enumerated, of rights which have not yet appeared, but which might be required to appear, takes on a new and exciting dimension.

THE "OTHER" RIGHTS

If the Ninth Amendment is to develop, the rights "retained by the people" will, in practice, be rights invented or adopted by the judges to serve new circumstances of the people. One of these could be the right to work. The argument has been made that not only income, but a feeling of social acceptance and personal usefulness, must be derived from one's work. One recognition of the right to work would be to confine very closely any governmental action to deny or deprive a person of a professional license, to dismiss him from a teaching position or a government job, or to do anything else which might effectively prevent him from working at his occupation or profession. The Court has gone part of the way in developing such requirements, and it has been urged to go further. A Ninth Amendment recognition of the right to work could furnish the basis for more effective procedural requirements when government challenges the employment of the individual.

If the premise were accepted that one must have work to participate fully in all the possibilities of a free society, the Court might conceivably ground an affirmative right to work in the Ninth Amendment. When it found the right to have been violated, it would then be the duty of the Court to order the state or federal government to provide suitable employment for the aggrieved petitioner.

The right to work can even be projected to a paradoxical conclusion. Suppose that all the promises of automation should come true, and that machines should obviate the necessity for many customary kinds of work. Society might then become, of necessity, a gigantic schoolhouse in which men and women would spend most of their lives in learning. Why not, then, a Ninth Amendment right to learn? Or even a right to play? Every school needs a playground.

Freedom of conscience is another right which could conceivably find a home in the Ninth Amendment. The Court recently presented a most interesting consideration of this problem in interpreting the matter of exemption from military service on the ground of "religious training and belief." The Court dealt with conscientious objectors whose religious views were unorthodox, and whose concepts of God were novel. The Court considered, and cited in its opinion, a series of startling thoughts on religion and the religious conscience. The opinion quoted such statements as that of Paul Tillich, speaking of the "god above God," and of "the power of being, which works through those who have no name for it, not even the name of God." Such views as these are the theological equivalents of the new scientific statements about the universe discussed previously.

The Court was careful to point out that none of the petitioners were outright atheists. But suppose they had been, and at the same time had subscribed to "the power of being" of which Tillich spoke? Their claim to freedom of conscience would be cut off from the statutory prescription that "religious training and belief" are the accepted grounds for exemption. This could be the kind of case which the Ninth Amendment might serve. A new freedom of conscience could be constructed to protect unorthodox thought, perhaps as an extension of the right of privacy, already partly grounded in the Ninth Amendment.

There is a procedural manner in which the Ninth Amendment might assume an important constitutional position. The Court has frequently used the due process clause of the Fourteenth Amendment to incorporate federal guarantees of freedom and apply them against the states. It has also found in this clause a source of fundamental rights independent of specific constitutional guarantees. The Ninth Amendment could be used to incorporate and apply against the federal government fundamental rights which have been announced under the broad equal protection and due process clauses of the Fourteenth Amendment. Something like this, as we have seen, has already taken place. The Court derived an equal protection clause from the Fifth Amendment by which to prevent federal racial discrimination in schools in the District of Columbia. The Ninth Amendment might have served better.

A striking possibility for such an evolution of the Ninth Amendment was illustrated in the Court's conclusion that seats in the House of Representatives must be apportioned among districts of equal size. The Court's opinion went to rather dubious lengths to justify the holding on the basis of Article I, Section 2, of the Constitution, which provides that the House of Representatives be chosen "by the people." The argument was historically grounded for the most part, and an equally compelling case, founded on the same history, was made in dissent. Had the Ninth Amendment been called into play, it might have served as the basis for more compelling reasoning. The Court had already at its disposal the "one person, one vote" rule which it had created under the equal protection clause of the Fourteenth Amendment to apply against the states. It could have termed that rule a fundamental constitutional principle, and incorporated it to apply against the federal government by way of the Ninth Amendment. Such a use of the Ninth Amendment could complete the Supreme Court's kit of constitutional tools by which to require that all fundamental rights apply evenly throughout the country, against both state and federal action.

One of the chief problems, if new rights are to be articulated under the Ninth Amendment, is that of ordering the process of change which this implies. The Court's role in such a process is not only to create new rights from the "emanations" of rights already stated, but to balance these rights against the necessities of government power. This is a dynamic process which is not likely ever to reach a point of stability and resolution, but guidelines must be established all the same.

It is apparent that the Court would exercise enormous discretion in announcing new interpretations of the rights "retained by the people" through the Ninth Amendment. Perhaps a broad consciousness of the process of constitutional change is the best limit on Court action, and the most likely foundation for acceptance of its new rulings. For if judges openly admit the necessity for change, and their role in bringing change about, there is built into the law, by the candor of the admissions, the necessity to examine thoroughly and to expose frankly the grounds for new departures.

We know at last that the search for unspecified rights in the Constitution is not a search for rights which "exist" already, and have only to be found and categorized for use. It is a search at the advancing perimeter of human experience for new constitutional devices to serve the ever-changing possibilities of human freedom. Should the Justices choose to activate it, the Ninth Amendment could become an important part of this process.

JOHN H. SCHAAR

Equality of Opportunity, and Beyond

I

Equality is a protean word. It is one of those political symbols—liberty and fraternity are others—into which men have poured the deepest urgings of their hearts. Every strongly held theory or conception of equality is at once a psychology, an ethic, a theory of social relations, and a vision of the good society.

Of the many conceptions of equality that have emerged over time, the one that today enjoys the most popularity is equality of opportunity. The formula has few enemies—politicians, businessmen, social theorists, and freedom marchers all approve it—and it is rarely subjected to intellectual challenge. It is as though all parties have agreed that certain other conceptions of equality, and notably the radical democratic conception, are just too troublesome to deal with because they have too many complex implications, too broad a scope perhaps, and a long history resonant of violence and revolutionary fervor. Equal opportunity, on the other hand, seems a more modest proposal. It promises that the doors to success and prosperity will be opened to us all yet does not imply that we are all equally valuable or that all men are really created equal. In short, this popular and relatively new concept escapes many of the problems and pitfalls of democratic equality and emphasizes the need for an equal opportunity among men to develop and be paid for their talents, which are of course far from being equal.

The doctrine itself is attractively simple. It asserts that each man should have equal rights and opportunities to develop his own talents and virtues

From "Equality of Opportunity, and Beyond," in Roland Pennock, ed., *Equality: Nomos IX*. Reprinted by permission of the publishers, Atherton Press, Inc. Copyright © 1967, Atherton Press, New York. All rights reserved.

and that there should be equal rewards for equal performances. The formula does not assume the empirical equality of men. It recognizes that inequalities among men on virtually every trait or characteristic are obvious and ineradicable, and it does not oppose differential evaluations of those differences. Nor is the formula much concerned with complex chains of normative reasoning: It is practical and policy-oriented. In addition, equal opportunity is not, in principle, confined to any particular sector of life. It is held to be as applicable to politics as to law, as suitable for education as for economics. The principle is widely accepted as just and generous, and the claim is often made that application of the principle unlocks the energies necessary for social and economic progress.

Whereas this conception of equality answers or evades some questions, it raises others. Who is to decide the value of a man's talents? Are men to be measured by the commercial demand for their various abilites? And if so, what happens to the man whose special gifts are not recognized as valuable by the buying public? And most important, is the resulting inequality, based partly on natural inequalities and partly on the whims of consumers, going to bury the ideal of democratic equality, based on a philosophy of equal human worth transcending both nature and economics?

These are serious questions, and it is my intention in this essay to probe their deeper meanings, as well as to clarify some major assumptions, disclose the inner spirit, and explore some of the moral and political implications of the principle of equal opportunity.

II

The first thing to notice is that the usual formulation of the doctrine—equality of opportunity for all to develop their capacities—is rather misleading, for the fact always is that not all talents can be developed equally in any given society. Out of the great variety of human resources available to it, a given society will admire and reward some abilities more than others. Every society has a set of values, and these are arranged in a more or less tidy hierarchy. These systems of evaluation vary from society to society: Soldierly qualities and virtues were highly admired and rewarded in Sparta, while poets languished. Hence, to be accurate, the equality of opportunity formula must be revised to read: equality of opportunity for all to develop those talents which are highly valued by a given people at a given time.

When put in this way, it becomes clear that commitment to the formula implies prior acceptance of an already established social-moral order. Thus, the doctrine is, indirectly, very conservative. It enlists support for the established pattern of values. It also encourages change and growth, to be sure, but mainly along the lines of tendency already apparent and approved in a given society. The doctrine is "progressive" only in the special sense that it encourages and hastens progress within a going pattern of institutions, activities, and values. It does not advance alternatives to the existing pattern. . . .

If this argument is correct, then the present-day "radicals" who demand the fullest extension of the equal-opportunity principle to all groups within the society, and especially to Negroes and the lower classes, are really more conservative than the "conservatives" who oppose them. No policy formula is better designed to fortify the dominant institutions, values, and ends of the American social order than the formula of equality of opportunity, for it offers *everyone* a fair and equal chance to find a place within that order. In principle, it excludes no man from the system if his abilities can be put to use within the system. We have here another example of the repeated tendency of American radicals to buttress the existing framework of order even while they think they are undermining it, another example of the inability of those who see themselves as radical critics of the established system to fashion a rhetoric and to formulate ends and values that offer a genuine alternative to the system. Time after time, never more loyally than at the present, America's radicals have been her best conservatives.

*   *   *   *

Secondly, it is clear that the equal-opportunity policy will increase the inequalities among men. In previous ages, when opportunities were restricted to those of the right birth and station, it is highly probable, given the fact that nature seems to delight in distributing many traits in the pattern of a normal distribution, and given the phenomenon of regression toward the mean, that many of those who enjoyed abundant opportunities to develop their talents actually lacked the native ability to benefit from their advantages. It is reasonable to suppose that many members of ascribed elites, while appearing far superior to the ruck, really were not that superior in actual attainment. Under the regime of equal opportunity, however, only those who genuinely are superior in the desired attributes will enjoy rich opportunities to develop their qualities. This would produce, within a few generations, a social system where the members of the elites really were immensely superior in ability and attainment to the masses. We should then have a condition where the natural and social aristocracies would be identical—a meritocracy, as Michael Young has called it.[1]

---

[1] Michael Young, *The Rise of the Meritocracy*, London: Thames and Hudson, 1958. Young's book imaginatively explores the conditions under which Jefferson's lovely dream of rule by the natural aristocracy turns into a nightmare of banality and outrage. The main condition, of course, is the dedication of virtually all creative energies to the goal of material abundance.

Furthermore, the more closely a society approaches meritocracy, the wider grows the gap in ability and achievement between the highest and the lowest social orders. This will happen because in so many fields there are such huge quantities of things to be learned before one can become certified as competent that only the keenest talents, refined and enlarged by years of devoted study and work, can make the grade.[2] We call our age scientific, and describe it further as characterized by a knowledge explosion. What these labels mean from the perspective of equalitarianism is that a handful of men possess a tremendous fund of scientific knowledge, while the rest of us are about as innocent of science as we have always been. So the gap widens: The disparity between the scientific knowledge of an Einstein and the scientific knowledge of the ordinary man of our day is greater than the disparity between a Newton and the ordinary man of his day.

Another force helps widen the gap. Ours is an age of huge, complex, and powerful organizations. Those who occupy positions of command in these structures wield enormous power over their underlings, who, in the main, have become so accustomed to their servitude that they hardly feel it for what it is. The least efficient of the liberal-social welfare states of our day, for example, enjoys a degree of easy control over the ordinary lives of its subjects far beyond the wildest ambitions of the traditional "absolute" rulers. As the commanding positions in these giant organizations come to be occupied increasingly by men who have been generously endowed by nature and, under the equal-opportunity principle, highly favored by society, the power gap between the well- and the poorly-endowed widens. The doctrine of equality of opportunity, which in its origins was a rather nervous attempt to forestall moral criticisms of a competitive and inequalitarian society while retaining the fiction of moral equality, now ironically magnifies the natural differences among men by policies based on an ostensibly equalitarian rationale. The doctrine of equal opportunity, social policies and institutions based on it, and advances in knowledge all conspire with nature to produce more and more inequality.

This opens a larger theme. We untiringly tell ourselves that the principle of equality of opportunity is a generous one. It makes no distinctions of worth among men on any of the factitious grounds, such as race, religion, or nationality, that are usually offered for such distinctions. Nor does it set artificial limits on the individual. On the contrary, it so arranges social conditions that each individual can go as high as his natural abilities will permit. Surely, nothing could be fairer or more generous.

---

[2]Success is a function of both inborn talent and the urge to do well, and it is often impossible to tell which is the more important in a particular case. It is certain that the urge to do well can be stimulated by social institutions. How else can we account for Athens or Florence, or the United States?

The generosity dissolves under analysis. The doctrine of equal opportunity, followed seriously, removes the question of how men should be treated from the realm of human responsibility and returns it to "nature." What is so generous about telling a man he can go as far as his talents will take him when his talents are meager? Imagine a footrace of one mile in which ten men compete, with the rules being the same for all. Three of the competitors are forty years old, five are overweight, one has weak ankles, and the tenth is Roger Bannister. What sense does it make to say that all ten have an equal opportunity to win the race? The outcome is predetermined by nature, and nine of the competitors will call it a mockery when they are told that all have the same opportunity to win.

The cruelty of the jest, incidentally, is intensified with each increase in our ability to measure traits and talents at an early age. Someday our measuring instruments may be so keen that we will be able to predict, with high accuracy, how well a child of six or eight will do in the social race. Efficiency would dictate that we use these tools to separate the superior from the inferior, assigning the proper kinds and quantities of growth resources, such as education, to each group. The very best training and equipment that society can afford would, of course, go to those in the superior group—in order to assure equality of opportunity for the development of their talents. It would seem more generous for men themselves to take responsibility for the matter, perhaps by devising a system of handicaps to correct for the accidents of birth, or even by abandoning the competitive ethic altogether.

Three lines of defense might be raised against these criticisms of the equality-of-opportunity principle.

It might be replied, first, that I have misstated the principle of equal opportunity. Correctly stated, the principle only guarantees equal opportunity for all to *enter* the race, not to *win* it. That is certainly correct: Whereas the equal-opportunity principle lets each individual "go as high as his natural abilities will permit," it does not guarantee that all will reach to the same height. Thus, the metaphor of the footrace twists the case in that it shows fools, presumably deluded by the equal-opportunity doctrine, trying to stretch hopelessly beyond their natural reach. But there is no reason to think that fat men who foolishly compete against Roger Bannister are deluded by a doctrine. They are deluded because they are fools.

These reservations are entirely proper. The metaphor of the footrace does misrepresent the case. But it was chosen because it also expresses some features of the case which are often overlooked. The equal-opportunity principle probably does excite a great many men to dreams of glory far beyond their real capabilities. Many observers of American life have pointed to the frequency of grand, bold, noble "first acts" in the drama of American life, and the scarcity of any "second acts" at all. The equal-opportunity principle, with its emphasis on success, probably does stir many men to excesses of hope for winning and despair at losing. It certainly leaves the losers with no external justification for their failures, and no amount of trying can erase the large element of cruelty from any social doctrine which does that. Cases like that of the footrace, and our growing ability to measure men's abilities, make it clear that the equal-opportunity principle really is not very helpful to many men. Under its regime, a man with, say, an Intelligence Quotient of ninety, is given equal opportunity to go as far as his native ability will take him. That is to say, it lets him go as far as he could have gone without the aid of the doctrine—to the bottom rung of the social ladder—while it simultaneously stimulates him to want to go farther.

Secondly, it might be argued that the equality-of-opportunity principle need not be interpreted and applied, as it has been in this treatment, within a setting and under the assumptions of social competitiveness. The principle could be construed as one that encourages the individual to compete against himself, to compare what he is with what he might become. The contest takes place between one's actual and potential selves, rather than between oneself and others.

This is an interesting, and hopeful, revision of the principle. It would shift the locus of judgment from society to the individual, and it would change the criteria of judgment from social utility to personal nobility. This shift is possible, but it would require a revolution in our present ways of thinking about equality, for those ways are in fact socially oriented and utilitarian. Hence, this defense against the criticisms is really no defense at all. It is irrelevant in the strict sense that instead of meeting the specific charges it shifts the question to a different battleground. It is an alternative to the existing, operative theory, not a defense of it. In fact, the operative doctrine, with its stress on overcoming others as the path of self-validation, is one of the toughest obstacles in the way of an ethic of personal validation through self-transcendence. The operative doctrine specifies success as the test of personal worth, and by success is meant victory in the struggle against others for the prizes of wealth and status. The person who enters wholeheartedly into this contest comes to look upon himself as an object or commodity whose value is set, not by his own internal standards of worth but by the valuations others placed on the position he occupies. Thus, when the dogma of equal opportunity is effectively internalized by the individual members of a society, the result is as humanly disastrous for the winners as

for the losers. The winners easily come to think of themselves as beings
superior to common humanity, while the losers are almost forced to think
of themselves as something less than human.

The third defense is a defense, though not a strong one. It consists in
explaining that the metaphor of the footrace oversimplifies the reality that
is relevant to an appraisal of the equal-opportunity principle. What actually
occurs in a society is not just one kind of contest but many kinds, so that
those who are not good at one thing need only look around for a different
contest where they have a better chance of winning. Furthermore, there is
not just one prize in a given contest but several. Indeed, in our complex and
affluent society, affairs might even be so arranged that everyone would
win something: There need be no losers.

This reply has some strength, but not enough to touch the basic points.
Although there are many avenues of opportunity in our society, their number is not unlimited. The theory of equal opportunity must always be implemented within a set of conventions which favors some potentialities and
discourages others. Persons who strive to develop potentialities that are
not admired in a given society soon find their efforts tagged silly, or
wrong-headed, or dangerous, or dysfunctional. This is inherent in any society, and it forms an insurmountable barrier to the full development of
the principle of equal opportunity. Every society encourages some talents
and contests, and discourages others. Under the equal-opportunity doctrine,
the only men who can fulfill themselves and develop their abilities to the
fullest are those who are able and eager to do what society demands they
do.

*   *   *   *

The formula of equality of opportunity, then, is by no means the warm
and generous thing it seems to be on first view. Let us now examine the
doctrine from another perspective.

III

The equal-opportunity principle is widely praised as an authentic expression of the democratic ideal and temper. I shall argue, to the contrary, that
it is a cruel debasement of a genuinely democratic understanding of equality. To argue that is also to imply, of course, that a genuinely democratic
conception of equality is not widely held in the United States.

*   *   *   *

The doctrine of equality of opportunity is the product of a competitive
and fragmented society, a divided society, a society in which individualism,
in Tocqueville's sense of the word,[3] is the reigning ethical principle. It

[3] *Democracy in America*, New York: Vintage, 1945, Vol. 2, pp. 104-5.

is a precise symbolic expression of the liberal-bourgeois model of society, for it extends the marketplace mentality to all the spheres of life. It views the whole of human relations as a contest in which each man competes with his fellows for scarce goods, a contest in which there is never enough for everybody and where one man's gain is usually another's loss. Resting upon the attractive conviction that all should be allowed to improve their conditions as far as their abilities permit, the equal-opportunity principle insists that each individual do this by and for himself. Thus, it is the perfect embodiment of the Liberal conception of reform. It breaks up solidaristic opposition to existing conditions of inequality by holding out to the ablest and most ambitious members of the disadvantaged groups the enticing prospect of rising from their lowly state into a more prosperous condition. The rules of the game remain the same: The fundamental character of the social-economic system is unaltered. All that happens is that individuals are given the chance to struggle up the social ladder, change their position on it, and step on the fingers of those beneath them.

A great many individuals do, in fact, avail themselves of the chance to change sides as offered by the principle of equality of opportunity.[4] More than that, the desire to change sides is probably typical of the lower and middle classes, and is widely accepted as a legitimate ethical outlook. In other words, much of the demand for equality, and virtually all of the demand for the kind of equality expressed in the equal-opportunity principle, is really a demand for an equal right and opportunity to become unequal. Very much of what goes by the name of democratic sentiment—as that sentiment is molded within the framework of an individualistic, competitive society and expressed in the vocabulary of such a society—is really envy of those who enjoy superior positions combined with a desire to join them.[5]

This whole way of thinking leads effortlessly to the conclusion that the existence of hierarchy, even of oligarchy, is not the antithesis of democracy but its natural and necessary fulfillment. The idea of equality of opportunity assumes the presence of a mass of men of average talents and attainments. The talents and attainments of the superior few can be measured by comparison with this average, mass background. The best emerge from the democracy, the average, and set themselves over it, resting their position securely on the argument from merit and ability. Those on top are automatically justified because they owe their positions to their natural

---

[4] Some civil rights leaders are suspicious of open enrollment plans to combat *de facto* segregation for precisely this reason.

[5] "The greatest obstacle which equality has to overcome is not the aristocratic pride of the rich, but rather the undisciplined egoism of the poor." Proudhon, as quoted in James Joll, *The Anarchists*, Boston: Little, Brown, 1964, p. 67.

superiority of merit, not to any artificial claim derived from birth, or wealth, or any other such basis. Hence, the argument concludes, the workings of the equal-opportunity principle help the democracy discover its own most capable masters in the fairest and most efficient way. Everybody gains: the average many because they are led by the superior few; the superior few because they can legitimately enjoy rewards commensurate with their abilities and contributions.

So pervasive and habitual is this way of thinking today that it is virtually impossible to criticize it with any hope of persuading others of its weaknesses. One is not dealing with a set of specific propositions logically arrayed, but with an atmospheric condition, a climate of opinion that unconsciously governs articulate thought in a variety of fields. Something like this cluster of opinions and sentiments provides the framework for popular discussion of the origins and legitimacy of economic inequality. We are easily inclined to think that a man gets what he deserves, that rewards are primarily products of one's talents and industry, secondarily the consequences of luck, and only in small part the function of properties of the social-cultural structure. Somewhere around three-fourths of all personal wealth in the United States belongs to the richest fifth of our families.[6] There is no evidence, in the form of major political movements or public policies, that this distribution shocks the American democratic conscience— a fact suggesting that the American conscience on this matter simply is not democratic but is, rather, formed by the rhetoric of equal opportunity. Similarly, the giant public and private bureaucracies of our day could not justify for a minute their powers over the lives of men if the men so used did not themselves believe in the justness of hierarchy based on merit— merit always defined as tested competence in a special subject matter, tested mastery of a special skill or craft. Most modern writers on the theory of democracy accept this argument for elitism and point out happily that no serious moral or political problems arise so long as avenues for the movement of members into and out of the hierarchies are freely provided. The principle of equal opportunity, of course, does just that.

* * * *

All that can be said against this orientation is that a genuinely democratic ethic and vision rejects oligarchy *as such*. The democrat rejects in principle the thesis that oligarchy of merit (special competence) is in some way different in kind from oligarchy of any other sort, and that this difference makes it nobler, more reasonable, more agreeable to democracy, than oligarchies built on other grounds. The democrat who understands his com-

---

[6] Oscar Goss, "The Political Economy of the Great Society," *Commentary* (October, 1965), pp. 31-37, at p. 37.

mitment holds oligarchy itself to be obnoxious, not merely oligarchy of this or that kind.

The argument for hierarchy based on merit and accomplished by the method of equal opportunity is so widespread in our culture that there seems no way to find a reasonable alternative to it. We automatically think that the choice is either-or: *either* hierarchy and orderly progress *or* anarchy and disorderly stalemate. But that is not so. It is hardly even relevant. The fact that it is thought to be so is a reflection of the crippling assumptions from which modern thought on these matters proceeds. It is thought that there must be hierarchies and masses, elites and non-elites, and that there can be no more democratic way of selecting elites than by the method of equal opportunity. The complexity of affairs demands elites; and democracy and justice require selection of those elites by merit and equal opportunity.

Of course there must be hierarchy, but that does not imply a hierarchical and bureaucratic mode of thinking and acting. It need imply no more than specialization of function. Similarly, the fact that complexity demands specialization of function does not imply the unique merit and authority of those who perform the special functions. On the contrary: A full appreciation of complexity implies the need for the widest possible diffusion of knowledge, sharing of views, and mutual acceptance of responsibility by all members of the affected community.

Of course there must be organization, and organization implies hierarchy. Selection of the hierarchs by the criterion of merit and the mechanism of equal opportunity seems to reassure the worried democrat that his values are not being violated. But hierarchy may or may not be consonant with the democratic spirit. . . .

Before there can be a democratic organization, there must first be a democratic mentality—a way of thinking about the relations among men which stresses equality of being and which strives incessantly toward the widest possible sharing of responsibility and participation in the common life. A democratic orientation does not grow from and cannot coexist with the present bureaucratic and "meritorian" ethic. It is an alternative to the present ethic, not an expansion or outgrowth of it. When the democratic mentality prevails, it will not be too hard to find the mechanisms for implementing it.

IV

I hope my argument will not be interpreted as some sort of mindless demand for the abolition of distinctions or as a defense of the ethic of mutual aid against the ethic competition. The argument was mainly negative in intention, attempting to show that the idea of equality of opportunity is a poor tool for understanding even those sectors of life to which the notion of equality is applicable. It is a poor tool in that, whereas it seems to defend equality, it really only defends the equal right to become unequal by competing against one's fellows. Hence, far from bringing men together, the equal-opportunity doctrine sets them against each other. The doctrine rests on a narrow theory of motivation and a meager conception of man and society. It reduces man to a bundle of abilities, an instrument valued according to its capacity for performing socially valued functions with more or less efficiency. Also, the doctrine leads inevitably to hierarchy and oligarchy, and tries to soften that hard outcome by a new form of the ancient argument that the best should rule. In all these ways, the idea of equality of opportunity constitutes a thorough misunderstanding of a democratic conception of equality.

It is not the primary task of this essay to set forth a genuinely democratic conception of equality: that is a work for another time. Still, enough should be done in the second part of this essay to arrest the most obvious and most likely objections to the first part.

The equal-opportunity principle is certainly not without value. Stripped of its antagonistic and inequalitarian overtones, the formula can be used to express the fundamental proposition that no member of the community should be denied the basic conditions necessary for the fullest possible participation in the common life, insofar as those conditions can be provided for by public action and through the use of public resources. This formulation will take one some distance toward a democratic conception of equality, but it must be interpreted carefully, for it can easily turn into just another defense of the equal right to become unequal.

Still, the formulation does provide some useful guidelines. It obviously implies equality in and before the law. It also implies a far greater measure of economic equality than is the case today. The issue here is not material comfort. Nor does it have anything to do with the notion that justice is served when economic goods are allocated according to the actual work (in the customary definition) each man does. That is impossible. We may urge that each should contribute according to his ability; we must surely insist that each be provided for according to his need.

What the criterion of a substantial degree of economic equalization requires is the establishment of the material conditions necessary for a generous measure of freedom of choice for all members of the community and the establishment of the conditions necessary for relations of mutual respect and honesty among the various economic and social groups within a society. This is not some kind of levelling demand for equality of condition. It is no more than a recognition of the obvious fact that the great material inequality that prevails in America today produces too much brutishness, impotence, and rage among the lower classes, and too much nervous vulgarity among the middle classes. There is no assertion here that economic equalization is the sufficient condition for the democratic New Jerusalem. Rather, the assertion is negative. As Arnold put it, "equality will never of itself alone give us a perfect civilisation. But·with such inequality as ours, a perfect civilisation is impossible."[7]

The equality-of-opportunity principle, as formulated above, also implies the equal right of each member to share in the political life of the community to the fullest extent of his interest and ability. But this is the point at which the principle, no matter how carefully formulated, easily leads one away from a democratic view. The equal-opportunity principle as employed today in, for example, discussions of representation and voting rights, really does nothing more than fortify the prevailing conception of political action as just another of the various steps individuals and groups take to secure and advance their own interests and advantages. In this view, politics is but another aspect of the struggle for competitive advantage, and men need political power in order to protect and advance their private powers. This conception of politics is drawn from the economic sphere, and never rises above the ethical and psychological possibilities of that sphere.

When it is understood that the principle of equal opportunity is in our time an expression of the competitive, capitalistic spirit, and not of the democratic spirit, then the boundaries of its applicability begin to emerge. To the extent that competition is inescapable, or socially useful, all competitors should have the same advantages, and this the equal-opportunity principle guarantees. In any competitive situation, some will do better than others, and it seems just that those who do well should be rewarded more generously than those who do poorly. This too the principle guarantees.

The basic question, however, is not whether competition should be praised or condemned, but where and under what conditions competition is a desirable principle of action and judgment and where and under what conditions it is not. Some kinds of competition actually draw men more closely together whereas others produce antagonism and isolation. The problem is to distinguish between these kinds, encouraging the former and discouraging the latter. Peace is but a euphemism for slavery unless men's competitive energies are given adequate outlet. Most people probably have some need for both inward and outward striving. Perhaps the struggles against other people and the struggles within the self can be brought to some kind of balance in each individual and in society as a whole. Ideally, we might strive toward a truly pluralistic society in which

---

[7]Matthew Arnold, essay on "Equality" (1878), in *Matthew Arnold: Prose and Poetry*, ed. by A. L. Bouton, New York: Scribner's, 1927, p. 362.

nearly everybody could find a specialty he could do fairly well and where he would enjoy friendly competition with others. Judged by this imaginative possibility, our present social order is a mean thing. It is a kind of institutionalized war game, or sporting contest, in which the prizes are far too limited in kind, the referees and timekeepers far too numerous, and the number of reluctant and ill-adjusted players far too high. We need a social order that permits a much greater variety of games. Such a social order could, I think, be based on an effort to find a place for the greatest possible range of natural abilities among men. The variety of available natural abilities is enormous and worth much more exploration than any of the currently dominant conceptions of social order are willing to undertake. In the United States today, the fundamental justification of the equal-opportunity principle is that it is an efficient means for achieving an indefinite expansion of wealth and power. Many men are unsuited by nature for that competition, so that nature herself comes to seem unjust. But many of the injustices we regard nature as having perpetrated on individuals are actually no more than artifacts of the narrow view we take of nature's possibilities and a consequent distortion of the methods and ideals by which we attempt to transcend nature. For example, in defining intelligence as what I.Q. tests measure, we constrict the meanings of intelligence, for there are many modes of intelligence that the tests do not capture— nature is more protean than man's conception of her. Furthermore, having defined intelligence in a certain way, we then proceed to reward the people who have just that kind of intelligence and encourage them to use it in the pursuit of knowledge, which they are likely to do by building computers, which in turn give only certain kinds of knowledge. Thus our constricted definition of nature is confirmed by the methods we use to study nature. In this special sense, there might still be something to say for the eighteenth-century idea that society should imitate nature.

We must learn to ask questions like these about the method of competition and the principle of equal opportunity. The task is to define their proper spheres of action, not to treat them as blocks to be totally accepted or rejected. At the outer limit, it seems clear that whereas every society is to some extent competitive and competition in some spheres is socially and individually valuable, no society ought to exalt the competitive spirit as such, and the equal-opportunity principle that implements it. Both conceptions tend naturally toward selfishness unless carefully controlled.

V

In addition to equality of opportunity, there is another kind of equality that is blind to all questions of success or failure. This is the equality that obtains in the relations among the members of any genuine community. It is the feeling held by each member that all other members, regardless of their many differences of function and rank, belong to the community "as fully as he does himself."[8] Equal opportunity, far from strengthening this kind of equality, weakens it.

When this point is reached, when the discussion turns to the meanings of equality involved in a democratic conception of membership and a democratic conception of ruling and being ruled, the equal-opportunity principle—no matter how carefully formulated—begins to mislead. A fuller conception of equality is needed, one stripped of the antagonistic and privatistic overtones of the equal-opportunity principle. That fuller conception, in turn, requires a broader view of politics than is afforded by the "who gets what, when, how" perspective.

Political life occupies a middle ground between the sheer givens of nature and society on the one side, and the transcendental "kingdom of ends" on the other. Through political action men publicly strive to order and transform the givens of nature and society by the light of values drawn from a realm above or outside the order of the givens. Men, acting together, define the ideal aims of the common life and try to bend realities toward them. Through acting with others to define and achieve what can be called good for all, each realizes part of his own meaning and destiny. Insofar as man is a being that wants not merely to live but to live well, he is a political being. And insofar as any man does not participate in forming the common definition of the good life, to that degree he falls short of the fullest possibilities of the human vocation. No man can assign to another dominion over how he shall live his life without becoming something less than a man. This way of thinking about political action leads to an idea of equality whose tone and implications are very different from those of the equal-opportunity formulation.

Other features of political action lead in the same direction, and, specifically, require a rejection of all claims to rulership based on the ancient analogies between the art of ruling and other arts. When one contracts with a carpenter to build a house, he may assume that the carpenter's skills are sufficient to the work that is to be done. But when citizens elevate some among them to places of political authority the case is different. Politics has so few givens and so many contingencies and complexities, contains so many dangerous possibilities and so few perfect solutions, and is such a baffling mixture of empirical, prudential, and ethical considerations that no man or group of men has knowledge and skill sufficient for all

---

[8] John Plamenatz, *Man and Society*, New York: McGraw-Hill, 1963, Vol. II, p. 120.

situations. As John Winthrop said, no man can "profess nor undertake to have sufficient skill for that office."[9]

Winthrop's comment, grounded as it is on a solid understanding of the political vocation, is a just rebuke to all claims for political authority based on technical competence. Relations between politician and citizen are very different from those between craftsman and employer. Politicians cannot be said to serve or to execute the will of citizens in the way that craftsmen can be said to serve their employers. Nor can politicians claim authority over their work and over other persons engaged in that work on the grounds of technical competence. The relations between politicians and citizens, in sum, are relations among equals in a number of important senses. Above all, their relations are built on premises that, when properly understood, encourage genuine conversation among the participants, not merely the transmission of information and commands up and down a line. This way of thinking about the matter presumes equality among citizens in the sense most basic to a democratic understanding of the relations among the members of a political community—in the sense of equality of being—and hence presumes the widest possible participation in and sharing of responsibility for the policies that govern the whole community.

*   *   *   *

A proper view of equality still leaves wide scope for the existence of necessary and just superiorities and differences, but it brings a different mentality to their appraisal. Certainly, some things *are* better than others, and more to be preferred. Some vocations and talents are more valuable than others, and more to be rewarded. The implication here is only that the more highly skilled, trained, or talented man has no ground either for thinking himself a better *man* than his less-favored fellows, or for regarding his superiorities as providing any but the most temporary and limited justification for authority over others. The paradigmatic case is that of the relation between teacher and student. The teacher's superior knowledge gives him a just claim to authority over his students. But central to the ethic of teaching is the conviction that the teacher must impart to students not only his substantive knowledge but also the critical skills and habits necessary for judging and contributing to that knowledge. The teacher justifies his authority and fulfills his duty by making himself unnecessary to the student.

Perhaps this at least suggests the outlines of a democratic conception of equality and draws the boundaries of its applicability. The heart of such

---

[9] John Winthrop, "Speech to the General Court," July 3, 1645, in Perry Miller, ed., *The American Puritans: Their Prose and Poetry*, Garden City, New York: Doubleday Anchor, 1956, pp. 91-92.

a view of equality is its affirmation of equality of being and belonging. That affirmation helps identify those sectors of life in which we should all be treated in a common or average way, so that the minimal conditions of a common life are made available to all: legal equality, equal rights of participation in political life, equal right to those average material provisions necessary for living together decently at all. It also stresses the greatest possible participation in and sharing of the common life and culture while striving to assure that no man shall determine or define the being of any other man.

*   *   *   *

639   7